T0389642

Elementary Predicates and Related Categories

Linguistik Aktuell/Linguistics Today (LA)

ISSN 0166-0829

Linguistik Aktuell/Linguistics Today (LA) publishes original monographs as well as edited collections on synchronic and diachronic linguistics. Studies in LA engage with empirical phenomena and theoretical questions as these are currently discussed in linguistics with the aim to establish robust empirical generalizations within a universalistic perspective.

For an overview of all books published in this series, please see
benjamins.com/catalog/la

Volume 285

Elementary Predicates and Related Categories
by Ludovico Franco

Elementary Predicates and Related Categories

Ludovico Franco
Università degli Studi di Firenze

John Benjamins Publishing Company

Amsterdam / Philadelphia

DOI 10.1075/la.285

Cataloging-in-Publication Data available from Library of Congress:
LCCN 2024023815 (PRINT) / 2024023816 (E-BOOK)

ISBN 978 90 272 1499 7 (HB)
ISBN 978 90 272 4662 2 (E-BOOK)

John Benjamins Publishing Company · https://benjamins.com

Per Salomè, Carlo e Daniele

Table of contents

Preface

All chapters of this book, save one,[1] are derived from articles that were published in *Working Papers in Linguistics and Oriental Studies* – Quaderni di Linguistica e Studi Orientali (QULSO) at the University of Florence between 2017 and 2022. Each of the 'QULSO working papers' has undergone re-editing. I believe they collectively constitute a coherent corpus of empirical evidence that substantiates the theoretical framework outlined in recent research, warranting their inclusion in a monograph. All abbreviations employed adhere to the Leipzig Glossing Rules (https://www.eva.mpg.de/lingua/pdf/Glossing-Rules.pdf).

I would like to express my sincere gratitude to Rita Manzini and Leonardo Savoia, without whose insights this work would not have been possible, as well as to my close friend (and frequent co-author) Paolo Lorusso. Additionally, I extend my thanks to my friends and colleagues at the University of Florence and beyond: Benedetta Baldi, Lena Dal Pozzo, Rosangela Lai, Mihaela Marchis Moreno, Greta Mazzaggio, Irene Micali, Matthew Reeve, Giuseppe Rugna, and Mariarosaria Zinzi.

Finally, I express my gratitude to Elly Van Gelderen for her interest in my work and to an Anonymous Reviewer for their invaluable help in improving the content and the structure of this book. All errors and omissions are my own.

---

1. Chapter 4 presents a novel perspective, building upon the concepts introduced by Franco et al. (2021) regarding relators within the locative domain, and extending them to encompass both spatial and non-spatial relational nouns. The Uralic data utilized in this chapter are sourced from Franco et al. (2017), originally published in the *Proceedings of OLINCO – Olomouc Linguistics Colloquium 2016*. We express our gratitude to Lena Dal Pozzo, a native Finnish speaker, for checking all the Finnish data. Chapter 5 is an updated version of a paper titled "On the Morpho-Syntax of Existential Sentences in Romance-based Creoles," which was included in Working Papers in Linguistics and Oriental Studies. Originally co-written with Paolo Lorusso, this chapter only includes the sections we contributed, leaving out Lorusso's contribution, with full acknowledgment of his valuable input.

CHAPTER 1

Introduction

1.1 Theoretical background

In the generative approach, researchers can meaningfully investigate categories across linguistic domains. Distributed Morphology (DM), a *mainstream* research paradigm focused on understanding the internal structure of words, introduces a unique computational Merge operation, which not only governs constituent structure but also encompasses word formation, leading to the view of 'syntax all the way down' (cf. Halle & Maranz, 1993 and subsequent literature). According to DM, the mental lexicon comprises lexical roots and grammatical morphemes.

This perspective allows for meaningful inquiries into the cross-domain application of key syntactic notions such as locality, which refers to the constraints on syntactic operations. Locality, originally defined by the notion of a cycle and later by that of a phase (Chomsky, 2001a) restricts arbitrarily long-distance relations and determines the visibility of morphological domains to syntactic processing.

Recent research has used the opposition between *thought structuring* (syntactico-semantic chunk) and its *externalization* (morpho-phonological chunk) to argue for largely invariant syntactic structures, isomorphic to interpretation. This view emphasizes the uniformity of syntax and semantics but posits a potentially complete opacity between them, allowing for arbitrary matching of morpho-phonology and syntax (cf. Rizzi & Cinque, 2016; Cinque & Rizzi, 2010; Caha, 2009).

However, opacity at the externalization interface poses a significant obstacle to learnability. Acquisition relies largely on learning the lexicon, which also accounts for cross-linguistic variation (cf. Manzini & Wexler, 1987). If there is no transparent connection between externalization and its syntactico-semantic source, the matching between the two becomes challenging, potentially hindering the learning process.

Thus, we begin with the premise of a universal conceptual inventory, with categories recruited by language being universal. However, the linguistic lexicon cuts this inventory in a language-specific manner, contributing to language variation.

Our main focus is the junction of externalization processes and the syntactic processor. We will investigate (cross-categorial) syncretism, considering paradigms as having no theoretical status and using "syncretism" to basically refer to homophony outside of paradigms. Our goal is to outline an inventory of *primitives* shaping morpho-syntactic derivations.

Syncretism, an empirical issue crucially interacting with notions of paradigmatic organization, is addressed by DM, which views it as resulting from opacization operations. These operations blur syntactic full feature specification, leading to syncretisms and portmanteau morphemes.

Inspired by the insights of Manzini & Savoia (2007, 2011a,b), we aim to take a conservative view, where the lexicon precedes syntax, and explore how lexical items interact under syntactic Merge. Syncretisms spread beyond grammatical categories and paradigms, revealing underlying structures that transcend traditional linguistic boundaries. The interaction between syntactic computation and content-dependent features shapes syncretisms, highlighting the intricate relationship between syntax and morphology.

The present book showcases research in theoretical morphosyntax aimed at redefining the status of (functional) categories. It challenges the conventional notion that the functional lexicon is predetermined within the universal (computational) component of syntax, organized in a cartographic/nanosyntactic manner. Instead, we propose that functional categories are drawn from the same conceptual inventory as lexical ones. While the underlying conceptual organization is universal, the linguistic lexicon shapes it in language-specific ways, accounting for the majority of language variation. Language embodies thought processes by integrating cognitive functions such as perception, articulation, categorization, and inference into cohesive behaviour. This integration is not clearly captured by traditional linguistic research paradigms, which treat phonology, morphology, and syntax as separate modules with distinct internal structures. In contrast, generative research implies a much closer integration of these previously *compartmentalized* components.

Drawing on the works of Manzini & Savoia (2018), Manzini, et al. (2015), Manzini & Franco (2016), Franco & Manzini (2017a, 2017b), Franco et al. (2021), Franco & Lorusso (2020), Rugna & Franco (2022) among others, we embrace the position formalized by DM (see Marantz, 1997, 2007) that predicative contents are listed in the lexicon without categorization, as bare roots. Consequently, nouns, verbs, and adjectives are defined by merging a-categorial predicative content with nominalizing, verbalizing, or adjectivizing functional heads.

However, we diverge from DM's assumption that functional categories constitute a separate, potentially universal lexicon – a sort of "Platonic ontology" of natural languages (cf. Manzini & Franco, 2016). Instead, we argue that the externalization of predicative contents and functional features/categories pass through the same lexicon.

Thus, we aim to demonstrate that diverse lexical items, which instantiate grammatical relations in the clause or serve as classifiers within the nominal phrase, share the same syntax. In this syntax, elementary predicates function as *inclusion/subset/part-whole* relators (Belvin & Den Dikken, 1997) or classifying/individuating/evaluating items.

1.2 Oblique devices as 'part-whole, inclusion' predicates. Toward a morpho-syntactic account of 'case' syncretism

In our current framework, the concept of 'subset/inclusion/part-whole' predicates can be applied at both the X (lexical base) and XP levels in constituent structure. It is the various domains of application that give rise to phenomena such as *(plural) number* and *(oblique) case*. Indeed, Manzini & Savoia (2011a) explain the widespreaed syncretism between genitive singular and nominative plural in the inflectional paradigms of natural languages,[2] arguing that the 'plural' value has the same (syncretic) inclusion/subset content which characterize genitives, usually encoding a relation between a possessed entity (a part) and a possessor (the whole). Specifically, Manzini & Savoia propose that the inclusion predicate is construed as plural morphology if its scope is restricted to the noun it attaches to. It contributes plurality to an entity by isolating a subset of the set (or set of sets) of all individuals denoting a given entity.

The nominative plural = genitive singular syncretism is an example of syncretism *across* paradigms. Indeed, we posit that traditional data classifications offer surface-level generalizations useful for descriptive purposes but do not accurately reflect the true (computational) structure of language. In our work, we aim to demonstrate how 'subset/inclusion/part-whole' predicates can shape syncretism, extending well beyond paradigms and categories.

Manzini & Franco (2016), Franco & Manzini (2017a,b), Franco & Lorusso (2020) argue that, cross-linguistically, just like genitive inflections, dative morphemes function as part-whole/inclusion predicates, notated as ($\subseteq$). However, it's crucial to note that the inclusion relation should not be interpreted strictly in a mathematical sense but rather loosely, akin to 'zonal inclusion' (cf. Belvin & den Dikken, 1997). This fundamental context of occurrence can be illustrated in English with the preposition 'to,' as in (the books) to (peter).

---

2. As shown in Caha (2016), within Indo-European languages, one may find this syncretism for instance in Lithuanian, Romanian, Latin, Albanian, Old Irish, among others.

(1)   a.   I gave the books **to** Peter
      b.   [$_{VP}$ gave [$_{PredP}$ the books [[$_⊆$ **to**] Peter]]]]

Drawing from the works of Kayne (1984), Pesetsky (1995), Beck & Johnson (2004), Harley (2002), and others, it is posited that in (1), a possession/part-whole/inclusion relation exists between the dative (*Peter*) and the theme of the ditransitive verb (*the books*).

As suggested above and in line with the insights of Manzini & Savoia (2011b), the same (⊆) content is attributed to genitives. Consider English in (2a). The preposition "of" (or the *'s* genitive ending) establishes a possession relation between the selected argument, namely "the woman" (the possessor), and the head of the DP, namely "the children" (the possessum). The content of the *'s* case or the "of" preposition aligns with the same part-whole elementary predicate (⊆) assumed for datives. Therefore, in (2b), (⊆) takes its sister DP (the possessor) as its internal argument and its head N/D (the possessum) as its external argument – indicating that 'the children' are included in the domain of 'the woman'.

(2)   a.   The woman's children/the children **of** the woman
      b.   [$_{DP}$ the children [$_{PP⊆}$ **of** the woman]]

Therefore, also the widespread genitive/dative syncretism (e.g., in Romanian as shown in (3)) precisely corresponds to a shared lexicalization pattern of the (⊆) value (Manzini & Savoia 2011b, 2018). This perspective does not contradict languages like English, which have two distinct lexicalizations for 'to' (dative) and 'of' (genitive). In English, 'of' is specifically used for DP-embedding of (⊆), while 'to' is employed for sentential embedding of (⊆).

(3)   *Romanian*
      a.   (I)-l   am   dat   băieț-i-l-**or**/ fet-e-l-**or**
           him.it I.have given boy-MPL-DEF-OBL/girl-FPL-DEF-OBL
           'I gave it to the boys/ girls'
      b.   pahar-ul   băieț-i-l-**or** /fet-e-l-**or**
           glass-MSG.DEF boy-MPL-DEF-OBL /girl-FPL-DEF-OBL
           'the glass of the boys/ girls'

Less trivially, we may want to consider that the superficial identity of differential object marking (DOM) internal arguments and of goal datives involves no accidental homophony or syncretism, but rather an underlyingly identical structure of embedding. According to Manzini & Franco (2016), the widespread syncretism of dative and DOM is based on the fact that the same lexical content ⊆ is instantiated in both contexts. In other words, Manzini & Franco assume that object DPs highly ranked in animacy/definiteness require the same elementary predicate ⊆ for their embedding as goals. Specifically, while in (1) and (2) the two arguments of ⊆ are two DPs, in structure (4c) for sentence (4a) illustrating the Southern Italian variety of Canosa di Puglia, the two arguments of ⊆ are the object DP and an eventive constituent.

(4) a. sɔ   vvistə **a** kkur ɔmə
      I.am seen   to that man
      'I saw that man.'

  b. da-nn-illə **a** jiddə
      give-him-it to him
      'Give it to him'   *Canosa di Puglia*

  c. [$_{vP}$ v [$_{VP}$ vvistə [$_{PP⊆}$ a [$_{DP}$ kkur ɔmə]]]]

Hale & Keyser (1993) and Chomsky (1995) propose that transitive predicates arise from the incorporation of an elementary state or event into a transitivizing v layer. Within this framework, (4a) can be interpreted as 'I had a sight of that man', where 'that man' is the possessor or locator of the sight sub-event.[3] However, this sensitivity to the two-layered v-V structure characterizes only highly ranked referents. In contrast, indefinite or inanimate complements are embedded as accusative themes, as seen in structure (5a) for sentence (5a). In (5), 'see' functions as a single predicate, while its lowly-ranked complement does not display sensitivity to the presence of sub-events or states.

(5) a. sɔ   vvistə n ɔmə
      I.am seen   a man
      'I saw a man.'   *Canosa di Puglia*

  b. [$_{vP}$ v [$_{VP}$ vvistə [$_{DP}$ n ɔmə]]]

Based on the analysis presented here, languages featuring Differential Object Markers (DOMs) are those in which an argument with highly ranked referential properties must fulfill a role at least as prominent as that of the 'possessor' of the event and cannot be embedded solely as bare themes. This concept is illustrated in (6).

(6) DOM
    [$_{VP}$ ... [*(⊆) DP] ...] *where DP is highly ranked*
                      (subject to parametric variation, cf. Manzini et al. 2020)

This approach prompts several questions, primarily whether Differential Object Marking (DOM) can be universally linked to obliquization, and secondarily, what occurs in languages where DOM-marked objects are represented by an oblique

---

3. Note that Svenonius (2002) employs the internal articulation of the predicate in a different manner to predict datives with unergatives.

devices other than the dative (cf. Franco & Manzini 2017a,b), which we intend to explore in of the present work.

Franco & Manzini (2017b) extend the part-whole/inclusion proposal to another oblique item commonly expressed as a case inflection in natural languages (Caha, 2009), namely the instrumental case; in English, the instrumental is typically lexicalized by the preposition "with". Here, we use the umbrella term "instrumental" to encompass all semantic roles that can be denoted by "with"-like morphemes (cf. Stolz et al., 2006). Our starting point is Levinson's (2011) observation that possession relations may be indicated by "with", as exemplified in (7). The relation in (7) differs from that in (1)–(2), as the preposition "with" embeds the possessum, while the possessor serves as the head of the DP.

(7)   The woman **with** the children

Franco & Manzini (2017b) assume that instrumental inflections/adpositions signify the inverse relationship compared to genitives/datives, where the possessum, rather than the possessor, is in the oblique case. Therefore, for instrumentals, they employ the ($\supseteq$) label and content, as depicted in (8). Essentially, (8) indicates that the complement of "with" ('the children') is the possessum (a part) of the possessor (the whole) 'the woman'.

(8)   [$_{DP}$ the woman [$_{PP(\supseteq)}$ **with** the children]]

They also argue that with-type morphemes offer fundamental mechanisms for incorporating (i.e., including) additional participants (themes, initiators, etc.) into events (VP or vP predicates) – with specific interpretations derived through pragmatic enrichment (contextual, encyclopedic) at the Conceptual-Intentional interface.[4] They extend this proposition to explain the observation that instrumentals can be used cross-linguistically in triadic verb constructions, alternating with datives, as exemplified in (9) and (10) with English and Persian examples, respectively.

---

4. We assume a relevance-theoretic perspective on the notion of 'pragmatic enrichment' (Sperber and Wilson, 1995), positing that natural language expressions typically do not directly target fully specified concepts (*akin* to those in the language of thought). Instead, they guide the hearer in constructing an *ad hoc* concept specific to the occasion, thereby facilitating particular inferential effects relevant to that context. Verbal concepts, especially, rely on their complements within the verb phrase for interpretation, and the propositional structure conveyed by an utterance is established only once the concept addressed by the verb has been appropriately delineated for the given situation. Thus, the resolution of verbal *underspecification* is highly pragmatic, entailing both the refinement of the addressed concept and the evaluation of hypotheses generated through concept activation. This highlights how the lexicon, structural syntactic processes, and pragmatic inferences interplay in the interpretation of utterances (see also Marten, 2002).

(9) a.   He presented his pictures **to** the museum   [dative]
     b.   He presented the museum **with** his pictures   [instrumental]

(10) a.   Pesar sang-ro   **be** sag zad   [dative]
          boy   stone-DOM to dog hit.PST.3SG
          'The boy hit the dog with the stone'
     b.   Pesar sag-ro   **ba** sang zad   [instrumental]
          boy   dog-DOM with stone hit.PST.3SG
          'The boy hit the dog with the stone'

Franco & Manzini (2017b) also explain dative/instrumental syncretism, potentially including DOM objects, by arguing that the inclusion predicate (⊆) corresponding to 'to' or the dative case and its reverse (⊇), corresponding to 'with' or the instrumental case, might reduce to an even more basic content capable of conveying inclusion in either direction.

The part-whole/inclusion (⊆) proposal for obliques has been further elaborated in Manzini & Franco (2016), Franco & Manzini (2017a, b), and Manzini et al. (2015; 2020) to address the observation that formally identical genitive/dative DPs exhibit different interpretive behaviors. Additionally, cross-linguistically, syntactico-semantic differences may lead to different lexicalization patterns. For instance, while with Goal datives, the (⊆) relator establishes a relation between two arguments (the goal and the theme), with experiencer datives, the (⊆) relator introduces a relation between an argument (the experiencer) and an event (the VP) (cf. Manzini & Franco 2016, p. 230–231). This aligns with the Applicative literature (cf. Pylkkänen, 2008; Cuervo, 2003), which suggests that the same Appl(icative) head (externalized by dative/oblique) can attach at different points in the syntactic tree (High Appl *vs.* Low Appl heads).

When evaluating the proposal/framework for obliques presented here, it's essential to consider the alternatives. One prominent alternative involves morphology-internal explanations, as seen in generative grammar with DM. Within this framework, Calabrese (2008) focuses on absolute syncretism, where certain cases/case oppositions are entirely absent in some languages. Calabrese suggests that functional categories are represented by abstract feature clusters in syntax, realized by actual exponents only at the PF interface. His key proposal posits a markedness hierarchy of cases, with lower cases in the hierarchy being more likely to be blocked. This results in surface syncretism, which is readjusted by the morphological component (including the DM key rule of Impoverishment).

In the Cartographic stream of studies, extended to morphology by Nanosyntax, Caha (2009) proposes that the Case hierarchy is represented in Universal Grammar (UG) by a hierarchy of syntactic Case heads. Caha argues that this syntactic hierarchy explains the observed patterns of syncretism, with only contiguous heads being realized by the same forms, given an *ABA constraint (cf. Bobaljik, 2012; Franco, 2013, among others).

However, these approaches, while manipulating the notion of markedness hierarchy, do not analyze traditional cases or the traditional notion of case itself. Conversely, we aim to approach obliques (inflectional, prepositional, or others) while keeping Chomsky's (2001a) conclusions on the non-primitive nature of case in mind. Oblique case denotes elementary predicative content ('includes'/'is included by') when realized inflectionally on a noun. Consequently, there is no externally imposed hierarchy ordering the relevant primitives, but rather a conceptual network determined by the primitive predicates we use and the relations they establish with each other. Therefore, case hierarchies reduce to a binary split between direct case (reduced to the agreement system, cf. Chomsky, 2001a) and oblique case, which reduces to the part-whole operator. Other so-called cases can be analyzed into a case core (typically oblique) and additional structure, yielding something akin to the internally articulated PPs of Svenonius (2006) (cf. Franco et al. 2017 and Chapter 4 of this book), who syntactically reinterprets Talmy's (2000) Gestalt-like perspective.

1.3   Elementary predicates beyond categories

It is reasonable to assume that lexical contents (properties) are organized into subsets and supersets. Typical examples include natural kinds, where the lexicon of natural languages (presumably directly reflecting the organization of the conceptual system) names both specific and less specific kinds (e.g., Siamese, cat, etc.); a similar organization can be detected in predicates (e.g., slice, chop vs. cut). When it comes to properties externalized by so-called functional categories, the same subset/superset organization is generally accepted. For instance, in the organization of persons, speaker and hearer denotation are included in the superset participant, underlying possible morphological neutralization or syncretism (cf. Manzini et al. (2015), on Indo-Aryan). We have argued above that natural class syncretisms, highlighting a subset/superset organization of the functional lexicon, can be detected where traditional morphological approaches see only ad hoc rules. If we are correct, and there is a much larger set of syncretisms on natural classes than detected with traditional methods, this further supports our claim that the distinction between the substantive and functional lexicon is currently overstated.

The part-whole relation applies in a natural way both to inclusion proper, hence to the partitive, and to possession. Inherent possession (e.g., possession of a body part) is, in fact, best described as a part-whole relation. For material possession, we invoke the idea of 'zonal inclusion,' used by Belvin & den Dikken (1997) to characterize the verbal predicate 'have'. Therefore, the genitive case is an elementary predicate, expressing relational content very much as its adpositional counterpart 'of' or the verb 'have'. We have already seen that the $(\subseteq)/(\supseteq)$ content is predicative, and it can be realized by adposition or by nominal inflections (case). The $(\subseteq)$ content is a primitive of grammar, but it is not a case or a preposition; it is an elementary predicate. For instance, the inflectional realization of the $(\subseteq)$ predicate is conventionally called a case. But in present terms, case is definable at most as the crossing of the more elementary notions of atomic predicate and inflectional realization. As originally argued in Fillmore (1968), we see no differences between (oblique) cases and adpositions (cf. Manzini & Franco, 2016; Franco & Manzini, 2017b; Franco et al., 2015b).

In this work, which has a broad cross-linguistic focus, we will concentrate on the encoding of oblique/non-core participant at the clausal level. In Chapter 2, we will show that (serial) light verbs pattern with adpositions and case in realizing the $(\subseteq)$ predicate, which introduces obliques. In a word, we will show that $(\subseteq)$ predicates can be (light) verbs. That's why many authors (Svenonius, 2007; Wood, 2015; Franco, 2016, 2020; Franco et al., 2017, among others) envisage a strict syntactic parallelism between the category *Preposition* and the category *Verb*.

In our research, we provide a systematic description and analysis of relational light verbs, showing that the patterns of syncretism commonly attested for case/adpositions (e.g. comitative/instrumental, etc.) are replicated in the realm of serial verbs, for those languages employing such an oblique device. An analysis of this kind at least to our knowledge – is missing within the contemporary formal literature. Here, we show that the verbs most commonly used to introduce oblique participants are the light predicates *give* and *take*, precisely expressing transfer of possession/inclusion. We will focus on Pidgin and Creole languages. A series of relevant examples is provided below.

In many languages, the verb *give* lexicalizes both datives and benefactives. Consider the examples below from Thai (11) where *hâj* 'give', introduce datives and benefactives (cf. Muysken, 1999; Heine & Kuteva, 2002, for other relevant cross-linguistic examples).

(11) Dɛɛŋ sɔɔn lêeg   **hâj** Sùdaa **hâj** phyan.
      Dang teach arithmetic give Suda   give friend
      'Dang taught arithmetic to Suda for his friend.'   *Thai* (Bisang 1998, p.771)

Other languages encode the dative content only with the verb for *give*, as in Modern Mandarin Chinese (12).

(12) wo xie le yi-feng xin **gei** ta.
    1SG write ASP one-class letter to him
    'I wrote him a letter.'   *Modern Mandarin Chinese*

Mono-argumental (intransitive) datives can also be introduced by *give*, as shown in (24) for the Portuguese based creole São Tomense.

(13) e fa **da** ine.
    he talk give them
    'He talked to them.'
                    São Tomense CP (Romaine, 1988, p 56, *apud* Heine & Kuteva, 2002)

As expected under Franco and Manzini's (2017b) proposal, instrumental (and comitative) relations are usually lexicalized by *take* (namely, the inverse counter-part of *give*). Consider the Lahu (14), and Twi (15) examples below.

(14) yɔ á-cu-ka **yù** lɛ gɔ-cá câ ve
    3SG chopstick take part cabbage eat part
    'He eats cabbage with chopsticks.'   *Lahu* (Matisoff, 1991, p.434)

(15) o-**de** né nnípa fòro bépow.
    he-take his men ascend mountain
    'He ascends a mountain with his men.'   *Twi* (Lord, 1989, p.136)

What is more, that Manzini & Franco (2016) are on the right track in structurally encoding Patient DOM markers as relational predicates, can be grasped by the fact that Twi encodes DOM (definite) patients, with the same *take* (de) mor-pheme, as in (16).

(16) o-**de**   afoa ce boha-m.
    he-(take) sword put scabbard-inside
    'He put the sword into the scabbard.'   *Twi* (Lord, 1989, p.136)

This process appears to be quite productive in natural languages. For instance, Chappell (2015) has shown that DOM patients can be marked by "take" and "give" verbs in the micro-variation of Sinitic languages.

   In short, our aim is to provide a formal approach to such cross-categorial variation in argument marking, attempting to outline a unified morpho-syntactic template in which so-called 'cases' do not configure a specialized linguistic lexicon of functional features/categories. On the contrary, they help us outline an under-lying ontology of natural languages, from which they derive some of the most ele-mentary relations. Such primitive relations can be expressed by different lexical means (case, adpositions, light verbs, etc.). Evidence supporting our approach is illustrated by the fact that in many Romance varieties, there are predicates that effectively exclude (adpositional) DOM. In particular, possession verbs like "have," as illustrated in the Southern Italian dialect of Cirò Marina. Here, "tenere" ('have') excludes DOM (17b), while "tenere" ('hold') displays DOM with definite human objects in (17a).

(17) a. tɛnənə   a   kkirə ɣwaɲɲunə
        they.hold DOM those boys
        'They are holding those boys'
     b. tɛnənə   kirə ɣwaɲɲunə
        they.have those boys
        'Those boys are their sons'

It is natural to speculate that the pattern in (18) depends on the fact that the content of the verb "have" is the 'reverse' of the content of the dative preposition/ case (cf. Svenonius 2007, 2008). Since we have denoted the latter as (⊆), we may suggest (⊇) as the content of "have," as schematically indicated in (18). It would seem, therefore, that the grammar avoids duplication of the possession structure – or perhaps specifically the combination of the dative inclusion relator and its reverse. Recall that according to Franco & Manzini (2017b), (⊇) is also the content of instrumentals and comitatives, as externalized by the preposition "with" (Italian "con"). Most transparently, "the girl with a hat" expresses the same relation between the two arguments as "the girl has a hat" – which reverses the dative (or genitive) relation: "(give) a hat to the girl" or "the hat of the girl."

(18)   [$_{VP⊇}$ tɛnənə [(*P⊆) kirə ɣwaɲɲunə]]

Easily, this unified approach extends to applicative morphemes, which are the topic of Chapter 3. In his comprehensive typological survey, Peterson (2007, p.130ff) demonstrates that applicatives are frequently lexicalized by verbal morphemes whose core meanings are 'give' or 'take'. On the topic of *cross-categorial* syncretism, we will consider applicative-causative syncretism, which is a pattern of morpheme polysemy attested in many different natural languages. We will focus on data from P'orhépecha, an isolate language spoken in Mexico.

We interpret the causative-applicative syncretism as based on a shared syntactic configuration. Specifically, we argue that the syncretic morpheme under investigation is the 'applicative' counterpart of an adpositional/case elementary relator (Manzini & Franco, 2016; Franco & Manzini, 2017a, b), attaching instrumental or benefactive obliques (High Applicatives, cf. Pylkkänen, 2002, 2008) to the verbal spine. We follow Bellucci (2017) and Manzini & Savoia (2018) in assuming that causees in causative constructions can be introduced as obliques, linked to the same structural position as High Appls. The causative reading of the sentence is driven by interpretive means (cf. Franco & Manzini 2017a, b). This readily explains the possibility of encoding causative and applicatives with the same lexical items.

Incidentally, P'orhépecha provides evidence for a 'contentive' approach to grammatical relations. In various languages, body terms (prototypical part-whole devices) are recruited from the lexicon to encode oblique 'case-like' morphemes (cf. Heine & Kuteva, 2002). Hence, not only (serial) verbs, but also relational nouns, can be recruited from the lexicon to express elementary part-whole inclusion predicates. Capistrán Garza (2015, p.17ff) illustrates the morphosyntactic direct arguments in P'orhépecha that are introduced by a zero-marked nominative or by the 'objective' marker -ni, as shown in (20).

(20)   *P'orhépecha*
       tumpí eshé-s-Ø-ti   maríkwa-**ni**
       boy   see-PRF-PRS-3IND   girl-OBJ
       'The boy saw the girl.'

P'orhépecha has DOM, subject to animacy/definiteness parameters, as illustrated with the contrast in (21).

(21)   *P'orhépecha*
       a. xí xúska-s-Ø-ka   xáasï
           1SG sow-PRF-PRS-1/2IND broad.bean
           'I sowed broad bean(s).'
       b. Lúpi xwá-s-Ø-ti   chíiti   tsúntsu*(-**ni**)
           Lupe bring-PRF-PRS-3IND   2SG.POSS   pot-OBJ
           'Lupe brought your pot.'

The same marking is employed for arguments with a goal-like role, as in (22), replicating the widespread Indo-European DOM=DAT pattern illustrated in Manzini & Franco (2016).

(22)   *P'orhépecha*
       Pédru íntsku-s-Ø-ti   wíchu-**ni** Lúpi-**ni**
       Pedro give-PRF-PRS-3IND   dog-OBJ   Lupe-OBJ
       'Pedro gave Lupe the dog.'

Actually, the same *ni* is employed to express the lexical item 'chest'/'cavity', namely it convey a (relational, part-whole) body-part meaning. Very interestingly, this morpheme may also denote (*applied* as a verbal affix) a 'part of' the argument encoded in subject function, as in (23a, b), or 'an area of' the place where this argument is or becomes located, as in (23c).

(23)   *P'orhépecha*
       a. María p'á-**ni**-s-Ø-ti
           Maria touch-cavity-PRF-PRS-3IND
           'Maria touched her breast.'

   b. ṕorhóta xawá-**ni**-s-Ø-ti
      hole   deepen-cavity-PRF-PRS-3IND
      'The hole is deep.'
   c. xí   wekó-**ni**-s-Ø-ka   kawáru
      1SG fall-cavity-PRF-PRS-1/2IND ditch
      'I fell into the ditch.'

Therefore, our working hypothesis suggests that the map of functional categories needs to be redefined. This entails the recognition that the functional lexicon is not predetermined in the universal (computational) component of syntax. Rather, functional categories originate from the same conceptual inventory as lexical ones. They externalize properties and relations that are not fundamentally distinct from those expressed by the substantive lexicon. However, these properties and relations are typically more elementary, thus delineating the conceptual universe into broader classes compared to the exponents of lexical categories.

Chapter 4 precisely focuses on relational nouns (and, particularly, body terms), targeting so-called Axial Parts (cf. Svenonius, 2006, and subsequent literature) in the spatial domain and beyond. Basing on Franco et al. (2021) we show that location in languages is often externalized by the same cases/adpositions introducing genitive, dative, instrumental, i.e. non-spatial obliques (Blake, 2001; Caha 2009, 2017) and that there are two possible ways of accounting for this coincidence in the syntax (clearly, avoiding the conclusion that a mere morphological/accidental syncretism is involved): either the spatial meaning is primitive (Freeze, 1992; Den Dikken, 1995, among many others) and the relational/part whole meaning is derived – or vice versa (Levinson, 2011; Myler, 2014, 2016). We will provide evidence for the second approach. We will argue in favour of a derived status for locatives, by showing that locative properties, such as motion *vs.* state or directionality, cannot be part of the core meaning of Ps. Rather Ps are general relators, and the locative interpretation depends on their context of embedding (see Svenonius, 2002; Grimm, 2012). We will provide a set of crosslinguistic data, starting from the Uralic family (for which see also Franco et al., 2017), in support of our hypothesis.

Chapter 5 provides a comprehensive comparative overview of existential sentences in Romance-based Creoles. Based on our empirical findings, we offer a theoretical analysis of existential constructions that mimic 'transitive' possession. Specifically, we assume that the prevalence of a predicative possession strategy for existentials in Creoles is reflected in their syntax, wherein a possession configuration will be drawn. Essentially, we argue that the *contextual domain* of existentials (see Francez, 2007; 2009) can be encoded as the possessor of a (transitive) HAVE predicate (cf. Examples (17) and (18) above), including the *pivot* as its internal argument (cf. Manzini & Savoia, 2005), with the *coda*, which is optionally introduced as an adjunct, encoding a further possessor ('locative' inclusor) of the predicate (cf. McNally, 1992).

In the last two chapters of this work, we will focus on the morphosyntax of the DP, mainly focusing on Italian data. Drawing from Franco et al. (2015a), Manzini & Savoia (2017a, b, 2018), we adopt a nominal morphosyntactic framework for Italian/Romance, positing a category-less root ($\sqrt{}$) as the initial component, as proposed by Marantz (1997, 2007). Following the root ($\sqrt{}$), various types of morphemes, including derivational and inflectional ones, are positioned. Typically, inflectional morphemes succeed derivational suffixes. The root is construed as a predicate with an open argument place (the R-role), as discussed by Williams (1994), ultimately bound by a determiner or quantifier operator (as per Higginbotham, 1985). Gender and number specifications, referred to as Class, act upon the open argument x at the predicate. We hypothesize that they function as predicates themselves, constraining the content of the argumental variable, eventually governed by a determiner or quantifier.

Manzini and Savoia propose that the inflectional vowel in Italian occupies an Infl(ection) position, embedding the root ($\sqrt{}$) and the Class nodes, which encode gender ([feminine], [masculine], etc.) or number specifications ([singular], [plural], etc.). The content of the plural, as we have already pointed out, is conceptualized as the relation part-whole [⊆], signifying that the denotatum of the predicate can be partitioned into subsets[5] (cf. Manzini & Savoia, 2011a and

---

5. As stated in Champollion & Krifka (2016): "*One of the principal applications of mereology in semantics is the characterization of oppositions such as count-mass and singular-plural in terms of higher-order properties. For example, various authors have identified the properties of mass and plural terms like gold and horses with the notions of cumulative reference: if two things are gold then their sum is also gold (Quine, 1960), and if you add some horses to some other horses then you again get some horses (Link, 1983).*" Incidentally, one could apply the part-whole proposal to the Italian 'partitive' determiner *del/dei* (*dammi del pane* 'give me some bread', *ho visto dei ragazzi* 'I have seen (some) boys') assuming that the homophony with the Italian genitive adposition is far from being accidental (*contra* Cardinaletti & Giusti 2016). Indeed, the partitive determiner in Italian picks up solely (indefinite) plural and mass (*cumulative* entities in the sense of Quine 1960). Actually, mass and plural expressions show some interesting similarities, suggesting they should be analyzed in a similar way (cf. Franco et al., 2020). Chierchia (1998a, 1998b) claims that mass nouns are essentially just lexical plurals, so that the part/whole relation on the *denotata* of mass nouns coincides with the subset relation on the denotata of plurals. Savoia et al (2017), Franco et al. (2020) explored the shape of *singulatives*, which are morphemes that turn mass terms into count nouns (cf. Corbett, 2011; Grimm, 2012), cross-linguistically, exploring the morphosyntactic implications of their widespread syncretism with evaluative (diminutive) morphemes (Jurafsky 1996, Ott 2011, De Belder 2011, among others). Cross-linguistically, there are morphemes which act as the mirror image of singulatives, turning count nouns intro (aggregate) mass terms. Again, such morphemes exhibit quite often the same lexicalization as evaluative morphemes (in Romance, Bantu, Semitic languages). The fact that

subsequent literature). A schematic representation of their model is depicted in (24) for the nominal items *gatt-o/i* 'male cat/cats' and *gatta-a/e* 'female cat/cats'.

(24)   [[[*gatt* √] [fem]/[masc] Class] [ç] Infl *-a -e -i -o*]

Additionally, building on the insights of Borer (2003, 2014) and the findings of Savoia et al. (2017), we posit that identical lexical content can be conveyed through both inflectional and derivational morphemes, as well as through stand-alone lexical items. This phenomenon is observed in Romance languages, where inflectional morphemes have the capacity to introduce properties typically associated with derivational processes and vice versa. For example, they can induce category changes and denote size properties, as evidenced by contrasts such as *melo* 'apple tree'/*mela* 'apple' and *buco* 'hole'/*buca* 'pit' (cf. Franco et al., 2015a, 2020; Manzini, 2020).

Chapter 6 provides a unified characterization of Italian ethnic adjectives, assuming that the derivational morphemes shaping this kind of items are a derivational counterpart of the genitive adposition *di* (of) (and other kinds of obliques). The proposal advanced for ethnic adjectives can be broadly extended to relational adjectives in general (and to qualifying possessive adjectives).

Finally, in Chapter 7, we examine the interplay between evaluative morphology and kinship terms introduced by possessive adjectives in Italian. Our analysis reveals that the application of evaluative affixes influences the syntactic context in which kinship terms can be utilized; specifically, they cannot be introduced by a bare determiner when evaluative morphemes attach to the lexical root. We contend that this seemingly trivial empirical observation carries significant theoretical implications. The 'alteration' of the syntactic environment by derivational morphemes, such as evaluatives, lends support to the theoretical framework illustrated above, in which Merge operates on morphemes as its input, and individual morphemes are fully accessible to the syntactic computation.

---

there exist morphemes which are able (inflectionally, derivationally) to turn count nouns into mass terms is not without implication, as it weakens Borer (2005) assumption that countability is (exclusively) shaped by grammar in a constructionist fashion and that all nouns born mass in the lexicon (cf. Mathieu, 2012).

CHAPTER 2

Oblique serial verbs in Creole/Pidgin languages and beyond

This chapter focuses on the syntax of (argument introducing/valency increasing) serial verbs in Creole/Pidgin languages, providing empirical arguments for the model of grammatical relations advanced in a series of recent works by Manzini and Savoia (2011a, 2011b), Manzini and Franco (2016), Franco and Manzini (2017a,b), Manzini et al. (2015, 2020). These authors lay out an analysis of the syntax and interpretation of dative *to*, instrumental *with* and Differential Object Marking (DOM) relators, based on the assumption that these elements are predicates endowed with an elementary interpretive content interacting with the internal organization of the event. We assume that these oblique relators, expressing a primitive elementary part-whole/possession relation, may be instantiated also by serial (light) verbs in the grammar of natural languages. We provide a formal approach to cross-categorial variation in argument marking, trying to outline a unified morpho-syntactic template, in which so-called 'cases' do not configure a specialized linguistic lexicon of functional features/categories – on the contrary they help us outline an underlying ontology of natural languages, of which they pick up some of the most elementary relations. Such primitive relations can be expressed by different lexical means (e.g. case, adpositions, light verbs, etc.).

2.1 Serial light verbs as relators

Our main aim is to describe the syntax of (argumental) serial verbs of the type represented in (1) in Creole/Pidgin languages, providing empirical support for the model of grammatical relations advanced in a series of recent works by Manzini & Savoia (2011a, b), Franco et al. (2015b, 2021), Manzini et al. (2015), Manzini & Franco (2016), Franco & Manzini (2017a, b), Franco & Lorusso (2020, 2022), Rugna & Franco (2022), among others.

As we have seen in the Introduction, these authors lay out an analysis of the syntax and interpretation of obliques (genitive *of*, dative *to*, instrumental *with*, and Differential Object Marking (DOM) relators), based on the assumption that these elements are endowed with an elementary interpretive content (inclusion, part-whole, possession) interacting with the internal organization of the predicate/event. We focus on (light) serial verbs used as 'valency-increasing' devices (encoding benefactives, instrumentals, comitatives, etc.) and/or employed for specifying arguments, that is, to introduce (DOM) direct objects and indirect goal/recipient arguments in ditransitive constructions. In the definition of Aikhenvald (2006, p.1), *"A serial verb construction is a sequence of verbs which act together as a single predicate, without any overt marker of coordination, subordination, or syntactic dependency of any other sort [...] They are monoclausal; their intonational properties are the same as those of a monoverbal clause, and they have just one tense, aspect, and polarity value"*.

(1)   a.   Kêdê mêzê ê   ka xikêvê kata ũa **da** mi
           every month 3sg HAB write   letter one give me
           'Every month, he writes me a letter.'   *Principense* (Maurer, 2009, p.111)
      b.   Zon **toma** faka va   mpon.
           3sg take   knife slice bread
           'Zon sliced the bread with a knife.' *São Tomense* (Hagemeijer, 2000, p.45)

Our main idea is that the same elementary interpretive content (inclusion, part-whole, possession) proposed by the aforementioned stream of literature for obliques can be instantiated through (light) serial verb constructions. Indeed, the serial verbs in (1), taken from two Portuguese-based Creoles of West Africa, are light verbs with a fundamental meaning of 'transfer' of possession (GIVE/TAKE). In other words, we posit that oblique cases and adpositions serve as (language-specific) relational devices used to introduce oblique arguments (cf. Fillmore, 1968). There is nothing to prevent a given language from utilizing a serial (light) verb as a relational predicate for this purpose. We assume that the underlying syntax remains the same.

Formally, our aim is to propose an approach to cross-categorial variation in (oblique) argument marking, attempting to delineate a unified morpho-syntactic template in which so-called 'cases' or 'adpositions' do not constitute a specialized linguistic lexicon of functional features/categories – on the contrary, they aid in outlining an underlying *ontology* of natural languages, capturing some of the most fundamental relations. Such primitive relations can be expressed through various lexical means: case, adpositions, light verbs, applicatives, etc.

We briefly summarize below the core proposal, already outlined in the Introduction. In illustrating the model of grammatical relations proposed by Manzini, Franco & Savoia, we begin with the encoding of datives. Regarding dative "to," the line of analysis of ditransitive verbs initiated by Kayne (1984) posits that verbs like "give" take as their complement a predication whose content is a possession headed by "to." Following in part the works of Kayne (1984), Pesetsky (1995), Beck & Johnson (2004), and Harley (2002), we may state that in (2), a possession relation exists between the dative (Mary) and the theme of the ditransitive verb (the book). We characterize the content of "to" in terms of the notion of '(zonal) inclusion,' as proposed by Belvin & den Dikken (1997) for the verbal item "HAVE". We equate this content to an elementary part/whole predication and represent it as $\subseteq$, so that (2a) is structured as in (2b). In (2b), the result of the causative event is that the book is included by (possessed by) Mary.

(2) a. I give the book **to** Mary
     b. [$_{VP}$ give [$_{PredP}$ the book [[$_{\subseteq}$ **to**] Mary]]]]

In the tradition of studies in (2), the alternation between Dative Shift (as in "I give Mary the book") and DP-to-DP structures is not derived, but rather reflects an alternation between two distinct base structures. In many theoretical works, the head of the predication postulated by Kayne for English double object constructions is an abstract version of the verb 'have'.[6] Franco & Manzini (2017b) propose that this abstract "HAVE" head, assumed for Dative Shift, is the covert counterpart of 'with'. Indeed, the preposition "with" can overtly appear in English alternations of the type represented in (3).

(3) a. I entrusted the key **to** my neighbor.
     b. I entrusted my neighbor **with** the key.
     c. She assigned the task **to** her assistant.
     d. She assigned her assistant **with** the task.
     e. He awarded the prize **to** the winner.
     f. He awarded the winner **with** the prize.
     g. They allocated the budget **to** the department.
     h. They allocated the department **with** the budget.

Therefore, it is possible to propose the structure in (4) for (3b), mirroring the one in (2). We represent the relation expressed by "with" as ($\supseteq$), assuming that the possessum is the complement of P and the possessor is its external argument. In fact, we encounter a relation that is the 'mirror image' of dative structures where the possessor is the complement of "P$\subseteq$" and the possessum is its external argument.

(4) [$_{VP}$ entrust [$_{PredP}$ my neighbor [[$\supseteq$ **with**] the key]]]]

---

6. For instance, for Harley (2002) the head of the predication in an English Dative Shift sentence is an abstract preposition P$_{HAVE}$, for Beck & Johnson (2004), the head of the predication is an abstract verb HAVE. Pesetsky (1995) limits himself to an abstract characterization of the predicate head as G.

For the purpose of our work, it is relevant to consider that in Romance languages (as in Indo-European, more generally), the dative adposition/case is the preferred form for externalizing DOM objects (Bossong, 1985; Aissen, 2003; Malchukov, 2008; Manzini & Franco 2016, among others). We provide just one example from standard Spanish in (5a). According to Manzini and Franco (2016), the syncretism of dative and DOM is based on the fact that the same lexical content ⊆ is instantiated in both contexts, as observed in structure (5b) for sentence (5a). In other words, object DPs that are highly ranked in animacy/definiteness require the same elementary predicate ⊆ to introduce goals/recipients. Indeed, as seen in (2b), the arguments of ⊆ are the two DPs, respectively *Mary* and *the book*, with the former possessing the latter as a result of the event of *giving*. In (5b), on the other hand, one of the two arguments of ⊆ is again its object DP "el" (him) – however, it is not clear what its external argument might be.

Manzini & Franco (2016) adhere to the standard idea of (Hale & Keyser, 1993, 2002), Chomsky (1995), who propose that transitive predicates result from the incorporation of an elementary state/event into a transitivizing "v" layer. Within such a framework, (5b) can be interpreted as 'He/She causes him to have a call', where 'him' is the possessor of the 'call' sub-event. Therefore, the ⊆ relation holds for a DP (*el*) and for an elementary event 'the call' (see Torrego, 2010; Pineda, 2014 for different implementations of the same basic idea).

(5) *Spanish*
    a. lo/le llama   **a** el
          him s/he.calls to him
          'S/he calls him'
    b. $[_{vP} \, v \, [_{VP} \text{llama} \, [_{PP⊆} \, \textbf{a} \, [_{DP} \text{el}]]]]$

It is important to consider that this syntactic/configurational characterization of syncretism (here DOM=dative) substantially diverges from the views of current realizational frameworks within the realm of theoretical morphosyntax. For instance, in Distributed Morphology (DM), which represents the standard morphology framework in generative grammar, syncretisms result from the application of morphological rules after the output of the syntax, but before lexical insertion. The argument has been made more than once (Kayne, 2010, p.171; Manzini & Savoia 2011a) that the morphological rules of DM are powerful enough to generate essentially any lexical string from any underlying syntactic structure. Markedness hierarchies (Calabrese 1998, 2008) offer an interesting response to non-accidental syncretism patterns – since contiguity in lexicalization is made to depend on contiguity in the hierarchy. However, they face the same problem as any extrinsic ordering device: *is there any internal reason for the ordering?* Much the same can be said of the nanosyntactic Case hierarchy of Caha (2009) or Pantcheva (2011) (cf. Starke, 2017). On the contrary, we approach obliques (inflectional/prepositional, etc.) with Chomsky's (2001a) conclusions on the non-primitive nature of case in mind. Oblique case is the name given to elementary predicative content when realized inflectionally on a noun. Correspondingly, syncretism depends on shared content, namely ⊆/⊇ in the instances discussed, and there is no externally imposed hierarchy ordering the relevant primitives, but rather a conceptual network determined by the primitive predicates we use and the relations they entertain with each other. Calabrese's markedness hierarchies or nanosyntactic functional hierarchies are not necessary because syncretism depends essentially on *natural class* (cf. Müller, 2007). Seen from this perspective, case hierarchies take on rather different contours.

In essence, they reduce to a binary split between direct case (reduced to the agreement system as in Chomsky, 2001a) and oblique case, reduced to the part-whole operator, whose lexicalization can be sensitive to the c-commanding relation between the possessor and the possessum.[7]

In this chapter, we essentially argue that serial (light) verbs in Creole languages may function as ⊆/⊇ relators, providing support for the model of grammatical relations outlined in the Introduction. Crucially, the model we are interested in distinctly predicts that paradigms do not exist within the competence of speaker-hearers; in other words, linguistic data are organized in a non-paradigmatic fashion – just like generative syntax never quite achieves a match to traditional constructions such as *passive* or *ergative*, etc (see Manzini et al., 2015, Manzini, 2017). Primitives are too finely grained, and the combinatorial possibilities afforded by Universal Grammar are too numerous to perfectly align with descriptive (macro)classes.[8]

The remainder of the chapter is structured as follows. In Section 2.2, we introduce some basic features of serial verb constructions, focusing particularly on their function as oblique devices. In Section 2.3, we examine the morphosyntax of ditransitive structures in certain Creole/Pidgin languages that utilize serial verbs for their encoding, as well as the expression of instrumental (and comitative) relations through TAKE predicates. We demonstrate that the syntactic and morpho-lexical regularities observed in the expression of these grammatical rela-

---

7. From this perspective, other non-core (spatial) cases are analysable into a case core (typically oblique) and some additional structure, yielding something similar to the internally articulated PPs of Svenonius (2006) (cf. also Franco et al., 2017), who (syntactically) reworks the Gestalt-like perspective of Talmy (2000). See Chapter 4 for relevant discussion.

8. The concept is quite straightforward, although Chomsky has reiterated it numerous times in the context of syntax (Chomsky 1981). However, what may not be widely recognized is that this principle should also apply to morphology and morpho-lexical variation.

tions in Creoles/Pidgins provide strong support for the framework of (oblique) case/adpositions outlined earlier. Section 2.4 briefly discusses the phenomenon of DOM serial verbs.

2.2 Background on serial verbs constructions

Serial verb constructions are widespread not only in Creole languages but also in the languages of West Africa, Southeast Asia, Amazonia, Oceania, and New Guinea (Aikhenvald, 2006). Muysken and Veenstra (1995, p.290) provide a schematic illustration of a series of definitional criteria to identify a serial verb construction. They argue that such constructions must contain two (or more) verbs that: (i) share only one external argument subject; (ii) have at most one expressed direct object; (iii) have one specification for TAM and only one possible negative item; (iv) lack intervening coordinating conjunctions or subordinating particles; (v) have no intervening pauses. Therefore, serial verb constructions consist of sequences of verbs that function together as a single predicate, without any overt markers of coordination, complementation, or other types of syntactic dependency (see Jansen et al., 1978; Zwicky, 1990; Aikhenvald, 2006; Muysken & Veenstra, 2006, among others).

Indeed, serial verb constructions are frequently represented in the formal literature (cf. Lefebvre, 1991; Aboh, 2009, among others) as mono-clausal. This is because they exhibit the intonational properties of a clausal unit, and all the verbs involved share the same TAM values.[9] Interestingly, as reported in Muysken & Veenstra (1995) and Aikhenvald (2006), generally one verb is fixed (usually it is a light verb), while the other can be freely selected from a certain semantic or aspectual class. In (6), adapted from Muysken & Veenstra (1995), we outline the main functions of the light verbs recruited in serial verb constructions:

(6)   locational   *go*   direction away (allative)
                     come   direction towards (ablative)
                     be/stay   locative
       argument   *give*   benefactive, dative, object
                     take   instrumental, comitative, object
                     say   finite complementizer

---

9. Some authors have assumed a correlation between the availability of serial verbs construction in a given grammar and the lack of derivational verbal morphology. Baker (1991, p.79) explicitly says that: *"Notions which are expressed by Serial Verb Constructions [...] in the Kwa languages of West Africa correspond to a large degree to those which are expressed by derivational verb morphology in the Bantu languages of East Africa".*

aspectual	*finish*	perfective
	return	iterative
	be/stay	continuative
degree	*pass*	comparative
	suffice	enough

As previously mentioned, argument (or valency-increasing) serial verbs are the focus of the present chapter. We will exclusively concentrate on GIVE and TAKE serial verbs of the type illustrated in (1).

Stewart (1963) was the first to observe that overt subjects and objects in serial verb constructions are semantically related to both verbs. For instance, in (1a), the object 'letter' is an object of both the light predicate "give" and "write". Similarly, the pronoun "he" is the subject of both predicates. Baker (1989) addresses this observation from a theoretical viewpoint, assuming that verb serialization is a unified phenomenon based on 'argument sharing'.

In essence, Baker argues that the two verbs in a serial construction share the same subject and the same object (e.g., the DP "letter" in (1a)). The internal argument is theta-marked by both verbs. The first verb directly theta-marks the object NP under structural sisterhood, while the second verb theta-marks the same NP less directly, via predicational theta-marking.

Den Dikken (1991) and Muysken & Veenstra (1995) convincingly show that Baker's argument sharing hypothesis is untenable on empirical grounds. Consider, for instance, the data in (7)–(8), respectively from Haitian and Saramaccan.

(7) Jan **bay** Pol liv   la **bay** Mari.
     John give Paul book the give Mary
     'John gave the book to Paul for (to give to) Mary'
                              Haitian (Muysken & Veenstra, 1995, p.298)

(8) A   **de** wan bunu mujee **da** en.
     3sɢ be a   good woman give 3sɢ
     'She is a good woman for him.' *Saramaccan* (Muysken & Veenstra, 1995, p.298)

In (7), there is no subject argument sharing. Conceptually, here it is interpreted as 'it is John who gives the book to Paul, who gives the book to Mary'. In (8), the first verb ('be') does not license an object theta role, so argument sharing is blocked. Note that in the Applicative framework (Pylkkänen, 2008), both the participant introduced by the GIVE verb in the second position in (7) and (8) can be rendered as High Applicatives (beneficiaries, experiencers, cf. Section 3.1). Aboh (2009) argues that light serial verbs of the TAKE and GIVE type are merged into an aspectual projection within the functional domain of the matrix lexical verb.

We will address Aboh's proposal in more detail in Section 3.2, specifically focusing on instrumental TAKE serial verbs.[10]

Finally, we must note that a core point of our proposal, already made explicit in Section 1, is that there is a structural analogy between serial verbs and adpositions/oblique cases in natural languages. Muysken & Veenstra (1995) argue against this idea, relying on two empirical observations. First, serial verbs usually allow stranding, as illustrated in (9), while adpositions do not in many languages (including Creoles/Pidgin).

(9)   San Edgar **teki** ___ koti a brede?
      what Edgar take   cut the bread
      'What did Edgar cut the bread with?'

                              Sranan (Muysken & Veenstra, 1995, p. 292)

We believe that this argument is not decisive, especially considering that preposition stranding is allowed in various languages. Just consider an example from English in (10).

(10)   Who did you speak with __?

The second observation relies on the availability of 'predicate clefts' in Creole/Pidgin languages. Predicate clefts are constructions in which a copy of a verb appears in sentence-initial position (cf. Koopman 1984 and subsequent literature), as illustrated in (11).

(11)   Na **teki** Edgar **teki** a nefi koti a brede
       FOC take Edgar take the knife cut the bread
       'Really with the knife Edgar cut the bread.'

                              Sranan (Muysken & Veenstra, 1995, p. 292)

The primary function of predicate clefting is to emphasize the verbal action. Muysken & Veenstra (1995) assume that prepositions cannot undergo 'predicate cleft', thus highlighting an asymmetry between adpositional items and serial verbs. Indeed, there is evidence that light serial verbs of the TAKE and GIVE type disallow predicate clefting in many Romance-based creoles, as highlighted, for instance, in Hagemeijer & Ogie (2011) and Hagemeijer (2011) for the Portuguese-based Creole São Tomense. Furthermore, predicate clefting of (complex) adpositions and

---

10. Another proposal put forth by Seuren (1990) and Corne et al. (1996) is to consider serial verb constructions as covert (asyndetic) coordinate structures with two juxtaposed finite clauses. For instance, an example like (1b) would be rendered as 'He takes the knife and slices the bread'. However, Jansen et al. (1978), Sebba (1987) (cf. also Muysken & Veenstra, 1995; Collins, 1997; Syea, 2013, among others) demonstrate that serial verb constructions never display the island effects associated with coordinated structures since Ross (1967).

adverbial particles is possible in various Creoles/Pidgins, as shown in (12) with a Jamaican Creole example involving the item "bak" ('back'). Thus, we again believe that this argument is not robust enough to distinguish between (light) serial verbs and adpositions.

(12) A **bak** mi wind **bak** di kasset
      cop back 1SG wind back the cassette
      'I am putting the cassette back (i.e. not forward)'
                        Jamaican Creole (Veenstra & den Besten, 1994:308)

In assuming a clear symmetry between adpositions and verbs, we align with Svenonius (2007) and Wood (2015), who essentially argue that the only difference between adpositions and verbs is that the latter is endowed with a temporal dimension (i.e., a TP layer). Svenonius (2007, p. 83), citing Chinese as an example, claims that: "*in tenseless serial verb languages [...] it can be difficult to distinguish between verbs and prepositions.*" Building on this fundamental insight, in the next section, we will attempt to explain the syntactic behavior of argumental serial verbs in Creole/Pidgin languages.

2.3   Goal, benefactive and instrumental serial verbs in Creole/Pidgin languages: On the (a)symmetry of 'give' and 'take'

2.3.1   GIVE serial verb as ($\subseteq$) predicates

Invariantly, the serial light verb GIVE appears in the second position, following the lexical verb and the direct object, introducing the recipient/goal/beneficiary, as illustrated in (13) for several Creoles/Pidgins. The data in (13) demonstrate that this pattern appears consistently across different substrates and lexifiers.

(13) a. Amu da wan kuzu **da** bo
          I   give a   thing give you
          'I gave you something.'   *Fa d'Ambu* (Post, 1995, p. 200)
      b. Kêdê mêzê Maa ka xikêvê kata ũa **da** mi (= 1a)
          every month Maa HAB write   letter one give me
          'Every month Maa writes me a letter.'   *Principense* (Maurer, 2009, p. 121)
      c. Siera bai shuuz **gi** Taam
          Sarah buy shoes give Tom
          'Sarah bought shoes for Tom.'
                        Jamaican Creole (Farquharson, 2013 APiCS structure dataset, 8–135)

d. I   buy chok   **give** you.
    1SG buy congee give you
    'I buy/bought congee to you.'
                    Singlish (Lim & Ansaldo, 2013 APiCS structure dataset, 21–118)
e. Ijénie   ka   pòté   mango **ba**   Ijenn
    Eugénie PROG bring mango give Eugène
    'Eugénie is bringing the mangos to Eugène.'
                                    Guadeloupean Creole (Ludwig, 1996, p. 282)
f. am a   kan goi   mais mi   ris **gi**   sini
    3SG PST HAB throw corn with rice give 3PL
    'He threw corn and rice to him'
                            Negerholland (De Josselin de Jong, 1926, p. 18)

It is intuitively possible to argue that the serial verb GIVE serves as the counterpart of the dative preposition "to" and/or the benefactive preposition "for". However, these are not the sole uses of GIVE serial verbs, as they are also capable of encoding experiencers and mono-argumental (intransitive) datives in various languages, as illustrated respectively in (14) and (15) with examples from Ndyuka and São Tomense.

(14) A   nyanyan sweti **gi**   me tee
      DET food   please give me very.much
      'I like food very much'   *Ndyuka* (Goury & Migge, 2003, p. 131)

(15) e fa **da** ine.
      he talk give them
      'He talked to them.'
                    São Tomense (Romaine, 1988, p 56, *apud* Heine & Kuteva 2002)

Therefore, GIVE serial verbs seem to perfectly correspond to the contexts in which the dative preposition "a" of Romance languages appears, as illustrated in (16), with Italian data.

(16) *Italian*
      a. Ho dato un libro **a** Gianni   [dative]
          'I gave a book to Gianni'
      b. Ho comprato le scarpe **a**/**per** Gianni   [benefactive]
          'I bought the shoes for Gianni'
      c. Ho parlato **a** Gianni   [intransitive dative]
          'I spoke to Gianni'
      d. Quel cibo piace **a** Gianni   [experiencer]
          'Gianni likes that food'

The use of the GIVE serial verb is not limited to Creoles/Pidgins, as we have outlined in the Introduction. In several non-Creole languages, the verb GIVE serves as the lexicalization for both datives and benefactives. Take for instance Example (17) from Thai (reproduced from Example (11) of the Introduction), where "hâj" 'give' introduces both datives and benefactives (see Aikhenvald, 2006 for a typological overview, and Muysken & Veenstra, 1995; Heine & Kuteva, 2002 for other cross-linguistic examples).

(17) Dɛɛŋ sɔɔn lêeg   hâj Sùdaa hâj phyan.
     Dang teach arithmetic give Suda give friend
     'Dang taught arithmetic to Suda for his friend.'   *Thai* (Bisang, 1996, p. 571)

In other languages, the verb for GIVE in the second position seems to encode dative content only, as illustrated in (18) for Modern Mandarin Chinese (cf. Example (12) of the Introduction).[11]

(18) wo xie le yi-feng xin **gei** ta.
     1SG write ASP one-class letter to him
     'I wrote a letter to him. Not: I wrote a letter for him'
                          Modern Mandarin Chinese (Sun 1996, p. 44)

Based on the discussion in section 1 and the empirical evidence provided above, we posit that the (serial) light verb GIVE aligns with the adposition "to" in English, "a" in Romance languages, or inflectional dative case in realizing the ($\subseteq$) predicate. The serial verb for GIVE is an elementary predicate signaling the transfer of possession and heading a projection in which the theme (possessum) is its sister and the recipient (possessor) is its complement, as illustrated in (19) for Example (13a).

(19)

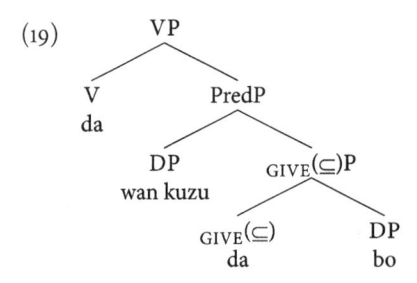

---

11. There appears to be an implicational hierarchy at work. According to APiCS feature 86, with GIVE, it is possible to encode datives and benefactives, datives only, but not benefactives only. Thus, the dative content of the verb GIVE must be 'lexicalized' in order to also trigger a benefactive meaning.

We are aware that many different Creoles/Pidgins can also utilize a double object construction with a goal-theme order for ditransitives, as exemplified in Principense in (20) (cf. Example (13b)).

(20) Kêdê mêzê Maa ka xikevê mi kata ũa.
      every month Maa HAB write 1SG letter one
      'Every month Maa writes me a letter.'   *Principense* (Maurer, 2009, p. 121)

Bruyn et al. (1999) assume that double object constructions are universally available in Creole/Pidgin languages, arguing that they are the unmarked option in Universal Grammar and linking them to language acquisition.[12] From this perspective, they follow a creolization schema along the lines of Bickerton (1981, 1984, 1989)'s *Bioprogram Hypothesis*. However, Michaelis and Haspelmath (2003) have shown that double object constructions can be absent from the grammar of individual Pidgins/Creoles, attempting to support a *substrate* explanation.[13]

For the purpose of the present analysis, we can assume that for Creole/Pidgin languages that exhibit a surface dative (or, better, GIVE) alternation like Principense in (20)–(13b), both of the main approaches taken by the generative literature on *Dative Shift* are compatible with our discussion.

A first possibility is to consider Freeze (1992)'s ideas, or the earliest transformational accounts of Dative Shift (cf. also Larson, 1988), assuming that leftward movement of the Goal argument derives the double object construction. Given that the structure in (19) is actually the same as the base structure of Freeze, we assume that nothing prevents a Dative Shift derivation from taking place starting from it.

A second possibility is to adopt the view that Dative Shift structures actually involve a different base-generated structure – along the lines of Kayne (1984) and subsequent literature – and to argue that the Dative Shift alternation is closely comparable to the alternation between '*He presented his pictures to the museum*' and '*He presented the museum with his picture*' illustrated in (3)–(4) (cf. Levinson, 2011; Franco & Manzini 2017b).

Regarding the lexical semantic motivation for the parallelism between dative/*to* adpositions and GIVE serial verbs, we may follow Givón (1975), who argued – within the framework of generative semantics – that GIVE can be analyzed as inducing a possessive relationship. From this perspective, the goal/recipient can be considered as representing a 'reference point,' and the theme as the

---

12. Snyder and Stromswold (1997) demonstrated that children typically develop the ability to produce double object datives several months earlier than they acquire to-datives.

13. Specifically, Michaelis and Haspelmath (2003) show that creoles in India, Indonesia and Melanesia do not have Double Object Constructions, regardless of their lexifiers.

'target' (of possession) found within the goal/recipient's domain. We believe that this view is coherent with the structure outlined in (19).

Givón also assumes that when the theme, which is manifested in the goal/recipient's domain, is not a thing/entity, but rather identified as the event profiled by the main verb, what GIVE conveys is the 'manifestation' (i.e., possession, inclusion) of the event in the recipient's (experiential) domain, resulting in its interpretation as an experiencer or beneficiary. This view aligns with the analysis provided in Manzini and Franco (2016) for dative experiencers. A sentence like the one in (14) for Ndyuka can be interpreted as expressing that 'liking the food' is an elementary event/state in the 'zonal inclusion/possession' domain of *me* and can be represented as in (21).

(21)

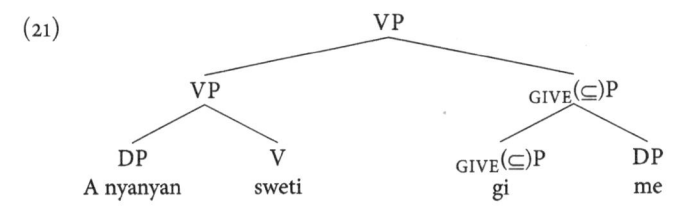

A similar structure/interpretation can also be provided for beneficiaries, as illustrated in (22), where a GIVE(⊆) predicate takes the result VP as its external argument and the beneficiary DP as its internal argument. In fact, a sentence like (13c) can be paraphrased as 'Sarah causes the result of 'buying the shoes' and 'Tom owns/possesses this result/has this result in his domain.'

(22)

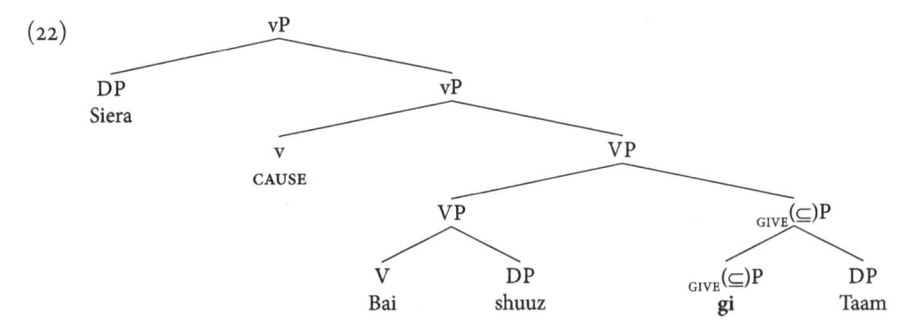

This line of analysis for GIVE is also generally compatible with the applicative literature (cf. Pylkkänen, 2008; Cuervo, 2003; Boneh & Nash, 2012, among many others), which considers it not coincidental that the same 'oblique' morphology found to express goals also introduces experiencers/beneficiaries. In the Applicative literature, this corresponds to the observation that the same Appl head (externalized by a dative/oblique) can attach at different points in the sentential spine. The low Applicative head establishes a relation between two arguments (namely the goal and the theme, cf. (19)), while the high Appl head introduces a relation between an argument (experiencer/beneficiary) and an event (the VP) (cf. (21)–(22)).

Regarding an example like São Tomense in (15), involving an intransitive (unergative) dative/GIVE construction, we propose again, following Manzini & Franco (2016), that in this instance the two arguments of GIVE($\subseteq$) are its complement DP and an eventive constituent. Intuitively, both transitive and unergative predicates can be paraphrased as consisting of a causative event and an elementary predicate associated with an eventive name, as shown in (23)–(24).

(23) ho chiamato Gianni > ho fatto una chiamata a Gianni [transitive]
      'I called Gianni'   'I made a call to Gianni'

(24) ho telefonato a Gianni > ho fatto una telefonata a Gianni [unergative]
      'I phoned Gianni'   'I made a phone call to Gianni'

As we have seen above, Hale & Keyser (1993), Chomsky (1995) formalize this intuition about the complex nature of transitive predicates by proposing that they result from the incorporation of an elementary state/event into a transitivizing predicate (CAUSE). In minimalist syntax, the transitivizing predicate is typically integrated into the structure in the form of a v functional head. Within such a conceptual framework, it is evident what we mean when we say that GIVE($\subseteq$) in (15) takes as its arguments the (elementary) state/event and the DP. Thus, (15) can be informally rendered as 'He caused them to be on the receiving end of some talk', or more directly 'He caused them talk', corresponding to a v-V organization of the predicate, as represented in (25) (cf. also the discussion in Section 2.4 below).

(25)

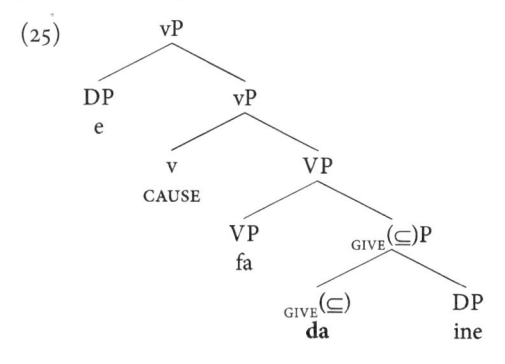

We argue that, despite the complex organization of the predicate in a v-V fashion, direct complements (e.g., of 'call' in (23)) are embedded in a canonical transitive structure comprising a nominative agent and an accusative theme. In other words, 'call' in (23) behaves as a single predicate, with its complementation structure displaying no sensitivity to the presence of (potential) sub-events/states within it (cf. Svenonius, 2002 on Icelandic). On the contrary, the dative with 'talk' in (15) results from the sensitivity of argument structure to the finer event articulation of the predicate, in which the oblique DP is perceived as the 'possessor' of a sub-event/state.

Finally, note that sometimes what are labeled GIVE serial verbs in the literature (cf. APiCS feature 86) actually behave as matrix predicates, introducing a CAUSE/v layer on their own. Consider the examples in (26).[14]

(26) a. Isti belu   **da** sabe kung ile ki   esta teng lugar
        this old.man give know DOM 3SG comp DEM COP place
        'The old man told him that this was the place'

                                    Batavia Creole (Maurer, 2011, p. 73)

    b. Pírmi yo ta-**dále**   prestá mi motor   konéle
        often 1SG IPFV-give borrow my motorcycle DOM.3SG
        I lend her/him frequently my motorcycle.

                                    Zamboanga Chabacano (Forman, 1972, p. 204)

Here, the verb for GIVE is in the first position and does not introduce an argumental DP, contrary to what we have seen in the examples we have provided so far. The example in (26a) can be rendered in a Romance language like Italian with a causative structure like the one illustrated in (27), using a *fare* (make) auxiliary.

(27) Il vecchio **fa** sapere a lui...
     'The old man told him...'   *Italian*

Actually, it is not uncommon to use the verb GIVE as an auxiliary in complementary distribution with *fare/faire* in causative-like predicate in Romance, as illustrated in (28) (cf. also Cuervo 2010 on Spanish).

(28) *Italian*
    a. il caldo **da** fastidio a Gianni
        'the heat annoys Gianni'
    b. il caldo **fa** male a Gianni
        'the heat hurts Gianni'

Thus, examples like the (26a) can be structurally rendered as in (29). They clearly do not match the 'argumental' use of GIVE serial verbs that are the topic of our discussion.

(29) [$_{VP}$ **da** [$_{VP}$ sabe ...]]

---

14. Note that the examples in (26) display DOM arguments marked with a 'with' adposition (e.g. *kung/kon*). This is a typical feature of Romance (Spanish/Portuguese) based Creoles of South-East Asia (cf. the discussion of the Kristang data in Franco and Manzini, 2017b).

2.3.2 TAKE serial verbs as (⊇) predicates

Considering ditransitive constructions again, based on the considerations above, it is possible to hypothesize that we can also find the 'reverse' of the verb GIVE involved in ditransitive constructions, specifically in a configuration where the 'reverse' of GIVE introduces the possessum, as in expressions like 'I presented the museum with pictures' (cf. the example in (4)) and the discussion in the Introduction. Franco & Manzini (2017b) show that this is not an uncommon strategy among natural languages (see Heine & König 2010). Just consider, for instance, an example from Chamorro in (30), where the only strategy available to encode ditransitives is precisely by means of an instrumental adposition meaning 'with', in a 'reverse' possessor–possessum configuration.

(30) Ha   na'i i   patgon **ni** leche
     he.ERG give ABS child   INST milk
     'He gave the milk to the child.'   *Chamorro* (Topping, 1973, p. 241)

Finding a similar pattern at work also with Creoles/Pidgins would provide substantial arguments in favor of a view suggesting that Dative Shift structures actually involve a different base-generated configuration, in which the possessor is structurally higher than the possessum. Namely, we are asking ourselves if – also in the domain of serial verbs – we can encounter a relation that is the 'mirror image' of datives/GIVE(⊆), where we have seen that the possessor is the complement of the 'inclusion/sub-set' relator and the possessum is its external argument.

Clearly, the best candidate for the role of the 'double' of GIVE is the verb TAKE, which stands in lexical semantic opposition to it. As we have seen in Section 2.2 (cf. (6)), TAKE serial light verbs are widely employed in Creole/Pidgin languages to encode instrumental and comitative participants. Thus, they are sorts of counterparts to the adpositions meaning 'with' elsewhere (cf. Stolz et al., 2006). Interestingly, TAKE serial verbs are widely used in Creole/Pidgin ditransitives, as illustrated in (31), with examples showing that this strategy is at work independently of the substrate and the lexifier.

(31) a. Mon **pran** en lit   donn Napoleon
         1SG take one liter give Napoleon
         'I give one liter to Napoleon.' *Seychelles Creole* (Bollée & Rosalie, 1994, T2)
     b. Mwen **pran** liv   bay Pòl.
         1SG   take book give Paul
         'I gave the book to Paul.'   *Haitian* (Lefebvre, 1998, p. 291)
     c. À   **tek** nayf giv yù
         1SG.SBJ take knife give 2SG.OBJ
         'I gave you the knife.'   *Nigerian Pidgin* (Faraclas, 1996, p. 75)

Sometimes both a GIVE and TAKE strategy for encoding ditransitive can be at work in the grammar of a given language, as shown in (32) with an example from Nigerian Pidgin (cf. 31c).

(32) À   kuk nyam **giv** yù
      1SG.SBJ cook yam   give 2SG.OBJ
      'I cooked yam to you.'   *Nigerian Pidgin* (Faraclas, 1996, p. 141)

The pattern illustrated above for Nigerian Pidgin is not an exotic feature to be ascribed to Pidgins/Creoles only. Indeed, the same strategy, with both GIVE and TAKE involved in ditransitives, is available, for instance, in Vietnamese, as illustrated in (33). Note that nothing prevents a given language from also instantiating a double object pattern in its grammar, as illustrated in Vietnamese (33c).

(33) a. Nó đưa   cái chảo **cho** con voi
          3SG deliver CL pan give CL elephant
          'It delivers the pan to the elephant.'
      b. Ông-ấy **lấy** tiền   đưa   bà-ấy
          He   take money deliver she
          'He gives her money.'
      c. Nó đưa   con voi   cái chảo
          3SG deliver CL elephant CL pan
          'It delivers the pan to the elephant.'   *Vietnamese* (Hanske, 2007)

There are two common features to highlight in the TAKE ditransitives illustrated above: (i) the verb for TAKE consistently appears in the first position, preceding the matrix verb; (ii) it always introduces the possessum. In this respect, it is the mirror image of the serial verb GIVE introduced in Section 2.3.1, which is always in the second position and consistently introduces the possessor. At the same time, TAKE verbs cannot be treated as the instrumental adposition of Chamorro in (30), which mirrors the *'I presented the museum with pictures'* configuration. Indeed, while it is true that TAKE verbs always introduce the possessum, they are never 'sandwiched' between the possessor and the possessum.

At first sight, one may entertain the idea of hidden coordination with two independent predicates, such as a structure of the type 'he takes the book and gives him (it)' for the examples in (31). However, it is suspicious to find that a coordinating particle never shows up in this context, despite the fact that an overt coordinator is usually employed at the VP level in those languages displaying a ditransitive TAKE serial verb construction, as illustrated in (34) for Seychelles Creole. Furthermore, we have not found any resumptive pronouns encoding the theme/possessum in Creoles/Pidgins employing TAKE ditransitives. Resumptive pronouns are usually employed in analogous coordinate structures in Romance, as illustrated in (35) for French (cf. also Syea, 2013 for a full set of compelling arguments against a coordination analysis, based on data from Indian Ocean French Creoles). Typically, constructions like (31) satisfy all the core requirements of serial verb constructions, behaving semantically and phonologically as a single unit.

(34) Marcel in manz banan e i 'n lir zournal
      Marcel PRF eat banana and 3SG PRF read newspaper
      'Marcel ate a banana/bananas and read the newspaper.'
                    Seychelles Creole (Michaelis and Rosalie 2013 APiCS: 56–138)

(35) Il prend le livre et **le** lui donne
      'he takes the book and gives it to him'   *French*

A possible solution to account for TAKE ditransitives in Creole languages would be to assume that we are dealing with a base structure of the type represented in (36) for the Haitian sentence in (31b), with the TAKE constituent moving to a preverbal position, matching a base configuration of the type '*I provide the museum with pictures*'. The target of movement could be a Topic position within the IP domain, as suggested by Belletti (2004, 2005). A possible representation is shown in (37).

(36) $[_{VP}$ bay $[_{PredP}$ Pòl $[[\supset_{take}$ **pran liv**$]]]$

(37) $[_{TopicP} \supset_{take}$ **pran liv** $[_{VP}$ bay $[_{PredP}$ Pòl $[[\supset_{take} \text{pran liv}]]]]]$

Such an interpretation could elegantly account for the (a)symmetry of GIVE and TAKE in ditransitive constructions. However, it would be suspicious to find information-driven movement to be obligatory without any overt instances of the base structure surfacing cross-linguistically.

    In fact, we have not found any instance of TAKE serial verbs in second positions.[15] Furthermore, the sequence TAKE – DP – Matrix Verb – (DP) is the only

---

15. The sole exception to this pattern seems to be represented by Tetun Dili (Malayo-Polynesian creole), as reported in Lovestrand (2017). The example in (i) is a typical instrumental serial verb structure with 'take' in first position. The example in (ii) is a grammatical sentence in Tetun Dili, with the same two verbs in the opposite order.

(i)   abó   **lori** tudik ko'a paun
      Grandparent take knife cut bread
      'Grandfather cut the bread with the knife.'
(ii) abó   ko'a paun **lori** tudik   *Tetun Dili* Hajek (2006, p. 244)
      Grandparent cut bread with knife

Note, however, that Hajek (2006, p. 244) states that when the serial verb *lori* appears after the main verb, it seems to be subject to a grammaticalization process, as it follows "*post-verbal TAM markers, always appears in the same position as an oblique PP, and cannot omit or front objects.*"

one consistently employed to introduce instrumental and theme arguments in Creoles/Pidgins, as illustrated in (38)–(39) for the Portuguese-based Creole Angolar.

(38) *Instrument-*TAKE
      N   **tambu** faka kota situ
      1SG take   knife cut meat
      'I cut the meat with a knife.'   *Angolar* (Maurer, 2013, APiCS structure dataset).

(39) *Theme-*TAKE
      Kathô **tambu** n'kila rê pê kosi   bega
      dog   take   tail his put under belly
      'The dog put his tail under his belly.'
                                 Angolar (Maurer, 2013, APiCS structure dataset).

Thus, we propose a different account in which the serial verb TAKE is actually inserted into the sentential spine to convey a causative meaning. Intuitively, ditransitives can be paraphrased with a causative predicate introducing the transfer of possession, as illustrated in the Italian minimal pair in (40). Crucially, the 'lexical' verb in the causative structure in (40b) is the verb for HAVE.

(40) *Italian*
      a.   Gianni ha dato una mela a Maria   [Ditransitive]
      b.   Gianni ha fatto avere una mela a Maria   [Causative]
           both: 'Gianni gave an apple to Maria'

Actually, in many different languages, verbs meaning HAVE (i.e. encoding predicate possession) are rendered via a HOLD/TAKE counterpart. This is a widespread pattern in Romance languages. Italian *avere* (HAVE) for instance is rendered in many Southern Italian dialects through the lexical item *tenere* (HOLD/TAKE), as shown in (41) for Cirò Marina (Calabrese) (see the discussion in Chapter 5).

(41) **tɛnənə**   kirə ɣwaɲɲunə
      they.have those boys
      'They have those boys' = 'Those boys are their sons'
                                 Cirò Marina (Manzini & Savoia 2005)

The relationship between HOLD and TAKE verbs is supported by the behavior of the *ba* morpheme in Chinese on historical grounds (cf. Ziegeler 2000), which we will briefly introduce in Section 2.4, addressing DOM TAKE serial verbs. Additionally, it's worth noting that in Italian, when one wishes to express 'transfer of possession,' both *tenere* (HOLD) and *prendere* (TAKE) can convey the same meaning, as illustrated by the minimal pair in (42). Moreover, Heine & Kuteva (2002) demonstrate that TAKE verbs can be utilized cross-linguistically to encode causative predicates, as illustrated in (43) for Twi and Yuruba (cf. also Kim, 2012 on English, and the discussion in Section 2.4). The causative=instrumental syncretism with applicative morphemes that we will discuss in Chapter 3 can also be a case in point.

(42) *Italian*
    a. Tieni queste chiavi
    b. Prendi queste chiavi
       both= 'Takes this keys'

(43) a. o **de** gwañ a-ba.
       He take sheep PFV-come
       'He has brought a sheep.' = 'He made a sheep come.' *Twi* (Lord, 1993, p.137)
    b. ọ̀rọ̀ Múyìíwá **mú** mi ṣẹ̀ ọ̀rẹ́ mi
       matter Muyiwa take me offend friend my
       'Muyiwa's affair made me offend my friend.' Yoruba (Oyelaran, 1982, p.110)

Assuming that the structure for ditransitives introduced by TAKE verbs is inherently causative, matching the Italian sentence in (40b), we suggest the representation in (44) for Creole/Pidgin TAKE ditransitives. (44) structurally reproduces the Haitian sentence provided in (31b).[16]

---

16. Note that in Haitian also a verb like 'show' can trigger a TAKE ditransitive as illustrated in (i).

  (i) Men **pran** liv la **montre** Jan.
      I take book the show John
      'I showed the book to John.' *Haitian* (Muysken & Veenstra, 1995, p.297)

Thus, one could object that 'montre' in (i) is a full verb, standardly projecting a VP. However, in many languages verbs meaning SHOW are employed as light serial verbs introducing goals and beneficiaries, as illustrated in (ii) for the verb *kyèré* 'show' in Twi. Thus, it seems that a representation like (43) can be adequate also when a SHOW item is involved.

  (ii) a. o kasa **kyèré** me
         he speak show me
         'He spoke to me.'
      b. wò tòw túo **kyèré** borohene
         they fire gun show governor
         'They fire guns for/in honor of the governor.' *Twi* (Lord, 1993, p.31–32)

Further notice that, as reported, in Carstens (2002) the verb SHOW in serial construction (in Haitian Creole, Saramaccan and Sranan) is able to determine a different pattern, in which the complement of 'take' can be the recipient (the possessor). Consider the example in (i).

  (iii) Jan pran Mari **montre** liv la
       John take Mary show book the
       'John show the book to Mary' *Haitian Creole* (Muysken & Veenstra, 1995, p.300)

(44)

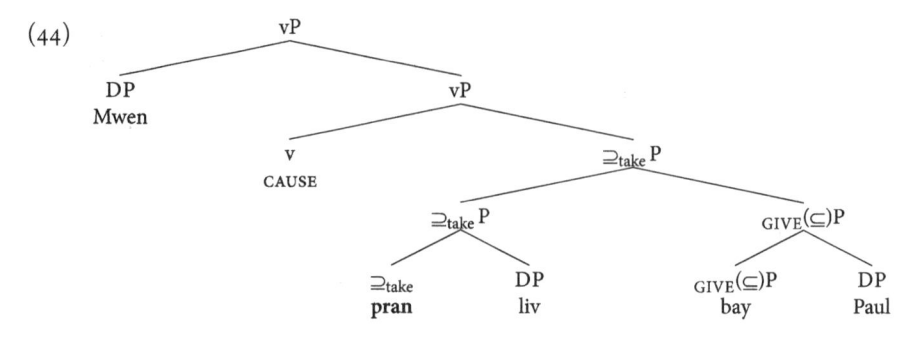

The representation above can be paraphrased as: "I cause 'having/holding/taking a book' and Paul owns/possesses this result". Crucially, we assume that the structure is the same as the one provided for benefactives in (25). The strict 'dative' interpretation is conveyed by the 'holding'/⊇take nature of the predicate. Further note that in Italian, it is quite odd to use the benefactive preposition "per" when a HAVE 'lexical' predicate is embedded under a causative layer, as illustrated in (45b). In such a case, the dative preposition "a" seems to be required.[17]

(45)   *Italian*
    a.   Ho fatto cucinare i ravioli **per** Gianni
        'I had the ravioli cooked for Gianni'
    b.   Ho fatto avere i ravioli ??**per/a** Gianni
        'I gave the ravioli to Gianni'

The discussion above allows us to easily address TAKE serial verbs in their "standard" use as instrumentals. Recently, Jerro (2017) proposes an analysis of the widespread syncretism between instrumental applicative morphology and causative morphology in Bantu, assuming an operation that adds a novel layer (and the associated participant) into the causal chain denoted by the event. Specifically, Jerro's idea is that this new causal layer can be interpreted as either

---

In such case, as acknowledged by Carstens (2002), SHOW clearly seems to act as a transitive verb selecting for a theme argument. What is the role of 'take' in such constructions? We can say that, in these contexts, it behaves like those adpositions/case introducing a benefactive meaning, where such meaning is triggered by the animacy feature of the argument it introduces (here, *Mari*). An instrumental=dative syncretism is well documented from a crosslinguistic viewpoint (cf. Franco & Manzini, 2017b). For instance, Classical Greek can be unambiguously interpreted as expressing either Recipient/Benefactive or Instrument on the basis of animacy: with inanimate nouns (apart from toponyms) the dative functions as an instrumental, while with animate nouns it has the typical functions of datives/benefactives (cf. Luraghi, 2003). Thus, from a structural viewpoint TAKE in (ii) would have the representation we provide for instrumentals in (47) below.

17. Note that this is coherent with what it is reported in the APiCS feature 86, namely that GIVE serial verbs are not able to lexicalize the benefactive meaning alone.

initial in the overall causal structure – deriving a causative reading – or intermediary – deriving an instrumental reading. We will come back to this issue in Chapter 3.

Actually, instrumental relations are quite often encoded by TAKE lexical items in Creoles/Pidgins, as shown in (46). The TAKE verb is again consistently in the first position. This pattern seems to arise independently of the substrate and the lexifier.[18]

(46) a. Apre ou **pran** goni   (ou) toufe pwason.
          Then 2sG take jute.bag 2sG choke fish
          'Then you choke the fish with the jute bag.'
                                    Seychelles Creole (Bollée & Rosalie, 1994, p.222)

      b. I   **pwan** vwati touché Lapwent.
          3sG take car   arrive La.Pointe
          'S/he went to La Pointe by car.' *Guadeloupean Creole* (Ludwig, 1996, p.248)

      c. eli ja **tomá** faka kotrá kandri
          3sG PFV take knife cut   meat
          'She cut the meat with a knife.'   *Kristang* (Baxter, 1988, p.212)

      d. Ê   **toma** faka va   mpon.
          3sG take   knife slice bread
          'He slices the bread with a knife.'   *Sao Tomense* (Hagemeijer, 2000)

      e. Kofi **teki** a   nefi koti a   brede.
          Kofi take DET knife cut DET bread
          'Kofi cut the bread with a knife.'   *Sranan* (Winford & Migge 2008, p.710)

We propose, of course, that the instrument relation expressed by TAKE verbs can be reduced to a ($\supseteq$) relation, similar to 'causative/possession' TAKE(S). This yields a structure of the type in (47), where ($\supseteq$)TAKE takes as its internal argument the DP instrument, while its external argument is the VP event. The only difference between causative and instrumental TAKE serial verbs can be reduced to a matter of projection. Following Chomsky (2013, 2015, 2020), indeed, we may assume that the difference between causatives and instrumental TAKE serial verbs relies on labeling. Upon Merge with a VP/XP, a ($\supseteq$)TAKE may label the resulting constituent, conveying a causative interpretation, essentially as indicated in (44) above. Alternatively, the resulting constituent may be labeled by V so that

---

18. While it is commonly assumed that serial TAKE verbs in Haitian and the other Atlantic creoles have their origin in the serial verb constructions of West African languages (see Aboh, 2009), there is very scarce evidence that those in the Indian Ocean Creoles come from the same source (see Bickerton, 1984; Syea, 2013, 2014). Bickerton (1984) argues that they are the result of language creation guided by an innate bioprogram. Syea (2013) assumes an influence of the lexifier, arguing that they are modelled on French imperative constructions and are the result of internal linguistic changes.

(⊇)TAKE is interpreted as an instrumental. The structure that we provide in (47) can be actually interpreted as: 'he causes 'bread cutting' and this resultative (sub)event includes a knife'.

(47)

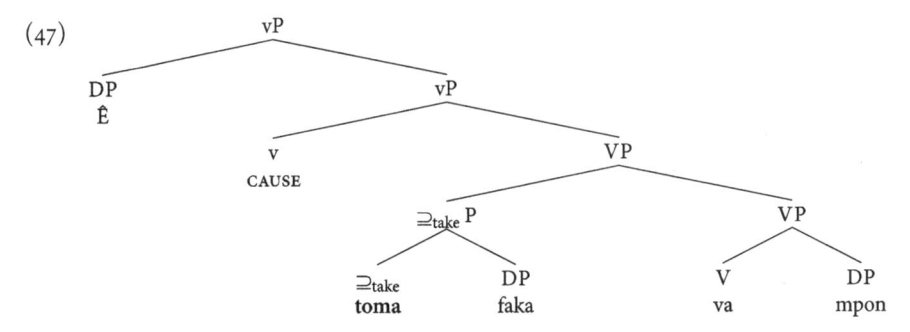

We consider instruments to be inanimate objects of (⊇)TAKE included in a caused event. In other words, the general interpretation of (47) is that the object of (⊇)TAKE could be a 'simultaneous/concomitant' of the VP result state. However, the VP event is in turn embedded under a causation predicate; in this context, it is interpreted with the inanimate object playing the role of 'instrument of' the external argument (the initiator of the event) in vP.

Naess (2008, p.99) assumes that "*An instrument is [...] involved in two separate, though connected, instances of causation: the agent's causing movement or change in the instrument, and the instrument triggering an effect on the patient [...] It is this intermediate role in a causal chain that gives the instrument the properties of being 'a Patient and a Causer at the same time'*". Baker (1992, p.28) has a similar conception of instruments since he assumes that "*[...] semantically, the instrument is a kind of intermediate agent-theme. If I cut the bread with a knife, then I act on the knife, such that the knife changes location. The knife thereby acts on the bread such that the bread goes into a new state*". According to Marantz (1984, p.246), in sentences like 'Elmer unlocked the porcupine cage with a key', "*[...] a key is an intermediary agent in the act of unlocking the porcupine cage; Elmer does something to the key, the key does something to the cage, and the cage unlocks*". On the other hand, in sentences like 'Elmer examined the inscription with the magnifying glass', "*the magnifying glass is an indispensable tool in Elmer's examination of the inscription, but it is not an intermediary agent in the examination*".

In our account, following Franco & Manzini (2017b), we are proposing to revert the characterization of instruments of the type proposed by Naess and Baker: an initiator triggers a causative event in which an inanimate argument plays a subordinate causation (i.e. instrument) role, as illustrated in (49) for the sentence in (48).

(48) John broke a window with a stone

(49) John caused a broken window and this (sub)event included a stone.
> John caused a stone to cause the result of a broken window

An important point revolves around the consistent encoding of take verbs in first position within serial constructions. In the literature this question has been approached from various perspectives (cf. Lovestrand, 2018). Muysken (1988) suggests that the verb order pattern in SVCs is forced by some extra-syntactic factor such as temporal iconicity, semantic principles, or morphological patterning. A similar perspective is the one in Durie (1997, p.330), who posits that the invariance of *take* serial verb sequencing in SVO and SOV languages suggests that serialization constraints cannot receive a general explanation through syntactic accounts alone.

Tai (1985, p.50) discusses serial verbs in Chinese and proposes a principle of "temporal sequence" asserting that *"the relative word order between two syntactic units is determined by the temporal order of the states they represent in the conceptual world."* Also Li (1993, p.500), addressing again Chinese, assumes that the linear order reflects the real-world temporal relation between the subevents represented by these verb phrases: *"one must take hold of the instrument before doing anything with it."* Li (1993, p.502) further specifies that *"the constituents involved must be verbal"* to be constrained by a linear condition. Note that Tai (1985) argues that if the subevents of a multiverb construction are truly simultaneous/concomitant, the verb order should be interchangeable. The inference is that fixed verb orders imply that the (sub)events could not be conceptualized as simultaneous/concomitant, possibly weakening the proposal of Franco and Manzini (2017b) for instrumental relations.

We can assume that verb order patterns in *take*-constructions reflect the impact of (extra-syntactic) temporal iconicity. If two verb phrases pertain to (sub)events happening sequentially, the order of verb phrases in serial verb construction become fixed in the temporal order (cf. Lovestrand 2017, 2018). Nevertheless, we may see that if the verb phrases are related to simultaneous (sub)events, they can become fixed in either order (see Lovestrand 2017). The serial verb USE, employed with an instrumental value, is a case in point (cf. Heine and Kuteva 2002). Consider the examples below, taken from Lovestrand (2017). In (50)–(51), *Use* is inserted into the structure, just like *take*, in first position. On the contrary, in (52)–(53), it appears in a position linearly similar to *with*-adpositions.[19]

---

19. The fact that we are dealing with serial constructions is confirmed by possible presence of a proclitic in both verbs. Consider the example in (i).

(i) n=pun bobay   n=pake sandal
3SG=kill mosquito 3SG=use thong
He killed the mosquito with a thong.   *Taba* (Bowden, 2001, p.299–300)

(50) yígbèci **lá** èbi tun etsu
thief   used knife stabbed chief
'A thief stabbed the chief with a knife.'   *Nupe* (George, 1975, p.316)

(51) sùk **cháy** phráa khôon tônmáy
Sook use machete cut   tree
Sook chopped down the tree with a machete.   *Thai* (Filbeck, 1975, p.120)

(52) Dong bekin mati tikus   **pake** batu
3PL   make die mouse use   stone
'They killed the mouse with a stonè.'
Kupang Malay (Jacob & Grimes, 2011, p.342)

(53) Nyoman namplak Ketut **ngganggo** lima
Nyoman AV.hit   Ketut AV.use   hand
'Nyoman hit Ketut with his (own) hand.   *Balinese* (Lovestrand, 2017)

Based on the behavior of 'use' serial verbs, we can assume that the representation we have provided for 'take' serial verbs is essentially correct. A principle of temporal iconicity can possibly explain the fact that it occurs always in first position in serial constructions,[20] while 'use' serial verbs allow a structure which minimally differs from the one we have proposed in (47) for 'take' instrumentals, in which the (sub)event described in the serial construction are perceived as simultaneous/concomitant (in a way similar to *with* adpositions). A representation for the Kupang Malay example in (52) is provided below in (54).

(54)

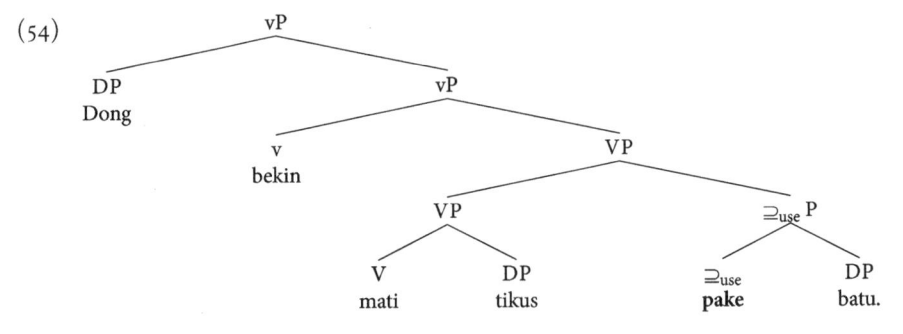

We believe that our analysis of TAKE serial verbs has the merit of being more economical compared to the one proposed by Aboh (2009). Aboh assumes that, in examples like those in (46), the lexical verbs merge with the theme to form a VP. The latter merges with a v-appl head, which introduces the instrument DP in its specifier. This vP in turn merges with a v-ext, responsible for the introduction

---

20. A similar principle can be advocated for "give" serial verbs, consistently appearing in the second position, which precisely encode a (temporally forced) transfer of possession.

of the subject external argument, in order to form a higher vP. This vP merges with an aspectual AspP. Under aspect licensing and the EPP, the lexical verb raises to Asp° to check its aspect features, followed by movement of the instrument to Spec,AspP. AspP further merges with a functional F head to form FP, which merges as the complement of the TAKE verb, itself merged under a higher aspect head. He argues that since F° has no PF content, we find in many serial verb languages the order TAKE – DP – matrix verb. A sentence like (46d) would be derived as in (55).

(55) $[_{TP}$ Ê $[_{AspP}$ $[_{Asp°}$ toma $[_{FP}$ $[_{AspP}$ faka $[_{Asp°}$ va $[_{vP}$ t Ê $[_{V-ext}$ t va $[_{vP}$ t $_{faka}$ $[_{v-appl}$ va $[_{VP}$ va mpon]]]]]]]]]]]]

Aboh (2009) argues that TAKE heads a projection in the functional field between T and V, while the lexical verb merges inside the VP-shell. In a nutshell, he proposes that TAKE is a functional (or light) verb that has no (internal) theta-role to assign.[21] This is fairly counterintuitive. TAKE can be consistently used as a lexical predicate in languages employing serial verbs construction. Just consider some examples from Twi, a Kwa language spoken in Ghana. The item *de* is a serial verb directly matching the behavior of *with* adpositions, as illustrated in (56). Indeed, *de* is able to introduce, among others, instrumental, means and comitative meaning.

(56) a. o **de** enkrante tya duabasa   [instrumental]
          he de sword   cut branch
          'He cut off a branch with a sword.'

      b. o **de** aivu enni nada anya ade   [means]
          he de theft and fraud get   thing
          'He has become rich with theft and fraud'

      c. o **de** né nnípa fòro   bépow   *comitative*
          He take his men   ascend mountain
          'He ascends a mountain with his men.'   *Twi* (Lord, 1993, p.67)

Crucially, as shown in (57), *de* can also be used as a 'stand-alone' predicate to introduce a 'have/hold/take' meaning (at least from a diachronic point of view, cf. the discussion in Lord 1993, p.68ff). Namely, it is fully able to assign a theta role on its own and is not purely an aspectual device devoid of lexical content.

---

21. Mazzoli (2015) has shown that TAKE serial verbs in Nigerian Pidgin can encode also a modal meaning, together with their 'standard' instrumental/possessee meaning, assuming that a grammaticalization path is currently at work in that language. However, she does not provide any evidence of an aspectual value of Nigerian Pidgin TAKE verbs.

(57) a. ɔkɔm **de** me
          hunger takes me
          'I am hungry.'
      b. ɔno ná ɔ **de**   kúró yi
          he FOC he possess town this
          'He is the possessor of this town.'   *Twi* (Lord, 1993, p. 68)

Moreover, there is no strong cross-linguistic evidence for an overt realization of the abstract functional head F° responsible for the licensing of the instrumental/comitative participant. We would expect that this functional head should show up in the grammar of some languages (i.e., in the form of a case morpheme, adposition, etc.). However, we have found no evidence of such a morpheme in the grammar of Pidgin and Creole languages based on the analysis of the data included in the APiCS feature 85. Thus, we follow the classic view (cf. Aikhenvald, 2006) that serial verbs introduce (peripheral) arguments and mark them as obliques.

Finally, we briefly address comitative TAKE serial verbs. The possibility to encode comitative relations with TAKE verbs is attested among Creoles/Pidgins, as shown in (58). More generally, this possibility is widely attested among natural languages, as documented in (59).[22]

(58) a. mi e **teki** Meri go na foto
          I ASP take Mary go to town
          'I go to the town with Mary'   *Sranan* (Jansen et al., 1978, p. 138)
      b. i **teik** mi go
          he take me go
          'He took me with him.'   *Cameroon Pidgin English* (Todd, 1982, p. 153)

(59) a. o **de** né nnípa fòro   bépow   (= 51c)
          He take his men ascend mountain
          'He ascends a mountain with his men.'   *Twi* (Lord, 1993, p. 137)
      b. u a   paa u **lwo**
          3SG PERF come 3SG take
          's/he came with him/her'   *Supyire* (Carlson, 1991, p. 204)

---

22. In serial-verb constructions, comitative is more often expressed by a verb whose basic meaning corresponds to English *follow* (cf. Chinese *gēn* 'to follow' as in *wo gēn tā shuohuà* 'I am conversing with him'; Bisang (1992: 182). Cf. Heine and Kuteva (2002) for more data. Consider also the sentence in (i) from Nigerian Pidgin English.

(i) im go **folo** dèm dans
     3SG FUT follow 3PL dance
     S/he will dance with them   *Nigerian Pidgin English* (Faraclas 1996: 80)

For the sake of this work, we can maintain the same structure as in (47) for sentences like the ones represented above (cf. also Bruening, 2012). In a sentence like (59a), (ⵣ)TAKE takes as its internal argument the comitative 'né nnípa' and as its external argument the VP event. Therefore, we predict again an interpretation under which the comitative participant is included in/part of the event 'ascending a mountain'. Substantially, the TAKE comitatives illustrated above are interpreted as such because the argument introduced by the (ⵣ) predicate is human. An instrument interpretation results when the two arguments of P(ⵣ) are an inanimate DP and a caused VP. Quite straightforwardly in (59)–(58), the object of (ⵣ)take is a sentient being, blocking an instrument reading (cf. Franco & Manzini, 2017b for further arguments and a review of the literature on the topic).

2.4   DOM serial verbs

In many languages, TAKE serial verbs are recruited from the lexicon to encode Patients/Themes. Lord (1993) demonstrates that the utilization of serial verbs for encoding patients is conditioned by their referential properties, namely it can be related to a scenario of Differential Object Marking (DOM). We provide below examples from Twi and Mandarin Chinese.

Lord (1993, p.111–112) presents the following data from Twi. For ditransitive verbs, there are two possible configurations for indefinite patients, as illustrated in (60). In (60a), we have a double object construction. In (60b), we have a TAKE serial verb introducing the theme in a ditransitive structure, just like in the sentences illustrated above in (31).

(60) a. o **ma** abofra no akutu
          he give child the orange
          'He gives the child an orange.'
      b. o **de** akutu **ma** abofra no
          he take orange give child the
          'He gives the child an orange'   *Twi* (Lord, 1993, p.111–112)

However, if the theme NP is definite, only the *de* construction is grammatical, as illustrated in (61).

(61) a. *ɔ ma me siká   nó
          he gave me money DEF
      b   ɔ de sika   nó ma me
          he take money DEF gave me
          'He gave me the money.'   *Twi* (Lord, 1993, p.112)

Mandarin Chinese further provides an example of the evolution of a DOM marker from the verb 'take' (cf. Li & Thompson, 1976, 1981). In sentences like (62), there are two word order possibilities: SVO, as in (62a), and SOV, as in (62b). The SOV order triggers object marking with the verbal item *bǎ*, meaning 'take/hold', which requires the object to be definite.

(62) a. háizi tàng yīfu   le
          child iron clothes ASP
          'The child ironed some clothes.'
      b. háizi **bǎ** yīfu   tang le
          child bǎ clothes iron ASP
          'The child ironed the clothes.'   *Chinese* (Li & Thompson, 1976, p. 458)

Chinese *bǎ* sentences have attracted a great deal of interest in the theoretical literature (cf. e.g. Sybesma, 1999; Huang, Li, & Li, 2009; Kuo, 2010, among many others). We leave their full treatment to future research. Here we just want to point out a striking similarity with Creole/Pidgin languages. As documented in the Atlas of Pidgin and Creole Language Structures (APiCS) Chapter 1 (https://apics-online.info/parameters/1.chapter.html), the vast majority of Creole/Pidgin languages (practically all of them) employ an unmarked SVO order in declarative sentences. Whenever a patient/theme argument is encoded through a serial verb meaning TAKE, the order switches to SOV, as documented in (63)–(66). This is the same pattern reproduced in many Sinitic languages, where the bǎ morpheme is in complementary distribution with GIVE serial verbs and instrumental/comitative adpositions (cf. Chappell, 2015 for a detailed survey).[23]

(63) a. no Ngola   ka zi   kai   no   kota mionga
          we Angolar HAB make house POSS.1PL side see
          'We, the Angolars, used to build our houses on the sea side.'
                                              Angolar (Maurer, 2013, APICS dataset)

---

23. We have found scarce evidence, among Creoles/Pidgins, of GIVE verbs recruited to introduce the object. Early Sranan provides a possible example of this pattern in (i), where the serial verb optionally encodes highly ranked (i.e pronominal) arguments. In this case, interestingly, the SVO order is not switched to an SOV order. It would be possible to assume that GIVE in (i) is the counterpart of Romance *a* adpositions introducing recipients and DOMs.

(i) Mi sa dini (**gi**) ju
     1SG FUT serve give 2SG
     'I will serve you'   *Early Sranan* (Schumann, 1783, p. 31) apud Bunting (2009)

    b. Kathô **tambu** n'kila rê pê kosi bega.
        dog   take   tail his put under belly
        'The dog put his tail under his belly.'

                    Angolar (Maurer, 2013, APICS dataset).

(64) a. kooknot bring   ail
        coconut bring.forth oil
        'The coconut produces oil.'   *Creolese* (Rickford, 1987, p. 131)
    b. ii **tek** ii   teel put bitwiin ii   fut
        3sg take poss.3sg tail put between poss.3sg foot
        'He put his tail between his legs'
            Creolese (Devonish & Thompson, 2013, APICS dataset)

(65) a. Mene ka kopa pêxi na fya   sempi
        Mene HAB buy fish LOC market always
        'Mene always buys fish at the market.'
    b. kasô **pega** ponta urabo pwê ubasu bwega
        Dog take point tail   put under belly
        '[...] the dog put its tail under his belly.' *Principense* (Maurer, 2009, p. 115ff)

(66) a. À   plant nyam
        1sg.sbj plant yam
        'I planted yams.'
    b. À   **tek** nyam kot
        1sg.sbj take yam   cut
        'I cut the yam.'   *Nigerian Pidgin* (Faraclas, 1996, p. 71)

We have not been able to find any explanation for the encoding of internal
arguments through the use of TAKE in Creoles/Pidgins, as evidenced by Examples (63)–(66) above, where it seems to function similarly to DOM marking
triggered by the referential properties of the items involved in the serial verb construction. Therefore, a comprehensive discussion of this topic is left for future
research, which may involve collecting first-hand data. However, the data from
Twi and Chinese presented earlier are quite suggestive. Hence, in the following
section, we attempt to outline a tentative explanation for TAKE-DOMs. We have
seen above in Section 2.3.2 that a TAKE item can easily include a holding, having,
or possession meaning (cf. Lord, 1993; Heine, 1997).[24]

    Ziegeler (2000) links the holding/possessing meaning of Chinese *bǎ* with
its function as an expression of 'high transitivity', namely the rendering of the

---

24. According to Heine (1997) these meanings encoded by TAKE items can be taken in terms
of a 'pragmatic extension/implicature': taking an object implies a physical acquisition (possession) of it.

events encoded by *bǎ* sentence in terms of a causal {cause-result} chain. Ziegeler (2000:822) precisely claims that: *"[...] possessors are not normally encoded as agents, though the action which brought about the resulting state of possession, such as grabbing or taking, implies the prior actions of an agent"*. Namely *Bǎ* sentences presuppose a state sub-event in which the object argument is affected as the result of the 'possessor/agent's' prior agency; Ziegeler (2000) shows that *bǎ* is introduced in constructions similar to have/get-causative in English introducing a perfect/passive participle, as in (67) (cf. Kim, 2012; Legate, 2014; Manzini, 2017).

(67)   Yuehan **bǎ** the xiu-hao   le
      John   **bǎ** car repair-RC ASP
      'John has his car repaired'

Mandarin Chinese Ziegeler (2000:884)

The sentence in (67) can be glossed as 'John has his car repaired', which is ambiguous between a resultative expression indicating that 'John did the repair work himself, and a causative expression indicating a present habitual situation in which he regularly takes it elsewhere to be mended'. A causative TAKE verb is used also in Twi as illustrated in (43), repeated in (68) for ease of references.

(68)   (= 43)
      o   **de**   gwañ a-ba
      He take sheep PFV-come
      'He has brought a sheep.' = 'He made a sheep come'

Twi (Lord, 1989, p.137)

As previously discussed, we adhere to the standard concept proposed by Hale and Keyser (1993) and Chomsky (1995), which posits that transitive predicates arise from incorporating an elementary state/event into a transitivizing *v* layer. As highlighted in Section 2.1, Manzini and Franco (2016) demonstrate that in Indo-European languages, patient arguments can be encoded as possessors of an elementary state-(sub)event embedded within a causative *v* layer (cf. (5b)). We may hypothesize that in languages like Chinese, the *v* layer can be represented by a (⊇)TAKE predicate. The external argument is depicted as a possessor of a resultant state. The referential properties of the internal argument may account for this distinct type of encoding. For example, Ziegeler (2000) considers the affectedness of the direct object as a significant parameter in Chinese. This aligns with the observation that affected items typically denote a lasting change in an event participant (cf. Beavers, 2011; Von Heusinger & Kaiser, 2011).

Therefore, we tentatively propose a structure akin to the one depicted in (69) for Nigerian Pidgin in (66b), interpreted as 'I have the jam cut'. The external argument functions as the possessor of the resultant state/sub-event.

(69)

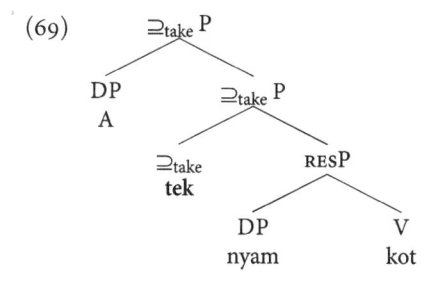

This is merely a preliminary glimpse into a potential analysis of 'transitive' TAKE serial verbs, a topic we intend to delve into further in future research.

In fact, supporting evidence for our characterization of TAKE as a DOM 'possession' predicate can be found in the observation that many Romance varieties feature predicates that effectively preclude (adpositional) DOM. As we have outlined in the Introduction, one such example is possession 'hold', as demonstrated by the Southern Italian dialect of Cirò Marina (cf. 41). In this instance, the verb tenere 'have' excludes the dative DOM adposition *a* (70b), while the (semantically heavier) verb tenere 'hold' exhibits DOM with definite human objects in (70a), as we have already pointed out (cf. examples in (17) in the Introduction).

(70) a. tɛnənə   **a**   kkirə ɣwaɲɲunə
          they.hold DOM those boys
          'They are holding those boys'
      b. **tɛnənə**   kirə   ɣwaɲɲunə
          they.have those boys
          'Those boys are their sons'   *Cirò Marina* (Manzini & Savoia 2005)

It is reasonable to conjecture that the pattern in (65) arises from the inverse relationship between the content of the verb 'have', which introduces a (⊇) relation, and the content of the dative preposition/case, namely (⊆). Therefore, we may propose the representation in (71) for the sentence in (70b).

(71) [$_{VP2}$ tɛnənə [(*P⊆) kirə ɣwaɲɲunə]]

Therefore, it seems that the grammar avoids duplicating the possession structure – or perhaps specifically the combination of the dative (⊆) inclusion relator and its (⊇) reverse. Recall that according to Franco & Manzini (2017b), (⊇) is also the content of instrumental and comitative adpositions, as externalized by the preposition 'with' (Italian 'con'). Most transparently, 'the girl with a hat' expresses the same relation between the two arguments as 'the girl has a hat' – which reverses the dative (or genitive) relation: '(give) a hat to the girl' or 'the hat of the girl'.

2.5   Conclusion

This chapter addressed the syntax of argument-introducing or valency-increasing serial verbs in Creole languages, providing empirical arguments for the model of grammatical relations advanced in a series of recent works by Manzini & Savoia (2011a,2011b, 2018), Manzini & Franco (2016), Franco and Manzini (2017a,b), Franco & Lorusso (2020, 2022), and Rugna & Franco (2022). These authors present an analysis of the syntax and interpretation of dative 'to', instrumental 'with', and Differential Object Marking (DOM) relators, based on the assumption that these elements possess a fundamental interpretive content that interacts with the internal organization of the predicate/event. Following this line of reasoning, we must assume that these oblique relators, expressing a primitive elementary part-whole relation, may also be instantiated by *serial light verbs* in the grammar of natural languages. We have proposed a formal approach to cross-categorial variation in argument marking, aiming to outline a unified morpho-syntactic template. In our framework, so-called 'cases' do not constitute a specialized linguistic lexicon of functional features/categories; rather, they assist in outlining an underlying ontology of natural languages, from which they derive some of the most elementary relations. Such primitive relations can be expressed by various lexical means: case, adpositions, light (serial) verbs, and applicatives, as we will explore in the next chapter.

CHAPTER 3

A syntactic interpretation of the applicative-causative syncretism

We consider the applicative-causative syncretism, which is a pattern of morpheme polysemy attested in many different natural languages. We basically interpret the causative-applicative syncretism as based on a shared syntactic configuration. Specifically, we argue that the syncretic morpheme under investigation is the 'applicative' counterpart of an adpositional/case elementary relator (Manzini & Franco 2016; Franco & Manzini 2017a,b), attaching instrumental or benefactive obliques (High Applicatives, cf. Pylkkänen 2002, 2008) to the verbal spine. We follow Bellucci (2017), Manzini and Savoia (2018) in assuming that causees in causative constructions can be introduced as obliques, linked to the same structural position as High Appls. The causative reading of the sentence is driven by interpretive means (cf. Franco & Manzini 2017b). This readily explains the possibility of encoding causative and applicatives with the same lexical items.

3.1 The applicative-causative syncretism

In this chapter, we delve into the applicative-causative syncretism, a pattern of morpheme polysemy that is in attested in various natural languages. The applicative is typically defined as *"a construction in which a verb bears a specific morpheme which licenses an oblique, or non-core, argument that would not otherwise be considered a part of the verb's argument structure"* (Jeong 2007, p.2). Baker (1988) and Bresnan & Moshi (1990) argue that the extra-arguments associated with applicative morphemes typically encode benefactive or instrumental participants. Typologically, however, applicative constructions commonly license other theta-roles, such as goal, locative, and source relations (Baker, 1992; Peterson, 2007, among others).

In current generative literature, the term 'applicative' (Marantz, 1993; Pylkkänen, 2002, 2008; Cuervo, 2003, 2010, among others) is also used to refer to oblique or indirect objects of the verb that precede the theme or patient object in languages like English without an overt applicative marker. For instance, Marantz (1993) assumes that English double objects of the type 'I gave Mary a letter' actually instantiate applicative structures with a covert applicative morpheme.

We analyze the syntax of those languages that have morphological devices that change verbs into their causative forms, and in which such causative morphemes happen to have the same lexical shape as an applicative, introducing a non-core (oblique) argument. The applicative=causative syncretism is quite widespread from a cross-linguistic point of view, as documented in McDonnell (2013). Consider the data in (1) to (3), where the applicative=causative morpheme is highlighted in bold.

(1) a. Habimana y-a-men-a   igi-kombe
       Habimana 1.SBJ-PST-break-IPFV 7-cup
       'Habimana broke the cup.'

    b. Habimana y-a-men-**esh**-eje   umw-ana igi-kombe
       Habimana 1.SBJ-PST-break-CAUS-PFV 1-child   7-cup
       'Habimana made the child break the cup.'

    c. Habimana y-a-men-**esh**-eje   igi-kombe in-koni
       Habimana 1.SBJ-PST-break-APPL-PFV 7-cup   9-stick
       'Habimana broke the cup with a stick.'   *Kinyarwanda* (Jerro, 2017, p.753)

(2) a. kucing mangan iwak
       cat   eat   fish
       'the cat ate fish'

    b. aku mangan-**i** kucing iwak
       1SG eat-CAUS cat   fish
       'I fed the cat fish'

    c. pelem nyeblòk-**i** gentèng ómah-ku
       mango fall-APPL roof   house-1SG.POSS
       'a mango fell on the roof of my house'

    a'. ès nyair
        ice melt
        'the ice melted'

    b'. aku nyair-**aké** ès
        1SG melt-CAUS ice
        'I melted the ice'

    c'. aku masak-**aké** Karolina jajan
        1SG cook-APPL Karolina cake
        'I baked Karolina a cake'   *Javanese* (Hemmings, 2013, p.168ff)

(3) a. Xwánu xwá-s-Ø-ti   tsíri
       Juan   bring-PRF-PRS-3IND corn
       'Juan brought some corn.'

    b. María xwá-**ra**-s-Ø-ti   Xwánu-ni tsíri
       Maria bring-CAUS-PRF-PRS-3IND Juan-OBL corn
       'Maria made Juan bring some corn.'

   c. xí   tsúntsu-ni xwá-**ra**-s-Ø-ka-ni   its
      1SG pot-OBL   bring-APPL-PRF-PRS-1/2IND-1SG.SBJ water
      'I brought some water with a pot.'

P'orhépecha (Capistrán Garza, 2015, p.145ff)

The examples in (1) illustrate the causative=instrumental applicative syncretism in Kinyarwanda, a Bantu language spoken in Rwanda (Kimenyi, 1980; Jerro, 2017). In this language, the applicative morpheme –ish/-esh introduces both a causative and an instrumental applicative reading. The example in (1a) shows a canonical transitive sentence with an external and an internal argument, while the verb bearing the –ish/-esh morpheme in (1b) and (1c) introduces three participants. In (1b), the reading is causative: an agent causes the child to break the cup. Conversely, in (1c), we are faced with an instrumental reading: an agent directly acts on the cup, using a stick to break it. As extensively illustrated in Jerro (2017), the causative=instrumental syncretism is very pervasive in Kinyarwanda. Jerro (2017, p.753) argues that: *"neither traditional analyses of causatives nor applicatives can naturally be extended to syncretic morphemes such as –ish since causativization is an operation that adds a new causer subject, while applicativization is an operation that adds a new object."* The question is: do the features of the added participant ensure that the instrumental is a direct object? We will show that there are languages in which it is possible to assume an oblique status for the extra-participant licensed by the applicative morpheme.

In Javanese (Austronesian), the applicative morpheme *–(n)i* encodes a locative relation (2c). As illustrated in Hemmings (2013), this item is also used as a causative morpheme with verbs of an underlying transitive nature, especially ingestive verbs such as 'eat', 'drink', and 'smell', as in (2b). This suffix also functions as a causative with intransitive verbal roots, typically those denoting states or 'inactive situations' (Shibatani & Pardeshi, 2002). Additionally, the suffix -*aké* is commonly used as a causative marker with intransitive verbs that denote a change of state like 'open' and 'melt', as shown in (2b'). The suffix *–aké* also encodes benefactive relations, as illustrated in (2c').

Finally, the examples in (3) illustrate the causative=instrumental applicative in P'orhépecha, a language isolate spoken in the North-Western region of Michoacán in Mexico. The suffix *–ra* (and its allomorphs, cf. Capistrán Garza, 2015) introduces both a causative (3b) and an instrumental reading (3c). Note that the added participants, namely the causee in (3b) and the instrument in (3c), bear an oblique *–ni* inflection. This is crucial for assuming that the applied argument retains oblique status (cf. Section 3.3 and 3.5). We will mainly use P'orhépecha to illustrate our analysis of the causative=applicative syncretism.

In his typological survey, Peterson (2007) assumes that there are two kinds of applicative/causative syncretism ('isomorphism' in his terminology): benefactive/malefactive applicative/causative and comitative/instrumental applicative/causative. We have seen, with the examples from Javanese, that we may also find locative-applicative/causative syncretism. Peterson (2007) argues that there is a 'dividing line' between benefactive applicatives and causatives, marked by the semantics of the verbal predicate involved: only intransitive (unaccusative) predicates would be turned into causatives by the 'benefactive applicative'. According to Petersen, transitive predicates cannot encode a causative reading when they bear a benefactive applicative marker. Peterson (2007, p.133–134) says that: "*benefactive constructions are often based on a schema of giving, and because of this, benefactive constructions often require that there be associated with the event they depict the normal participants in a giving frame. In particular, there must be a giver, a recipient, and, crucially, there must be a gift to be transferred. Hence, an intransitive base event will not have enough participants to work in the construction, but a transitive base event will.*"

Actually, cross-linguistic data do not seem to support Peterson's claim. As shown in Sneddon (1996), the Indonesian benefactive-applicative morpheme –*kan*, illustrated in (4), can encode a causative meaning with a set of transitive verbal roots, as in (5).

(4) a. pelayan mengambil segelas   air
        waiter   take   a.glass.of water
        'The waiter took a glass of water.'
    b. pelayan mengambil-**kan** tamu segelas   air
        waiter   take-APPL   guest a.glass.of water
        'The waiter brought the guest a glass of water.'
                                    Indonesian (Sneddon, 1996, p. 80)

(5) a. wanita itu mencuci pakaian saya
        woman that wash   clothes 1SG
        'That woman washes my clothes.'
    b. saya mencuci-**kan** pakaian wanita itu
        1SG wash-CAUS   clothes woman that
        'I have my clothes washed by that woman.'
                                Indonesian (Sneddon, 1996, p. 74, 76)

Peterson proposes an externalist explanation for the instrumental applicative=causative isomorphism. He claims that: "*as long as a language allows causees to be inanimate, then the possibility of interpreting an inanimate causee as an instrument is available; this seems like a minor extension to make*" (Peterson 2007, p.135–136). We recognize that Peterson's intuition is on the right track in assuming that instruments are nothing else than inanimate causee-like arguments (cf. Franco & Manzini, 2017b, and the discussion in Section 3.5). However, we will try to avoid a shift of meaning and potential grammaticalization patterns in accounting for the syncretism between the causee role and the benefactive/instrumental/(locative) one in those languages that make use of verbal affixes to encode them. Instead, we will provide an explanation based on the idea that the construction involved may share the same syntax and that syntax drives those interpretations that are (structurally) allowed.

To our knowledge, there are no formal syntactic attempts trying to capture Caus=Appl. Recently, Jerro (2017) provides a semantic analysis of the syncretism between instrumental applicative morphology and causative morphology in Kinyarwanda, assuming an operation that adds a novel layer (and the associated participant) into the causal chain denoted by the event. Specifically, Jerro's idea is that this new causal layer can be interpreted as either initial in the overall causal structure – deriving a causative reading – or intermediary – deriving an instrumental reading. Jerro leaves a precise syntactic implementation of his proposal for his future research. In this Chapter, we will show that the causal nature/interpretation of the morpheme adding a new participant to an event is actually possible given a very basic 'inclusion' relation instantiated by the applicative/causative morphology. Franco & Manzini (2017b) dubbed this loose relation 'concomitance' with an event. We adhere to their view, assuming that a 'concomitant argument' can be variously interpreted as the causee, the instrument, the beneficiary of a given event, under the right syntactico-pragmatic conditions.

The rest of this Chapter is structured as follows. In Section 3.2, we provide some theoretical background for our proposal, assuming that the syntactic projections of predicates and functional features/categories are mediated by the lexicon, which organizes these contents in different language-specific manners. In Section 3.3, we introduce our interpretation of applicatives, arguing that they are not qualitatively different from oblique cases, adpositions, or serial verbs, as we have seen in the previous Chapter: all these items are different lexical realizations of a relational 'inclusion' predicate, whose role is to add non-core participants to the verbal spine. In Section 3.4, we will provide a possible syntactic template for causatives, based on the idea that causees may be encoded as oblique (external) arguments put forth in recent work by Bellucci (2017), Manzini (2017), Franco et al. (2021). In Section 3.5, we formulate an analysis for the Appl=Caus syncretism, interpreting such phenomenon as relying on a shared syntactic configuration, based on data from P'orhépecha.

3.2   Theoretical background: Syncretism beyond paradigms/categories

As previously discussed, our working hypothesis, originating from the research of Manzini & Savoia (2011a), suggests a reconsideration of the functional categories' map. We propose that the functional lexicon is not precompiled in the universal (computational) component of syntax in a cartographic manner (cf. Cinque & Rizzi, 2010). Instead, we posit that functional categories are drawn from the same conceptual inventory as lexical ones.

Our core idea is that functional categories externalize properties and relations that are not fundamentally different from those realized by the substantive lexicon. They are merely more elementary, typically partitioning the conceptual universe into broader classes than the exponents of traditional lexical categories (i.e., nouns, verbs, adjectives, cf. Baker 2003). Essentially, we adopt a perspective in which the lexicon precedes syntax and projects it, aligning with the minimalist postulate of *Inclusiveness* (Chomsky, 1995; Manzini & Savoia, 2011a, 2018; Manzini, 2017). Consequently, understanding how the items projected from the lexicon, including the 'isomorphic' applicative and causative morphemes focused on in this study, interact with one another under syntactic Merge (effectively projecting syntactic structures) becomes paramount.

We start from the premise of a universal conceptual inventory; at the very least, the categories of the conceptual system recruited by language must be universal. While the underlying conceptual organization is universal, the linguistic lexicon cuts it in language-specific ways, accounting for the majority of language variation. Following again the framework outlined by Manzini & Savoia (2011a, 2018), Manzini et al. (2015), Manzini & Franco (2016), Franco & Manzini (2017a, b), Rugna & Franco (2022) among others, we adopt the position, formalized by Distributed Morphology (DM), that predicative contents are listed in the lexicon without any categorization (as bare roots). Therefore, nouns, verbs, and adjectives are defined by the merger of an a-categorial predicative content with a nominalizing, verbalizing, or adjectivizing functional head. However, unlike DM, we do not posit that functional categories form a separate, potentially universal lexicon, akin to a 'Platonic ontology' of natural languages (see Manzini, 2017; Manzini & Savoia, 2018). Instead, we argue that the externalization of predicative contents and functional features/categories passes through the same lexicon.

An empirical challenge closely linked to the organization of the lexicon is syncretism. As we have already pointed out, according to DM, syntax operates on abstract features, roughly corresponding to the descriptive categories of traditional grammar (Calabrese, 1998, 2008). Opacization operations, which obscure the full syntactic feature specification, give rise to syncretisms.[25] A stronger stance could potentially be taken – that syncretisms correspond to natural classes and operate outside the paradigms of traditional categories. (cf. Manzini & Franco, 2016).[26]

This is our perspective: while paradigms serve as the traditional framework for teaching and descriptive grammars, they arguably fall short of capturing the entirety of linguistic competence possessed by speaker-hearers. The theoretical framework embraced here posits that paradigms do not exist within the competence of speakers; rather, linguistic data are organized in a non-paradigmatic fashion. The granularity of primitives is too fine, and the combinatorial possibilities afforded by Universal Grammar are too vast to achieve a perfect match with 'descriptive' macro-classes.

In essence, our research in the present Chapter targets the intersection of externalization processes and the syntactic module, exploring the domain of cross-categorial syncretism. Our approach begins with the radical assumption that paradigms hold no theoretical status, not even as derived constructs. Thus, we employ the term "syncretism" to denote homophony/isomorphism outside of paradigms, as discussed by Francez & Koontz-Garboden (2016, 2017).[27] An alternative label

---

25. Specifically, under a realizational conception of the lexicon as assumed by DM, certain abstract feature clusters may be realized by certain phonological strings – with syncretisms being treated in terms of *Underspecification* and other morphological adjustments (i.e., *Impoverishment, Fusion, Fission*, see Noyer, 1992; Halle, 1997; Harley, 2008, inter alia).

26. The idea that syncretisms correspond to natural classes is certainly not novel. Jakobson (1936) assumes that syncretism can be taken to reveal the fine-grained structure of a set of underlying (binary) featural distinctions. In recent literature this idea is strongly associated with the work of Gereon Müller (cf. e.g. Müller 2007). This is deemed to be too strong a position face to empirical evidence – yet the conclusion is based on assuming/revising the traditional repertory of categories and features (cf. also Stump, 2001, 2002; Baerman et al., 2005; Grimm, 2011, among others).

27. Trying to broaden our understanding of cross-categorial syncretism, it is possible to consider also TAM morphemes as elementary predicates (Franco & Lorusso 2020). Aikhenvald (2008) has shown that, quite often, 'cases in disguise' crosslinguistically appear as verbal suffixes (expressing typical verbal-related categories).Actually, the idea of a part-whole rendering for imperfectives is far from being new. Comrie (1976:16) argues that: 'perfectivity indicates the view of a situation as a single whole (...) while the imperfective pays essential attention to the internal structure of the situation'. Comrie's approach pays attention to the internal temporal structure of the event, proposing that, in a sense, the perfective–imperfective contrast can be accounted for in terms of a whole vs. part–whole contrast. Bach (1986) further argues that a progressive operator in the verbal domain is the counterpart of the partitive operator in the nominal domain, both instantiating a part-whole/sub- set relation. Filip (1999) is even more radical in claiming that: 'the semantic core of many, possibly all, aspectual systems can be characterized in terms of the basic mereological notions 'part' and 'whole''' (Filip 1999, p. 158). Given

for the phenomena we investigate could be "polyfunctionality." However, our focus is not on identifying functionalist grammaticalization paths (cf. Heine & Kuteva, 2002); rather, we aim to detect an inventory of categorial primitives that shape morpho-syntactic derivations. Here, applicatives are our main target.

3.3   On the nature of applicative heads: Relations beyond categories

As emphasized in Section 3.1, applicatives are constructions utilized to license oblique/non-core participants within a sentence. Therefore, it is natural to associate applicatives with other devices commonly used cross-linguistically to introduce oblique arguments, such as cases and adpositions.

---

this, we think that translating a part-whole relational content for aspect into morpho-syntax can be a welcome result. Thus, the 'dative' morpheme in (i), which happens to be involved in the encoding of progressive periphrases in many Romance varieties and beyond (e.g. Jóhannsdóttir, 2012 for Icelandic) lexicalizes the same basic 'part-whole/inclusion' content. We clearly take the lexicon to be the locus of externalization (cf. Berwick and Chomsky 2011), pairing syntactico-semantic content with phonological content: we assume a steady ($\subseteq$) signature for all the occurrences of the 'dative' a (to, at) adposition of Italian. In (i), basically, we might say that a ($\subseteq$) part/whole relation hold of event pairs, saying that one event is 'part of' (or a stage of, cf. Landman, 1992) of a second event – or rather a set of events/an event type. Alternatively, we may want to say that the time of reference (or viewpoint, cf. Comrie 1976) expressed within the matrix (finite) verb phrase is 'part of' the embedded event introduced by the ($\subseteq$) relator.

  (i)   *Italian*
       a.   Gianni sta/è a studiare 'Gianni is studying'
       b.   [IP/TP Gianni è [($\subseteq$) a [VP studiare]]]

Note that, quite often, the fact that the same morpheme is involved in argumental and aspectual relation passes unnoticed. For instance, that the same morpheme expresses progressives and genitives in Punjabi (Manzini et al. 2015, 2019), as illustrated in (ii)–(iii), has attracted practically no interest in either the functionalist or the theoretical literature.

  (ii)   o   kutt-a   dekh-d-a/-i   si   [Progressive]
         s/he.ABS dog-ABS.M.SG see-PROG-M.SG/-F.SG be.PST
         'S/he was seeing a/the dog.'
  (iii) *Punjabi* muṇḍ-e-d-i/-īā   kita:b/kitabb-a   [Genitive]
         boy-OBL.M.SG-GEN-F.SG/-F.PL book.ABS.F.SG BOOK-ABS.F.PL
         'the book/the books of the boy'

We argue that, cross-linguistically, we are not dealing with accidental homophony between TAM morphemes and case-like relators, but we face with natural classes of morphemes. There is a 'contentive' motivation for syncretisms of this kind, based on a shared morphosyntactic template in which such items act as elementary part-whole (mereological) predicates linking events and/or entities (cf. Francez & Koontz-Garboden, 2016, 2017).

We adopt Fillmore's intuition (1968), which considers oblique cases as the inflectional equivalent of adpositions, and posit that applicatives are essentially adpositions or case morphemes attached (incorporated) to the main verb (cf. also Aikhenvald, 2008). This aligns with Baker's idea (1988), who suggests that applicatives result from the incorporation of a prepositional head into the verb via head movement. According to Baker, applicatives restructure the argument in such a way that the applied object is licensed as the direct object, while the direct object becomes an oblique. Baker also contends that applicatives are permissible with transitive verbs but generally prohibited with intransitive predicates. This restriction stems from the fact that intransitives lack Case to assign, potentially resulting in the applied object being unlicensed, which violates the Case Filter (Chomsky, 1981).

However, as demonstrated in P'orhépecha in (3c), the applied object "tsúntsu" bears the oblique inflection "-ni" (refer to Section 5 for a full description of the "-ni" morpheme in P'orhépecha). Thus, Baker's notion that applied objects are always licensed as direct internal arguments cannot be upheld (as already made explicit by Marantz, 1993; McGinnis, 1998, Pylkkänen, 2008, among others). Furthermore, unaccusatives are able to license applied objects in P'orhépecha, as illustrated in (6).

(6) a. tsakápu wekórhi-**ku**-s-Ø-ti   Xwánu-ni
        stone   fall-APPL-PRF-PRS-3IND Juan-OBL
        'The stone fell on Juan/near Juan.'
     b. mésa-ni   kweráta-**ku**-sïn-Ø-ti   ma xantsíri
        table-OBL be.missing-APPL-HAB-PRS-3IND one leg/foot
        'The table is missing a leg.'
     c. ú-**ku**-s-Ø-ti   ma k'waníntikwa María-ni
        do/make-APPL-PRF-PRS-3IND one shawl   Maria-OBL
        'S/he made Maria a shawl.'   *P'orhépecha* (Capistrán Garza, p. 122, 124)

In P'orhépecha, the applicative morpheme "ku" (and its allomorph "-chi") introduces participants with respect to whom a given event takes place. Thus, in (6a), the applied argument delimits the space/domain where the unaccusative event (the 'falling of the stone') is located, and Juan is not a patient-like participant. The same logic applies to (6b), where an unaccusative predicate expressing incompleteness introduces the (un)possessor ('the table') as an oblique/applied argument. The example in (6c) shows that the applicative morpheme "-ku" also canonically introduces beneficiaries: the item Mary, namely the participant for whose benefit the action takes place, is again encoded as an oblique.

Hence, it seems that Baker's original characterization of applicative arguments is not supported by the P'orhépecha data illustrated above. Nevertheless, we agree with Baker in assuming that applicatives are adpositional-like elements attached to the verbal spine. There is plenty of evidence that this is the correct characterization of applicatives on cross-linguistic grounds. For instance, Craig & Hale (1988) provide strong arguments in favor of an adpositional source for applicative markers in Amerindian languages. Moreover, as illustrated in Kimenyi (1980, cf. Peterson, 2007; Jerro, 2017), many applicative markers in Bantu languages are of manifestly adpositional nature. Consider the Kinyarwanda examples in (7), where the allative morpheme "mu" can appear as a preposition (7a) or as a morpheme cliticized (applied) on the verb (7b).

(7) a.   umwaana y-a-taa-ye   igitabo **mu** maazi
          child   he-PST-throw-ASP book   in   water
          'The child has thrown the book into the water.'
     b.   umwaana y-a-taa-ye-**mu**   amaazi igitabo
          child   he-PST-throw-ASP-APPL water   book
          'The child has thrown the book into the water.'

          Kinyarwanda (Kimenyi, 1980, p. 89, 94)

The same pattern holds in Oceanic languages. For example, Durie (1988) shows that in Mokilese, a Micronesian language spoken on Mwoakilloa, the instrumental morpheme "-ki" can appear as an applicative affix on the verb in (8a) or as a standalone adpositional item in (8b).

(8) a.   ngoah insengeh-**ki** kijinlikkoano nah pehno
          1SG   write-APPL letter   his pen
          'I wrote the letter with his pen.'
     b.   jerimweim koalikko pokihdij erimweim siksikko **ki**   suhkoahpas
          boy   big   hit   boy   little   with stick
          'The big boy hit the little boy with a stick.'   *Mokilese* (Durie, 1988, p. 8)

Furthermore, applicative items have the same shape as (serial) light verbs, discussed in the previous Chapter, in many different languages (cf. Peterson, 2007; Creissels, 2010). For instance, in Kwaza (an Amazonian isolate), the benefactive applicative marker "-*wady*" is actually the verb for "give" in that language, as shown in (9b).

(9) a.   Kudɛrɛ-'wã   mãmãñẽ-**wady**-da-ki.
          Canderé-OBL sing-APPL-1SG-DECL
          'I sang for Canderé.'
     b.   Wɛra-'wã haru'rai   **wady-wady**-taʔỹ-ra.
          Vera-OBL armadillo give-APPL-1SG-IMP
          'Give the armadillo (meat) to Vera for me.'

          Kwaza (van der Voort, 2004, p. 373)

In Chickasaw, a Native American language spoken in Southeast Oklahoma, a serial verb form (labeled *converbial form* in the descriptive literature) of the verb "ishi" meaning "take," as in (10a), can be attached to the main verb, and the resulting structure is that of an instrumental applicative, as illustrated in (10b).

(10) a. tali' **ish**-li-t   isso-li-tok
          rock take-1SG.ACT-CONV hit-1SG.ACT-PST
          'Taking a rock, I hit him.'
      b. tali' **isht**-isso-li-tok
          rock APPL-hit-1SG.ACT-PST
          'I hit him with a rock.'   *Chickasaw* (Munro, 2000)

We have seen in Chapter 2 that (light) serial verbs meaning GIVE and TAKE are commonly used as 'valency-increasing' devices, encoding benefactives, instrumentals, comitatives, goal datives, etc. We have argued that they are relational predicates employed to introduce oblique arguments, just like cases and adpositions. Given the cross-linguistic evidence provided above, nothing prevents a given language from using an applicative morpheme for this purpose. Sometimes the difference between an adposition and an applicative morpheme, or a serial verb and an applicative morpheme, is blurred, as highlighted above. We propose that the underlying syntax is nonetheless largely the same.

Oblique cases, adpositions, serial verbs, and applicatives represent different lexical realizations of relational predicates aimed at incorporating non-core participants into verbal predicates. We offer an analysis of the syntax and interpretation of obliques (such as genitive, dative, instrumental), suggesting that these elements carry elementary relational content (e.g., inclusion, part-whole) that interacts with the internal structure of the predicate or event.

Our approach to categorical variation in argument marking seeks to outline a unified morpho-syntactic component. Instead of treating 'cases,' 'adpositions,' or 'applicatives' as distinct categories within a specialized lexicon of functional features, we view them as providing insights into the fundamental structure of human language, capturing some of its most basic relations: these foundational relations find expression through a variety of lexical means, including case, adpositions, light verbs, and applicatives.

For clarity purposes, let's provide a brief summary once more of our central claim (already illustrated in the Introduction and in Chapter 2), concentrating on the morphosyntax of datives. Regarding the dative "to," our analysis follows the line of inquiry into ditransitive verbs initiated by Kayne (1984). This framework suggests that predicates like "give" take as their complement a predication characterized by possession, headed by "to." Building upon the work of Kayne (1984), Pesetsky (1995), Beck & Johnson (2004), Harley (2002), among others, we can argue that in sentence (11), there exists a possession relation between the dative (Jack) and the theme of the ditransitive verb (the book). We conceptualize the content of "to" in terms of the notion of "(zonal) inclusion," as proposed by Belvin & den Dikken (1997) for the verbal item "HAVE" (as also discussed in Kim, 2012). We associate this content with an elementary part-whole predication, denoted as $\subseteq$. Therefore, in (11a), the causative event results in *the book* being (zonally) included by Jack, as depicted in (11b) (see Manzini & Franco, 2016).

(11) a.   I give the book **to** Jack
      b.   [$_{VP}$ give [$_{PredP}$ the book [[$_{\subseteq}$ **to**] Jack]]]]

In the analysis outlined in (11), the variation between *Dative Shift* (as in "I give Jack the book") and DP-to-DP structures is not derived (as proposed by, for instance, Larson, 1988), but instead, it reflects an alternation between two distinct base structures. One possibility is to consider that the head of the predication proposed by Kayne for English double object constructions represents an abstract form of the verb "have." Franco & Manzini (2017a), Franco & Lorusso (2022) contend that this abstract "HAVE" head, posited for Dative Shift, corresponds covertly to the adposition "with" (as suggested by Levinson, 2011). Indeed, the presence of the "with" preposition is overtly evident in the English minimal pair provided in (12).

(12) a.   He assigned the project *to* his team.
      b.   He assigned his team *with* the project.

Therefore, it is conceivable to propose the representation in (13) for (12b), as a 'double' of the structure in (11b). We represent the relation encoded by "with" as ($\supseteq$), where the possessed/inclusee serves as the adposition's complement and the possessor/inclusor functions as its external argument. Essentially, we encounter a relationship that is the inverse of dative constructions where the possessor serves as the complement of $\subseteq$ and the possessed is its external argument.

(13) [$_{VP}$ assign [$_{PredP}$ his team [[$\supseteq$ **with**] the project]]]]

We also suggest that oblique case refers to the fundamental predicative content when it's expressed as an inflection on a noun. Moreover, syncretism is based on shared content, specifically $\subseteq/\supseteq$, in the instances under consideration (see Rugna & Franco, 2022 for an expansion of the set of elementary relators in natural languages). In particular, we assert that applicatives serve as $\subseteq/\supseteq$ relators, offering backing for the previously outlined model of grammatical relations. We will illustrate how the syncretism between applicative and causative forms is accommodated within this framework.

In the following section, we present an analysis of the syntax of causatives, which will assist us in establishing our analysis of applicatives. We will illustrate how causatives involve a process of obliquization of the causee. Given the oblique nature of causees, as well as instrumentals, beneficiaries, etc., it is foreseeable that natural languages may opt to project the same lexical elements in the syntactic component to express these types of meanings.

3.4   Causatives and the obliquization of the causee

Recently, Bellucci (2017), Manzini (2017), and Franco et al. (2021) have argued that *causees* in causative constructions can be analyzed as oblique agents, forming a syncretism of goals and agents in Italian (and potentially in other languages). Let's consider the data in (14).

(14) *Italian*
    a. Ho fatto pulire la stanza **a/da** Gianni
        'I made Gianni clean the room'
    b. Ho dato un libro **a** Gianni
        'I gave Gianni a book'
    c. Michele è stato ucciso **da** Gianni
        'Michele has been killed by Gianni'

The example in (14a) demonstrates that causees in Italian can be introduced interchangeably by the prepositions "a" or "da" (with potential restrictions not addressed here, cf. Folli & Harley 2007). The preposition "a" commonly introduces goals/recipients, as depicted in (14b). In (14c), we observe that the preposition "da" is associated with the expression of agents in passive constructions.

The data in (14) can be explained by assuming that in causative constructions, "a" phrases can be construed as agents (quirky subjects), forming a common lexicalization (a syncretism in our view, cf. Section 3.2) of goals and agents (cf. Franco et al., 2021).

Baker (1988) argues that causative constructions of the Italian type, as outlined in (14a), are derived by movement of the embedded VP to a position contiguous to the matrix causative verb, allowing for the incorporation of V into the causative predicate. Thus, we encounter a 'restructuring' (Rizzi, 1978) of the arguments of the embedded sentence: according to Baker, a complex predicate like "make-clean" in (14a), implying the presence of a causer, a causee, and a theme/patient, aligns them in the same fashion as ditransitive predicates, namely nominative-accusative-dative. However, ditransitives consistently interpret the dative as a goal. By contrast, the goal interpretation does not consistently characterize the causee (see Section 3.5, where we demonstrate, for instance, that the causee-instrumental syncretism extends beyond the realm of applicatives, cf. also Torrego, 2010). Crucially, a problematic aspect of Baker (1988) is that it does not provide an account for the "da"-encoded causee (the so-called "faire-par" construction in the literature, starting from Kayne 1975), where an embedded active verb is coupled with an external argument expressed through what appears to be a by-phrase (Baker 1988 p. 487).[28]

To address these challenges, we propose here that external arguments in complements of causative verbs undergo a process of 'obliquization' (Bellucci 2017), as depicted in (15).

(15) $[_{VP}$ fatto ... $[_{vP}$ v $[_{VP}$ pulire la stanza] $[\subseteq$ **a/da** Maria]]]

What we need to explain is why the complement structure in (15), featuring the oblique alignment of the external arguments, cannot be embedded under any other matrix predicate than the causative verb (or a restricted set of causative/direct perception predicates, cf. also Marchis Moreno & Franco, 2020). We follow Franco et al. (2021) in asserting that a matrix predicate with pure CAUSE content (e.g. *fatto* in (15)) directly selects a vP – or alternatively an IP lacking agreement properties and an EPP position. In either case, an embedded nominative subject is blocked, necessitating obliquization or existential closure of the external argument variable, as in (16) (see also Manzini 2017 on passives).

(16) *Italian*
      Ho   fatto pulire la   stanza
      I.have made clean the room
      'I had the room cleaned'

One might wonder why, among all verbal predicates, it is causative ones that select this kind of embedding. Franco et al. (2021, p.153) assume that "*causative constructions permit the formation of a hyper-complex predicate, expressing the direct causation (or perception) of a caused event. This must lie at the heart of their selection properties (as in other treatments it underlies VP-movement or V incorporation or complex predicate formation).*" In some languages, such as Italian, causativization allows for the movement of the embedded object to the matrix subject

---

28. Belletti (2017) reforms the VP-movement analysis of causatives so as to bring out the parallel with the smuggling analysis of passive. Thus the *a/da* phrase in (14) is constructed as the *by* phrase in Collins (2005). The external argument of transitive (or unergative) predicates embedded under causative verbs, for instance in (14), occupies the Spec, vP/Voice while being case-marked by the *a/da* dummy attached to the sentential spine. We follow Manzini (2017) in rejection the smuggling analysis of passive, as involving again movement of the VP and – generally – the 'dummy' nature of adpositional heads.

position, as shown in (17). Importantly, the oblique introducing the embedded external argument can be either *a* or *da*.

(17) *Italian*
      La stanza è stata fatta pulire (a/da Maria)
      the room is been made clean to/by Maria
      'One has had the room cleaned (by Mary)'

Based on the analysis of causative structures outlined above, we align with Franco et al. (2021) regarding the analysis of the free alternation between *a* and *da* in (14) or (17), which involves using the *a/da* phrase as an oblique agent or causer. This illustrates an instance of shared lexicalization (i.e., syncretism) of goals and agents, which becomes understandable when we assume that they share the same general content: the ⊆ relator. With this understanding, we can now delve into the causative-applicative syncretism and attempt to explain it in syntactic terms.

3.5 The nature of the cross-categorial syncretism: An analysis

We interpret the causative-applicative syncretism by assuming that the syncretic morpheme serves as the applicative counterpart of an adpositional or case relator ⊆. As demonstrated for Italian in Section 3.4, this relator is capable of introducing goals and causee/agents, among other roles (e.g., allative, locative, etc.), using the same lexical means. Let's consider the data from P'orhépecha in (3), repeated in (18) for ease of reference.

(18) a. Xwánu xwá-s-Ø-ti   tsíri   =(3)
          Juan   bring-PRF-PRS-3IND corn
          'Juan brought some corn.'
      b. María xwá-**ra**-s-Ø-ti   Xwánu-ni tsíri
          Maria bring-CAUS-PRF-PRS-3IND Juan-OBL corn
          'Maria made Juan bring some corn.'
      c. xí xwá-**ra**-s-Ø-ka-ni   tsúntsu-ni its
          1SG bring-APPL-PRF-PRS-1/2IND-1SG.SBJ pot-OBL   water
          'I brought some water with a pot.'

          P'orhépecha (Capistrán Garza, 2015, p.145ff)

The presence of the oblique marker "-ni" on causees and instrumentals in P'orhépecha, both encoded via the verbal affix "-ra," indicates their status as oblique participants. In contrast, the direct arguments in (18) remain unmarked. It's worth noting that P'orhépecha exhibits Differential Object Marking (DOM), influenced by animacy, specificity, and definiteness parameters. This variation explains why direct internal arguments may or may not occur with the oblique "-ni" inflection. In Examples (19a–c), the presence of the "-ni" morpheme on the internal argument conveys a definite reading, while its absence, as seen in (19d) with inanimate indefinite internal arguments, suggests a non-specific interpretation.

(19) a. Chalío pyá-s-Ø-ti   ganádu/ganádu-ni
          Chalío buy-PRF-PRS-3IND cattle/cattle-OBL
          'Chalío bought some cattle/the cattle.'

      b. xuchá arhá-s-Ø-ka   kurúcha/kurúcha-ni
          1PL   ingest-PRF-PRS-1/2IND fish/fish-OBL
          'We ate fish/the fish.'

      c. Páblu eshé-s-Ø-ti   yurhíri/yurhíri-ni
          Pablo see-PRF-PRS-3IND   blood/blood-OBL
          'Pablo saw blood/the blood.'

      d. xí pyá-a-ka   ma k'waníntikwa/k'waníntikwa-ni
          1SG buy-FUT-1/2IND one shawl/shawl-OBL
          'I will buy a shawl (non-specific/a particular one).'

                              P'orhépecha (Capistrán Garza, 2015, p. 31–32)

In P'orhépecha, there is no distinction between DOM and dative marking. Goal recipients are marked with the same "-ni" inflection, as illustrated in (20).

(20) xí ˏ íntsku-s-Ø-ka   itsî(-ni)   maríkwa-ni
      1SG give-PRF-PRS-1/2IND water-OBL girl-OBL
      'I gave the girl some water/some of the water.'

                              P'orhépecha (Capistrán Garza, 2015, p. 68)

In ditransitive constructions, the goal argument must be case-marked, whereas the theme/patient has the same DOM-like restrictions as the internal argument of monotransitive structures. Thus, goals in double object constructions are marked by the "-ni" morpheme, even if they are inanimate or indefinite, as illustrated in (21), where the theme is unmarked and the goal necessarily bears the "-ni" marker.

(21) a. inté acháati arhí-s-Ø-ti   ampé   ma anátapu*(-ni)
          that man   say-PRF-PRS-3IND (some)thing one tree-OBL
          'That man said something to a tree.'

      b. p'ikú-Ø   míkwa ma tsúntsù*(-ni)
          take.off/pull.off-IMP lid   one pot-OBL
          'Take the lid off a pot.'   *P'orhépecha* (Capistrán Garza, 2015, p. 69)

It is relevant to consider that, cross-linguistically, the 'oblique' dative adposition/case is the preferred externalization for DOM objects (Bossong, 1985; Aissen, 2003; Malchukov, 2008; Manzini & Franco 2016; among others). P'orhépecha is not an exception. We provide just one other example from Sardinian in (22a).

(22) a. appu tserriau   (a) un   ommini/su ɣani
I.have called DOM a   man the   dog
'I have called a man/the dog'   *Orroli* (Manzini & Savoia, 2005)

b. [$_{vP}$ v [$_{VP}$ tserriau [$_{PP⊆}$ **a** [$_{DP}$ un ommini]]]]

According to the analysis by Manzini & Franco (2016), previously outlined in the preceding chapters, the merging of dative and DOM (Differential Object Marking) occurs because of the instantiation of the same lexical content in both linguistic contexts. This phenomenon is exemplified in structure (22b) derived from sentence (22a). In (22b), object DPs exhibiting high animacy, definiteness, or specificity necessitate the same elementary oblique-introducing predicate, ⊆, for their incorporation, mirroring the pattern observed with goals/recipients and causees (as demonstrated in Section 3.4). For instance, in the scenario presented in (11b), the entities involved in ⊆ are two DPs – Jack and the book – where Jack is depicted as possessing the book resulting from the act of giving.

Following the theoretical framework proposed by Hale & Keyser (1993) and Chomsky (1995), which posits that transitive predicates arise from the merge of an elementary state/event into a transitivizing v layer (as we have seen in Chapter 2 for light serial verbs), the construction depicted in (22b) can be construed as 'I cause the man to have a call', where 'him' functions as the possessor of the 'call' sub-event. Thus, a relational bond is established between a DP (the man) and an elementary event 'the call', exemplifying the concept of ⊆ relation. Drawing parallels, we can infer a similar mechanism at play in P'orhépecha. For instance, a comparable representation can be applied to (19c), as depicted in (23).

(23) [$_{vP}$ v [$_{VP}$ eshé [$_{KP⊆}$ [$_{DP}$ yurhíri] $_{K⊆}$ ni]]]

We propose that, given the theoretical approach just represented above, it is possible to assume that all the NPs bearing the inflection *–ni* in P'orhépecha are oblique participants, requiring a relational predicate to be inserted into the verbal spine.[29] The arguments of adpositions, as in (24a), and applicatives, as in (24b,c), require the same *–ni* inflection.[30]

(24) a. María-eri kúchi wántiku-na-s-Ø-ti   Chalío-ni **ximpó**
          Maria-GEN pig   kill-PASS-PRF-PRS-3IND Chalío-OBL postp
          'Maria's pig was killed by Chalío.'

      b. imá acháati wántiku-p'i-**ra**-s-Ø-ti   pistóla-ni
          that man   kill-INDF.OBJ-APPL-PRF-PRS-3IND gun-OBL
          'That man killed (people) with a gun.'

      c. María-ni xanó-ku-s-Ø-ti   ma karákata
          Maria-OBL arrive-APPL-PRF-PRS-3IND one writings
          'A letter arrived for Maria.'   *P'orhépecha* (Capistrán Garza, 2015, p.106ff)

Building on the framework established by Franco & Manzini (2017b), we assume that adpositional or applicative elements, whether present in languages with or without inflectional obliques, delimit the basic contents such as (⊆) / (⊇), as exemplified in (25). This is exemplified in (24a), where at least two structural layers delineate the demoted agent "Chalío-ni ximpó" ('by Chalío'). The underlying layer constitutes the oblique *–ni* case inflection, serving as a (⊆) relator in our current framework, merely introducing an additional argument or participant into the event's framework. We attribute the specific agentive relation to the

---

29. An overlooked (yet crucial) observation, as previously noted in the Introduction, that bolsters the argument for a 'relational' content of this morpheme is its dual usage in expressing the lexical concept of 'chest' or 'cavity,' effectively conveying a relational, part-whole meaning. Additionally, when employed as a verbal affix, this morpheme can signify 'a part of' the argument encoded in the subject function, as demonstrated in (ia, b), or 'an area of' the place where this argument is situated or transitions to, as seen in (ic).

(i) a. María p'á-**ni**-s-Ø-ti
         Maria touch-cavity-PRF-PRS-3IND
         'Maria touched her breast.'

     b. p'orhóta xawá-**ni**-s-Ø-ti
         hole   deepen-cavity-PRF-PRS-3IND
         'The hole is deep.'

     c. xí wekó-**ni**-s-Ø-ka   kawáru
         1SG fall-cavity-PRF-PRS-1/2IND ditch
         'I fell into the ditch.'   *P'orhépecha* (Capistrán Garza, 2015, p.207ff)

30. As shown in Svenonius (2002, 2007) C-selection, as the determination of syntactic conditions on a dependent, hold only between a head and its complement. For example, a verb usually may determine idiosyncratic case on its internal arguments, but not its external arguments. Cross linguistically, adpositions quite commonly determine the case of a complement. Following Svenonius, this can only be demonstrated using language-specific diagnostics of c-selection We can assume that in P'orhépecha adpositions (and applicatives) consistently mark their complements as obliques.

Postpositional layer, which may be viewed as an Axial Part (AxPart) transposed to a non-locative domain (Svenonius 2006), or a category that is the *non-locative counterpart* of AxPart, as will be discussed in Chapter 4. The same rationale applies to instrumental (24b) and benefactive (24c) applicatives in P'orhépecha.

(25) ... [$_{PP}$ [$_{KP(2)}$ [$_{N}$ Chalío] -ni] ximpó]

Further specification of the reference of an oblique argument can involve additional layers. For example, in P'orhépecha, the applicative meaning can be augmented by adpositional or case inflection values. Specifically, instrumentals can be introduced as obliques through the postposition "ximpó" (26a), the instrumental case "-mpu" (26b), the applicative/causative "-ra" and its allomorphs, as previously demonstrated in (3b,c) and (18b,c), or by a combination of the applicative morpheme and case/adpositional devices, as seen in (26c,d).

(26) a. xí   ichárhuta-ni **ximpó** xwá-a-ka   p'atsímu
        1SG canoe-OBL   POSP bring-FUT-1/2IND reed
        'I will bring reed in the canoe/by canoe.'

      b. kachúku-s-Ø-ti k' wirípita kuchíyu-**mpu**
        cut-PRF-PRS-3IND meat   knife-INST
        'S/he cut some meat with the knife.'

      c. karákata-icha kará-**ra**-na-sïn-Ø-ti   lápisï-icha-ni **ximpó**
        writings-PL   write-INST-PASS-HAB-PRS-3IND pencil-pl-obl posp
        'Letters are written with pencils.'

      d. tsïntsîkata-icha ú-**ra**-na-s-Ø-ti   kuchára-**mpu**
        fence-PL   make/do-INST-PASS-PRF-PRS-3IND trowel-INST
        'The fences were built with a trowel.'

P'orhépecha (Capistrán Garza, 2015, p.114ff)

The availability of various means or layers to encode obliques is widespread cross-linguistically. Take, for example, the Italian pair in (27), where the same instrumental value can be expressed either by the adposition "con" or by the lexical string "per mezzo di" ('by means of', for which see Chapter 4).

(27) *Italian*
      a. Ha avvertito la fidanzata **con** un telegramma
        'S/He alerted the fiancée with a telegram'
      b. Ha avvertito la fidanzata **per mezzo di** un telegramma
        'S/He alerted the fiancée with a telegram' (lit. '...for mean of a telegram')

Now that we have provided evidence for the oblique status of the 'object' of applicative morphemes (at least in P'orhépecha), we can illustrate our analysis of the applicative=causative syncretism.

We follow Pylkkänen (2002, 2008) in assuming that there are two basic kinds of applicative arguments: a High Applicative which is introduced by a head attaching outside of VP and relating an individual to an event and a Low Applicative argument which is introduced by a head attaching below VP and relating two entities involved in a transfer of possession (i.e. in a 'giving environment'). As for interpretation, in the Applicative literature (Pylkkänen, 2008, p.13), instrumentals and benefactives are assumed to be encoded as High Appls, as opposed to Low Appls like goal datives: High Appl heads appear in an intermediate position between VP and v and express a relation between the oblique argument in their Spec and the VP event. Note that in P'orhépecha instrumental and benefactive applicatives represent the layer most closely associated to the verbal root: no other suffixes can be inserted between them.[31]

Based on the discussion of instrumentals (and benefactive) in Franco & Manzini (2017b), we propose that these relations can be reduced to an inclusion predicate notated as ($\supseteq$) (cf. the representation in (13)). This yields a structure of the type in (28), where the instrumental Appl($\supseteq$) takes as its two arguments the oblique DP instrument and the VP event.[32]

(28) a. xí   xwá-**ra**-s-Ø-ka-ni   tsúntsu-ni its
          1SG bring-APPL-PRF-PRS-1/2IND-1SG.SBJ pot-OBL   water
          'I brought some water with a pot.'

---

31. When benefactives, instrumental and causative meanings are lexicalized by different morphemes in natural languages, their ordering in the verbal skeleton is quite free, as shown by Buell & Sy (2006) for Wolof, undermining a cartographic/nanosyntactic approach to Appl=Caus. Note however that they are still the morphemes more tightly attached to the root and that no TAM markers can be inserted in between.

32. We want to adhere to the structure proposed in Franco & Manzini (2017b), in which the instrumental DP is the sister of the relator ($\supseteq$) and the VP event is its specifier. Nevertheless, we just point out that, standardly, applied instrumental participants are taken to be generated in Spec,ApplP (cf. Pylkkänen, 2008) right above V. Thus, we can imagine an alternative structure in which the ($\supseteq$) relation takes the VP event as its complement and the instrumental participant as its specifier. The same holds for causees, as illustrated in the structure in (31b). We leave this issue for future research of the topic.

b.

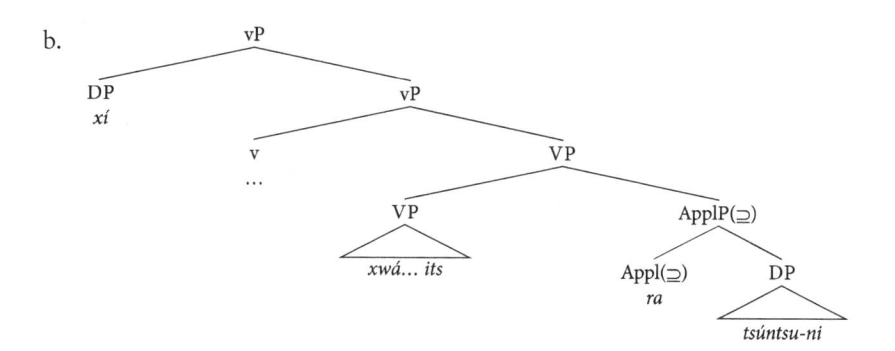

In (28), the (⊇) relation holds between 'a pot' and the event of 'water bringing,' indicating that such an event includes 'a pot.' Following the analyses of Alexiadou et al. (2015), Schäfer (2012), and Franco & Manzini (2017b), we assume that instruments are naturally associated with transitive events. However, nothing prevents applicative arguments from being introduced by unaccusative predicates (e.g., as causers, locatives, etc.), as demonstrated in (6a,b). Instruments are exclusively defined in the presence of an external argument introduced by vP (cf. also Bruening 2012).

Instruments are inanimate objects of ApplP/PP/KP (⊇) included in a caused event. The general interpretation of the structure in (28) is that the object of Appl(⊇) is a 'concomitant' participant of the VP result state (cf. the discussion in Section 3.1). Essentially, it asserts something like: "I caused 'brought water', and this (sub)event includes a pot." Namely, the VP result event is in turn embedded under a causation predicate; in this precise context, it is interpreted with the inanimate oblique playing the role of 'instrument of' the external argument in Spec, vP (the *initiator* of the event, cf. Marantz, 1984, Franco & Manzini, 2017b).

Given the characterization of instruments outlined above, it is evident how the same syntax as in (28) is capable of introducing the causee of causative constructions. As shown in Section 3.4, High Appls are responsible for adding an extra participant to an event, and the P'orhépecha morphemes –*ra* (with the allomorphs -*ta* and –*tara*) increase the valence of a predicate, introducing an argument construed as bearing a causee or instrument role.

As demonstrated in the previous section, causatives in Italian are expressed by a matrix predicate with pure CAUSE content, which selects directly a vP lacking a licensing slot for the expression of the causee as a direct argument (or an IP lacking agreement properties and an EPP position). Such impoverished environments crucially lack a structural case position for the external argument. Applicatives are precisely syntactic devices made available by Universal Grammar for the introduction of additional non-core arguments in the verbal spine when structural positions are unavailable.

The distinction between causees and instrumentals may also be blurred in languages introducing causees and instruments by means of adpositional devices. For instance, in Hindi, the causee usually surfaces as an instrumental (Ramchand, 2011). Moreover, consider the following Italian data.

(29) *Italian*

    a.   Il medico ha fatto guarire il paziente con le/*alle erbe
         'The doctor made the patient recover with the herbs'
         -> le erbe hanno guarito il paziente
         'The herbs cured the patient'

    b.   Il medico ha fatto guarire il paziente allo/dallo/#con lo specializzando
         'The doctor made the trainee cure the patient'
         -> 'lo specializzando ha guarito il paziente'
         'the trainee cured the patient'

    a'. Il principe ha fatto eliminare il rivale col veleno
         'The prince has the rival eminated by the poison'
         -> 'il veleno ha eliminato il rivale'
         'The poison eliminated the rival'

    b'. Il principe ha fatto eliminare il rivale al/dal/#con lo scagnozzo
         'The prince has the rival eliminated by the henchman'
         -> 'lo scagnozzo ha eliminato il rivale'
         'the henchman eliminated the rival'

In (29a, a'-b, b'), the causative predicates can be assumed to have 'inanimate causees' introduced by the (instrumental) adposition con. The fact that these participants can be interpreted as causees in such contexts is ensured by their ability to surface as the subjects of the base predicates from which causatives are derived, as illustrated in the examples in (28). Animate causees in the same environments are typically externalized by the adposition a/da (cf. Section 4). If they are introduced by the con adposition, the only possible reading is comitative, either subject or object-oriented (cf. Yamada, 2010). Thus, it is possible to assume that the instrumentally marked inanimate causees in (29) are nothing else than Differentially Marked Causees, based on an animacy scale. In any event, the link between causees and instruments is ensured by the Italian data provided above.

Nothing prevents multiple adjuncts in minimalist syntax (Chomsky, 1995), and both inanimate (instrument) and animate (canonical) causees can be present in the same sentence. Following Franco & Manzini (2017b, p.31) on the ergative-instrumental syncretism, we assume that both the causee and the instrument are adjoined at the VP level. Consider the example in (30a) and the possible representation in (30b). The interpretation is that of a complex causal chain of the type: 'the prince caused the henchmen to be involved in the killing of a rival and this same event involve the (use of) poison'.

(30) a. Il principe ha fatto eliminare il rivale col veleno al/dal/#con lo scagnozzo
'The prince had the rival eliminated with poison by the henchman

b.

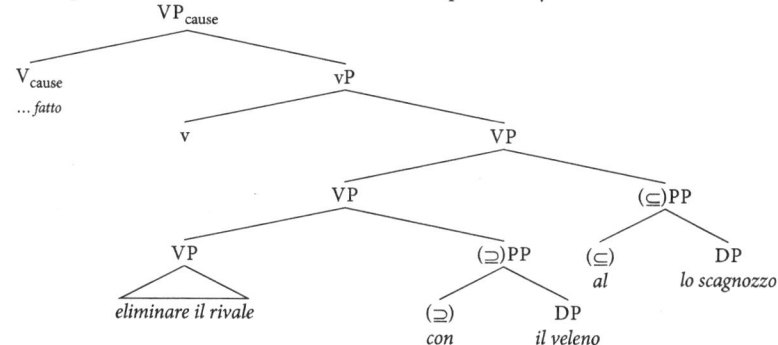

Hence, it is evident how applicative morphemes can be utilized to introduce causees and instrumental participants (and more generally, arguments associated with the high applicative projection). (High) applicatives serve as elementary relators linking an oblique argument to the event depicted by a VP. As discussed in Section 3.3, they are one of the possible devices provided by Universal Grammar to increase the valence of a predicate. Crucially, as previously noted in Cole (1983), the syncretism between instrumentals and causees extends widely beyond the realm of applicatives: instrumental adpositions and instrumental cases are often employed as the unmarked way to encode the causee in numerous languages (such as Hungarian, Kannada, Hindi, etc.).

Therefore, concerning the applicative-causative syncretism, we can posit that causees are inserted into the syntax as 'applied arguments' (similarly to instrumentals, beneficiaries, or other roles linked to the High Appl projection). A representation is provided in (31) for the P'orhépecha example in (18b). We assume that the structure is essentially the same as in (28).

(31) a. María xwá-ra-s-Ø-ti   Xwánu-ni tsíri
Maria bring-CAUS-PRF-PRS-3IND Juan-OBL corn
'Maria made Juan bring some corn.'

b.

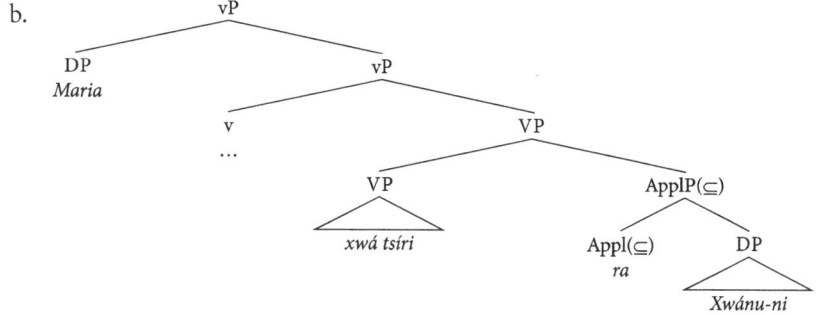

Following Franco & Manzini (2017b), the relationship (⊇) between the applied (causee) argument and the VP event in (31) implies inclusion in an event or concomitance with it. The causee applicative (⊇) is then embedded under a causation predicate (vP), similar to the instrumental applicative. The Appl literature (cf. Pylkkänen, 2008) assumes that instruments correspond to high Appls, generated in an intermediate layer between VP and vP, taking the applied argument in its specifier, not as its complement. Thus, one problem is whether the VP-adjunction structure we have proposed above for (high) applicatives can be shown to yield two differentiated causer and instrument meaning. Actually, we believe that the causative interpretation is derived from what the structure essentially conveys; for (31), it implies "Maria caused the inclusion of Xwánu (or Xwánu to be included) in the event of 'bringing corn.'" The fact that *Xwánu* is a human participant to the event favours its interpretation as the causee. Therefore, we think that the applicative data presented in this Chapter support Franco & Manzini (2017b)'s proposition that ⊆ / ⊇ are associated with vP or VP predicates (assuming the two-tiered structure of Hale & Kayser, 1993, Chomsky, 1995) as general 'oblique' participants.

Specifically, we can hypothesize that causees and instruments are differentiated based on a relatively fundamental ontology, which includes the ranking of event oblique participants in the animacy hierarchy: here, human vs. inanimate: instruments (*contra* causees) are consistently inanimate objects of P(⊇) included in a caused event, cf. Peterson, 2007).

3.6   Conclusion

This chapter has explored the applicative-causative syncretism, an often overlooked phenomenon of morpheme polysemy found in numerous natural languages. We have interpreted the causative-applicative syncretism as rooted in a shared syntactic structure. Specifically, we argue that the syncretic morpheme in question serves as the applicative counterpart to an adpositional or case elementary relator (Manzini & Franco 2016; Franco & Manzini, 2017b). This morpheme attaches instrumental or benefactive obliques (High Applicatives, cf. Pylkkänen 2002, 2008) to the verbal spine. Building on the work of Bellucci (2017) and others, we posit that causees can also be introduced as obliques, potentially occupying the same structural position. The interpretation of the causative sentence is driven by semantics, while the syntax closely resembles that of the instrumental (cf. Franco & Manzini, 2017b). This explains the capacity to encode causatives and applicatives utilizing identical lexical material.

CHAPTER 4

Axial Parts beyond space

Relational nouns and grammatical categories

This chapter investigates the nature of Axial Parts (AxPs)/Relational nouns(RelN) and their relationship with Grounds in spatial expressions and beyond. We argue that the relation between AxPs and Grounds is predicative. We challenge the view that prepositions inherently encode spatial meanings, arguing instead that they function as general relators whose specific interpretation depends on the context. The Finnish locative system is examined as a challenge to existing accounts, and a novel structure with a "double inclusion layer" is proposed. Cross-linguistic evidence, mainly basing on Italian and Persian data, supports our analysis, showing that AxPs spread beyond spatial expressions and that prepositions act as general relators for the predicative content.

4.1 On the definition of Axial Part, PLACE & PATH

In accordance with Svenonius (2006), the linguistic category Axial Part (henceforth: AxP) delineates a component of the Ground (the reference landmark for location), which serves as a spatial *axis* for locating the Figure (the object whose location is at issue, cf. Talmy, 2000). AxP exhibits a hybrid behavior, sharing certain characteristics with nouns. Often, AxP is phonetically identical to Relation Nouns (RelN) denoting *body parts* (Roy, 2006) or other nominal entities with spatial relevance.

Before defining AxP, we need to provide some background on the spatial concepts of Figure & Ground and the way they have been applied to syntactic investigation. The terms 'figure' and 'ground' have been introduced by Leon Talmy (1985, 1988) and were adopted following insight from Gestalt psychology (cf. Svenonius, 2003, p. 433). Talmy (1985, p. 61) defines Figure & Ground as follows:

i.   The Figure is a moving or conceptually movable object whose path or site is at issue;

ii. The Ground is a reference-frame, or a reference-point stationary within a reference-frame, with respect to which the Figure's path or site is characterized.

The concepts of Figure and Ground are *relational*, as originally assumed in Svenonius (2003, 2006, 2007). Indeed, Figure and Grounds are positioned with respect to each other and it is very likely, as we will show below, to assume that the adpositions that connect them are sort of relators/predicates. For example, in the expression the keys on the table, the keys is the Figure, and it is positioned with respect to the Ground, the table, by the predication denoted by the adposition *on* (cf. Wood, 2015, p.173, from which the examples in (1) are taken). The Figure can be in motion, as in (1a), or at rest, as in (1b).

(1) a.   John threw the keys **on** the table.
     b.   John saw the keys **on** the table.

In (1a), the keys, acting as the Figure, are understood to traverse a Path, the endpoint of which is on the table, which acts as the Ground. In (24), the keys are at rest in a position on the table. Still, their relational content is expressed by means of the adposition on.

Svenonius (2006), employing various diagnostics (e.g., the absence of articles with AxPs compared to homophonous Rel Ns, inability to pluralize, modify, possibility of specification by a measure phrase, etc.), argues against considering AxPs (terms like "front," "beside," "behind," etc.) as a subset of nouns, particularly RelNs (as opposed to Sortal nouns, e.g., "a child of someone" vs. "*a person of someone") (Hagège, 2010, p.162–165; Barker, 1995). Scholars have proposed that AxP can be regarded as an independent category, positioned between nouns and prepositions (Pantcheva, 2011; Fábregas, 2007a; Roy & Svenonius, 2009; Cinque, 2010a; Franco, 2016, among others). Specifically, Svenonius (2006) posits that AxP projects a functional layer immediately dominated by a locative preposition (Place) and situated above the DP that introduces the Ground. Svenonius employs the term K(ase) to designate the element connecting the AxP to the Ground. Svenonius subscribes to what Borer (2005) terms "Neo-constructivism," suggesting that certain semantic dimensions are modelled by syntactic structure, while others stem directly from the lexical content of the item integrated into the syntactic framework.

The AxP vs. RelN contrast exemplifies this notion. A term like "front" in English is polysemous. When inserted under an N node in a syntactic derivation, "front" functions as a noun, capable of combining with plural morphology, determiners, etc. When inserted under an AxP node, it contributes to the functional structure of the extended projection of P. Essentially, Rel N and AxP would assume distinct syntactic configurations, as illustrated in (2), following the representation provided in Svenonius (2006).

(2) a. AxPart > *front*

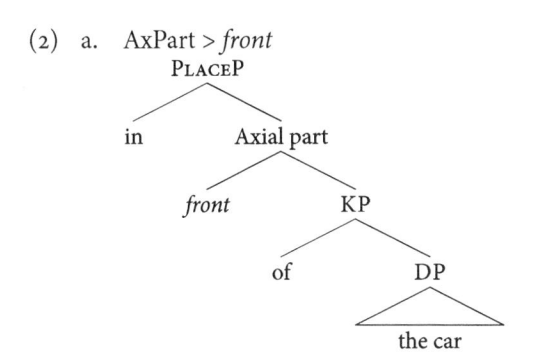

b. RelNoun > *(the) front*

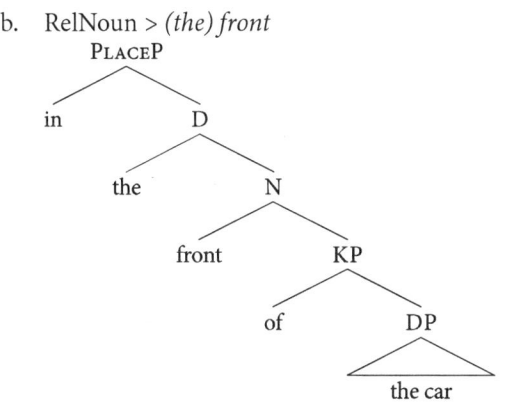

Example (2a) states that a given entity (acting as the Figure) would be situated in contact with the upper surface of the front section of the car (acting as the Ground), such as its hood or bonnet, while (2b) is primarily interpreted as indicating a given entity occupying one of the two front seats of a standard car, although it could alternatively suggest an entity located in a cargo area beneath the hood or bonnet of a rear-engine vehicle, for instance. In either scenario, as stated in Svenonius (2006), "in" is fitting as the entity is enclosed within a confined space.

In the cartographic literature, the domain above AxP within the PP structure has garnered significant attention in recent theoretical discussions (Zwarts, 1995; Koopman, 2000; den Dikken, 2010, on Dutch; Holmberg, 2002 on Zina Kotoko; Svenonius, 2003, 2007, across different languages). This domain is believed to encompass at least two primary components: PLACE (associated with static locational meanings) and PATH (associated with directed motion) (also discussed by Pantcheva, 2011; Romeu, 2013; Takamine, 2017, among others, who offer more comprehensive analyses).

Place elements provide information regarding the relationship between the Figure and the Ground (the reference landmark for the Figure's location, as discussed previously). This is exemplified in (3a), where the elephants represent the Figure and the boat serves as the Ground. In contrast, Paths offer details about a trajectory; they may specify whether a Place serves as a Goal (3b) or a Source (3c), and may also provide information on the orientation of a trajectory (3d) (cf. Pantcheva 2011; examples drawn from Svenonius, 2010, p. 127).

(3) a. The elephants remained in the boat.
     b. They cast a wistful glance to the shore.
     c. The boat drifted further from the beach.
     d. Their ears sank down several notches.

In cartographic theoretical framework, it's generally posited that Path occupies a higher structural position than Place, as demonstrated in (4) and (5). When both Path and Place are present, the Path layer is typically regarded as being structurally more distant from the Ground (cf. Baker 1988; also supported by evidence from Dutch in studies such as Koopman, 2000; Den Dikken, 2010).

(4) na to gma
     on to table
     "onto the table"   *Zina Kotoko* (Holmberg, 2002)

(5) sew-re-l-di
     bear-ERG-on-to
     "onto the bear"   *Lezgian* (Haspelmath, 1993)

In (6) below, we present a structure incorporating the Place and Path nodes, following Svenonius (2006) and subsequent research. It's important to note that AxP would likely be generated within a node positioned below Place.

(6) *"into the room"*

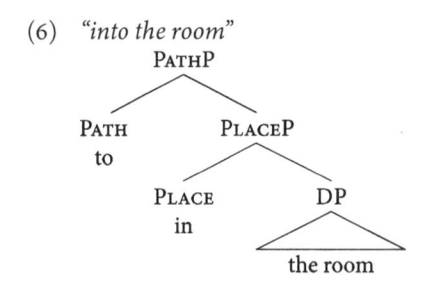

4.2   Space is not PLACE (nor PATH)

Expanding on the discussion of case systems, particularly obliques characterized as elementary predicates conveying part-whole or inclusion (possession) semantics, we can provide a systematic explanation of potential case syncretisms beyond case itself, within the realm of locative morphemes, without resorting to a layered structure.

Franco et al. (2021) offer a comprehensive analysis of this phenomenon, primarily focusing on Italian. In Italian, the preposition "a" ('at/to') introduces both states of being at/in (Place) and motion towards (Path), as exemplified in (7a), whereas "da" ('from') specializes in denoting motion originating from, as shown in (7b). However, this distinction holds true only for inanimate complements. With human referents, "da" is used for both states of being at/in, motion towards, and motion from (though the translation 'from' proves to be inaccurate), as depicted in (8). This demonstrates an instance of Differential Object Marking (DOM) within the adpositional locative domain (cf. Fábregas, 2015a, b).

From the examples in (8), we deduce that *da*'s inherent meaning lacks directionality and other spatially significant specifications (such as state/motion). If these were inherent to its core denotation, its compatibility with the various contexts presented in (8) would be difficult to reconcile.

(7)   *Italian*
    a.   Sono/vado a/*da   casa
        I.am/I.go   at/to/*from home
    b.   Esco   *a/da   casa.
        I.get.out *at/*to/from home

(8)   *Italian*
    Sono/vado/esco   **da**-l parrucchiere.
    I.am/I.go/I.get.out at/to/from-the hairdresser
    'I am at/I go to/I come from the hairdresser'

By the way, it's worth noting that this phenomenon is not exclusive to Romance languages, as evidenced by Persian examples in (9) and (10). In Persian, the use of a complex preposition is obligatory (as discussed by Pantcheva, 2006), such as "pish" (in front of, with, near) or "nazd" (before, beside, near), in similar contexts involving animate referents (resembling French "chez," as it will be discussed below). Conversely, inanimate referents are introduced by a simple preposition (e.g., "dar" for 'in', "be" for 'to', without taking the *ezafe*/linker morpheme, see our discussion of Persian in 4.8 below).

(9) *Persian*
     dar bazar   hastam/**be** bazar   miravam
     at   market I.am/ to   market I.go
     'I am in/at the market/ I go to the market'

(10) *Persian*
      pish-e   doctor hastam/miravam/*dar/*be doctor...
      near-LNK doctor I.am/I.go *at/*to   doctor...
      'I am at the doctor'/I go to the doctor'

According to the hypothesis, the preposition 'a' ('at/to') in (7a) carries the meaning of $\subseteq$, suggesting that the 'house' contains (or comes to contain) 'me' in a locative sense. This same content of $\subseteq$ should also apply to 'da' in (8), which encompasses similar contexts (cf. the interpretation of causees provided in Chapter 3). Supporting evidence for this conclusion can be found in the fact that the motion-from usage of 'da' is pronominalized by the same clitic as genitive/partitives, namely 'ne', as shown in (11). It's worth noting that motion-to and state-in are pronominalized by a dedicated clitic 'ci' meaning 'there/here', which is syncretic with the dative clitic in many Italian dialects, as discussed by Manzini & Savoia (2007), Kayne (2005, 2010).

(11) *Italian*
      a. **Ne**   esco   ora (dal   parrucchiere/da casa)
          from.it I.get.out now (from.the hairdresser/from home)
      b. **Ne**   vedo tre
          of.them I.see three'
          'I see three of them'

This raises questions about how we explain the differences in meaning between 'a' and 'da', given their shared interpretive content, as well as the issue of the DOM(-like) split. We will revisit these questions after presenting further evidence against 'a' and 'da' being inherently locative.

To begin, as elaborated in more detail by Franco et al. (2021), in the Central Italian variety in (12), 'da' encompasses the contexts discussed for Italian in (7)–(8), including motion-from (12c) and locative DOM (12b). Additionally, 'da' introduces dative complements (12a). Meanwhile, 'a' also exists in this language, introducing motion-to as seen in (12d).

(12) a. lo ðajo **da** mmi fratɛllo
          it I.give to my brother
      b. vajo/stɔnno lla **da** esso
          I.go/they.stay there to/at him
      c. vɛŋgo **da** su/ju   kkasa
          I.come from up/down home
      d. vajo **a**/*da ttɔdi
          I.go to   Todi

Avigliano (Umbria)

Considering a system like Italian (7)–(8) (or even English), one might consider the notion that the denotation of goals in ditransitive constructions is an extension of the motion-to (Path) content. However, (12) presents a direct counterexample to this assumption, as the goal can just as effectively be encoded by the same preposition found in motion-from contexts. The most straightforward analysis (supported by the occurrence of 'da' with highly-ranked objects) suggests that adpositions introduce elementary relations that extend beyond the locative domain; the locative meaning is contingent upon additional locative restrictions imposed on their relational core.

Additionally, Creole languages provide even more compelling evidence that prepositions are general relators, with specific locative interpretations emerging based on their embedding context. As documented in the Atlas of Pidgin and Creole Language Structures (Michaelis et al., 2013: APiCS feature 81), many Romance-based Creoles deviate from the Romance pattern, consistently marking motion-to and motion-from in the same way (regardless of DOM-like patterns). For example, Haitian Creole employs the relator "nan" to convey both motion-to and motion-from (13a–b). Thus, "nan" differs from French "dans" (to which it is formally related, cf. Wälchli & Zúñiga, 2006), which expresses motion-to and state-in but never motion-from.

(13) a. Jézi désann soti **nan** kannòt la
          J.   descend exit P boat DET
          'Jézi come out from the boat.'
      b. li tounin **nan** kannòt la
          he return P boat DET
          'he return to the boat'
          Haitian Creole

While Italian varieties utilize the preposition "da," many Romance languages, such as French or Catalan, denote motion-from using the genitive preposition "de" ('of'). Consider French Examples (14a–b); once again, a dedicated preposition (for DOM purposes) introduces highly ranked referents, namely "chez," as in

(14c) (a similar situation is illustrated with Persian above). *Chez* can be assumed to act as an Axial Part in the sense of Svenonius, also given etymological consideration (cf. Longobardi, 2001). The crucial observation here is that French "de" ('from') is drawn from the basic repertoire of relators in the language. Indeed, the genitive, like the dative, conveys notions of possession, inclusion, or part-whole relationships and is therefore ascribed the content of ⊆ in this analysis. Consequently, while the system's contours may be slightly reconfigured in French, they align with the conclusions drawn in connection with Italian.

(14) *French*
    a. Je viens **de** la maison/**de** Paris
        I come from the house/from Paris
    b. le livre **de** Marie
        the book of Marie
    c. Je suis/vais **chez** lui
        I am/go   at/to him

We follow Franco et al. (2021) to formally represent the different locative interpretations of *a* and *da* in Italian (*a* and *da* in Aviglianese, *à* and *de* in French, etc.) and to account for the fact that there are languages (e.g. Haitian Creole) which consistently use the same morpheme to convey a motion-to/state-in *vs.* a motion-from interpretation. Let's take Italian for example. As mentioned earlier, location can be conceptualized as inclusion within a given spatial area, thus it suffices to introduce a locative constraint on the relation of ⊆ to capture this notion, as shown in (15). However, this formulation fails to distinguish between 'a' and 'da'.

(15) *a, da*: P, ⊆ (Loc)

It appears that the most plausible explanation lies in the notion that the relevant interpretations are contingent upon the nature of the event. In telic events, 'a' ('to') signifies the location at the telos or endpoint of the event, i.e., at the result clause implied by it (Higginbotham, 2009), as exemplified by 'I go (to) home' in (7a) with the structure depicted in (16a) (for a discussion on unaccusatives as verbs endowed with a *v* layer, see Alexiadou et al., 2015). Conversely, 'da' ('from') implies a location outside the result or telos of the event, indicating its causal component, as illustrated by 'I get out from home' in (16b). This inference is supported by the observation that English 'from' also introduces causers, while Italian 'da' introduces both causers and agents (i.e., 'by'-phrases, cf. Manzini 2017, Chapter 3 above and the discussion around Section 4.5).[33]

(16)   a.   [$_{CAUSE}$ [$_{ResP}$ go [$_⊆$ (to) home]]]
     b.   [$_{CAUSE}$ [$_{ResP}$ get out] [$_⊆$ (from) home]]

Regarding locative DOM, explaining languages like French or Persian where complex prepositions such as "chez" specialize in locative inclusion with highly ranked referents isn't challenging.[34] This strategy is to locate the highly ranked referent with respect to an Axial Part which is the (noun-like) location directly embedded in the event structure.[35]

---

33. State-in, as the most basic locative relation, requires only that P embeds a location, as in (i), where the atelic predicate blocks the motion-to reading in Romance, but not the state-in reading.

(i)   Ho camminato a Roma'I walked in/*to Rome'

34. A similar selection of specialized locative prepositions occurs in many Italian dialects, such as "nnə/ndə" (found in Aidone, Sicily, according to Manzini & Savoia, 2005, etymologically linked to Latin "inde" meaning 'from there'), and in certain Ibero-Romance varieties (for instance, the use of "donde/adonde" with animate landmarks in Peruvian and Mexican Spanish, as discussed by Luraghi, 2011).

35. The French and Persian strategy, locating the highly ranked referent with respect to an Axial Part which is the (noun-like) location directly embedded in the event structure, is widely attested crosslinguistically. For instance, as illustrated in Nishina (2001), in Japanese there are different markers for locative. In (i) we provide locative markers encoding stative *vs.* dynamic situations.

(i)   a.   Taroo-wa   Tokyo-**ni**   sun-de   iru
          Taro-TOP Tokyo-LOC live-GER be
          "Taro lives in Tokyo."

     b.   Taroo-wa   Tokyo-**de**   hatarai-te   iru
          Taro-TOP Tokyo-LOC work-GER be
          "Taro works in Tokyo."   *Japanese* (Nishina, 2001, p.359)

The inflection -*ni* is employed with stative predicates, as illustrated in (ia), while the case morpheme –*de* is used with predicates encoding dynamic events, as illustrated in (ib). As to animacy, -*ni* is also the dative inflection by which an animate participant is marked, whereas -*de* cannot mark animate locatives directly (**Hanako-de*). In such cases, Japanese resorts to an Axial Part strategy, by means of a string meaning 'in the place of Hanako', as shown in (ii). Note that the Ground *Hanako* and the Axial part *tokoro* are linked, as expected, by a genitive case marker (here, *no*):

(ii)   Taroo-wa   **Hanako-no**   **tokoro**-de hatarai-te iru
      Taro-TOP Hanako-GEN place-LOC work-GER be
      "Taro works under Hanako."   *Japanese* (Nishina, 2001, p.360)

The Dravidian language Kuvi seems to behave like Japanese, but, in addition, it also disentangles between animate/inanimate datives, by means of the same Axial Part recruited for locatives. Consider the examples in (i). Inanimate datives and animate locatives are encoded by means of the same *ta/ taɳ* (meaning 'place') axial adposition.

More tricky is understanding the behaviour of Italian "da." The most compelling interpretation of the data in (7b)–(8) suggests that 'da' ('from, by') consistently implies location at the causal component of the event, thereby situated outside its telos. However, this interpretation is at odds with the structural analysis of motion-to interpretations. Consequently, we must infer that although 'da' is typically constrained to attach to 'v' (the causation node of the predicate), it does attach to the resultative complement of 'V' in specific instances when it selects a human location, as illustrated in (17a). The structure of motion-from contexts mirrors that introduced for non-animates in (16b), as shown in (17b) below.

(17) a. [vP v [VP vado [1SG [⊆ da [DP il parrucchiere]]]]
      b. [vP v [VP esco 1SG] [⊆ da [DP il parrucchiere]]]

In Franco et al. (2021), "da" has been analyzed as one of several exponents of the elementary predicate '⊆'; hence, both attachments in (17) are plausible for it. However, the lexical entry we might have considered based on motion-from (and agent/causer environments) proves overly restrictive for "da." Indeed, Italian "da" is not limited to selecting for "vP," but can also occur while selecting highly ranked referents with any attachment to the event.[36] This flexibility is summarized by the

---

(i) a. āyana-ki
         woman-DAT
         'to the woman'
     b. ilu   ta-ki
         house P-DAT
         'to the house'
     c. āyani   taṇ-a
         woman.GEN P-LOC
         'at the woman's place'
     d. ilut-a
         house-LOC
         'at the house'   *Kuvi*, Aristar (1996, p. 215)

36. Differential marking is a phenomenon normally studied in relation to the embedding of verbal objects. Nonetheless, it is attested in prepositional embedding as well. Interestingly, differential encoding of locative Grounds, where the feature animacy/human acts a relevant trigger is widely attested across genetically non-related languages (cf. the typological survey in Haspelmath, 2019). Differential Marking is also at work regarding the item linking AxP and the Ground (cf. Franco & Manzini, 2017a). This context is characterized by the alternation between the direct embedding of lexical DPs and the embedding of pronouns using the genitive preposition "di" ('of') in Italian. For instance, the use of the genitive "di" preposition is possible (and preferred) with person pronouns in (ib), whereas it is not used with lexical DPs, including human referents, as seen in (ia).

disjunctive set of lexical specifications in (18). According to (18), "da" can select a "vP" as its external argument, i.e., a causation event. It can also select an animate entity when the latter needs to be interpreted as a location (an object extended in space). Importantly, these two options are not mutually exclusive, as illustrated by (17b), namely motion-from with an animate location.

(18)   da: P, ⊆, selects vP/CAUSE or [Loc *mental state*]

In the lexical entry in (17) we have employed the two fundamental theta-roles suggested by Reinhart (2003), namely [cause] and [mental state], to indicate that Italian "da" requires one of them to be positively valued for one of its two arguments. This entry aligns with our understanding of light verbs or other elementary predicates. While these predicates have a clearly defined denotational core, the contexts in which they prove compatible are not entirely predictable and must be learned for each language.

(i)   a.   Il   cane corre verso   il/*del   suo padrone
           the dog runs toward the/of.the its owner
           'The dog runs toward its owner'

    b.   *Italian* Il   cane corre verso   (di) me/voi/lei
                 the dog runs toward of me/you/her
                 'The dog runs toward me/you/her'

Generally, within Italian syntax, there exists a group of AxP complex adpositions (such as "senza" for 'without' and "dopo" for 'after,' among others, as documented by Rizzi, 1988, p. 535–536) that incorporate a genitive "di" layer to enclose personal pronouns, specifically deictic elements (cf. Garzonio & Rossi, 2016). Conversely, non-deictic complements are directly embedded without this genitive layer. Rizzi (1988) further observes that this use of the genitive "di" can be extended to demonstratives (e.g., "verso di questo" for 'toward this'). This observation aligns with our understanding of the intricate relationship between animacy and definiteness scales in Differential Object Marking (DOM) within Romance languages (Manzini et al., 2020). Demonstratives, being inherently high on the definiteness hierarchy, exhibit the behavior noted by Rizzi. In present terms, the relevant Italian Ps, though normally selecting a DP complement, are allowed (and for some speakers/contexts forced) to syntactically encode their pronominal complements via a ⊆ (genitive) layer, as schematized in (ii), following Franco & Manzini (2017a). Consequently, elements ranking high on the definiteness scale (such as deictic pronouns) are syntactically rendered as possessors of the spatial (or temporal, etc.) Axis lexicalized by the preposition, which, in Svenonius's (2006) terms, as we have shown in Section 4.1, constitutes an AxP. It's worth noting the formulation in (ii) underscores the parallelism with the sentential DOM schema proposed by Manzini and Franco (2016). This syntactic alignment between the structures of prepositions and verbs aligns with recent literature (Svenonius, 2007, Wood, 2015, Franco 2020), which will be discussed in the subsequent sections.

(ii)   Differential Marking: *Italian Complex Ps* [AxP [(⊆) DP]] where DP = pronouns

This analysis of locatives leads us to the conclusion that the core obliques (cases, prepositions) of natural languages function as a system of elementary operators that link arguments to the verbal spine, indicating possession, inclusion of other DPs or events/states, or potentially establishing the reverse relationship with them.[37] In the next Section, we will provide some relevant data from Finnish locative system.

4.3   Finnish locative puzzles

4.3.1   The *l/s* series

Further evidence supporting our analysis comes from the examination of Finnish locatives, as presented in Franco et al. (2017). In this section, we will outline the most significant characteristics of the Finnish locative system and provide an overview of some previous theoretical perspectives on the topic. Finnish features six productive morphological cases that express location in a concrete sense (cf. Siro, 1964, p. 29 for a comprehensive overview, including relics of non-productive locative cases, which will not be considered in this work, cf. also Hakulinen, 1979; Häkkinen, 1996; Itkonen, 1997, among others). The Finnish spatial system is exemplified in (19) with the noun "talo" meaning 'house.'

The spatial case morphemes of Finnish can be understood as compositional; the illative -(h)Vn, for historical reasons, is related to -s, though a phonological process occurred in which 's' gradually weakened into 'h' and then disappeared in most instances (Huumo & Ojutkangas, 2006; Lehtinen, 2007). Comrie (1999) suggests that Finnish has two "series markers:" -s meaning 'in' and -l meaning 'on.' These series markers combine with the locative endings to express states, motion-to, and motion-from meanings.

---

37. We acknowledge that one may legitimately wonder what may be excluded from the denotation of such a wide-ranging relator as ⊆. We observe that precisely because of its very general denotation, the part/whole or inclusion predicate (whether it corresponds to a case inflection or to an adpositional head) does not have sufficient lexical content to characterize, say, specific (sub)types of possession, location, etc. Thus, in a language like Latin (the same) oblique case attaches to locations, possessors, goals e.g. *Romae* (Rome-OBL) 'in Rome, of Rome, to Rome (dative)'. However, there are no languages where the oblique case may denote, say, 'after' as opposed to 'before', 'on' as opposed to 'under', etc. To encode those meanings, natural languages precisely resort to more specialized relational nouns/Axial Parts.

(19)   Series   'in/at'   'to'   'from'
       -s (**internal**) -ssa (talo-ssa) -(h)Vn (talo-on) -sta (talo-sta)
                      inessive   illative   elative
       -l (**external**) -lla (talo-lla) -lle (talo-lle)   -lta (talo-lta)
                      adessive   allative   ablative
       Spatial case system of Finnish (Pantcheva, 2011, cf. Sulkala & Karjalainen,
       1992)

In Finnish, the primary spatial function of the so-called internal cases (denoted
by the -s series) is to indicate containment, indicating that one entity is positioned
within (or moving into or out of) a (typically three-dimensional) space.

(20)   *Finnish*
       Tyttö on   kirjastossa
       girl   is.PRS.3SG library.INE
       "The girl is in the library."

(21)   *Finnish*
       Tyttö meni   kirjastoon
       girl   go.PST.3SG library.ILL
       "The girl went to the library."

(22)   *Finnish*
       Tyttö tuli   kirjastosta
       girl   come.PST.3SG library.ELA
       "The girl came from the library."

The external cases (*-l* series) designate a relation of 'association', 'contact', etc.

(23)   *Finnish*
       Tyttö on   kirjastolla
       girl   come.PST.3SG library.ADE
       "The girl is at the library."

(24)   *Finnish*
       Tyttö meni   kirjastolle
       girl   go.PST.3SG library.ALL
       "The girl went to the library."

(25)   *Finnish*
       Tyttö tuli   kirjastolta
       girl   come.PST.3SG library.ABL
       "The girl came from the library."

4.3.2   Finnish adpositions

Finnish makes extensive use of adpositions to express local relations. These adpositions are linked to the ground by a genitive (26) or partitive (27) case morpheme. The adposition is inflected by the spatial case series reviewed in (19). The partitive tends to encode complements of prepositions, as in (27), while genitives encode complements of postpositions, as in (26) though this does not represent a fixed behavior. Some postposition take both series of spatial case (*s/l*) (e.g. *ede-* "above"), others take a series only (e.g. *perä-* "behind" > *-s* series).

(26)   *Finnish*
Järvi talo-n   lähe-llä.
lake house-GEN near-ADE
"The lake near the house."

(27)   *Finnish*
Järvi lähe-llä. talo-a.
lake near-ADE house-PART
"The lake near the house."

4.3.2.1   *Previous accounts: Pantcheva (2011)*

According to Pantcheva (2011), the series markers *-l* and *-s* lexicalize the AxP head, while the spatial case(s) above may lexicalize either the Place head or the Path head, which she decomposes into Goal and Source. The Illative morpheme *-(h)Vn*, which lacks the overt display of *-s*, lexicalizes AxP, Place, and Path (Goal). It's worth noting that within the nanosyntactic framework (Starke, 2009; Caha, 2009), Pantcheva assumes that a single morpheme can lexicalize a series of syntactic nodes.

However, Pantcheva's proposed model appears problematic on empirical grounds. In Finnish (and throughout the entire Uralic language family), adpositions appear to instantiate prototypical AxP. Specifically, they are frequently derived from body terms, as shown in (28), in which the body part term involved can be interpreted both nominally and adpositionally (see Suutari, 2006, for a comprehensive discussion), and are connected to the Ground via a K device (in Finnish, as we have seen, the genitive and partitive case).[38]

---

38. Note that a differential encoding of human Grounds by means of an Axial Part is attested also in Uralic (cf. the data in Section 4.2). For instance, in Finnish 'at' meaning 'location in the close vicinity' can be introduced by two different structures: (i) the adessive marker *–llA*; (ii) the postposition *luo-* 'at', which shows nominal inflection and is preceded by a genitive modifier. We consider the latter as an Axial Part along the lines of the discussion above. See the example in (i).

(28)   Lapsi nukku-u äidi-n   rinna-lla.
       Child sleep-3SG mother-GEN chest/breast-ADE
       "The child is sleeping in its mother's breast ~ lap ~ arms."   [nominal]
       "The child is sleeping beside its mother."   [adpositional]

                                                    Finnish (Suutari, 2006, p. 113)

Consider the examples provided earlier in (26)–(27). Adpositions clearly lexicalize the AxP node, yet the morphemes *-s* / *-l* persist. This raises the question: what do they lexicalize in such cases?

This situation presents an issue of 'overabundance' if we assume that both morphemes are AxPs competing for the same slot. One would expect *-l* and *-s*

   (i)   luona (ade.) – luo/luokse (– /transl.) – luota (abl.)   *Finnish*
         (a) 'at someone's', (b) 'very near to something'

The [+/–human] feature of the lexical item is highly relevant in triggering the use of the postposition *luo*. With [+human] referents the two structures can alternate without any change in the meaning of the sentence. Consider the example in (ii).

   (ii)   *Finnish*
          a.   Olen   Kaarinan   luona. / Olen   Kaarina-lla.
               Be.PRS.1SG Kaarina.GEN at.ADE / be.PRS.1SG Kaarina-ADE
               "I'm at Kaarina's place"
          b.   Menen   Kaarinan   luokse. / Menen   Kaarina-lle.
               Go.PRS.1SG Kaarina.GEN at.TRANSL / go.PRS.1SG Kaarina-ALL
               "I'll go to Kaarina's place."
          c.   Tulen   Kaarinan   luota. / Tulen   Kaarina-lta.
               come-PRS.1SG Kaarina.GEN at.ABL / come.PRES1SG Kaarina-ABL
               "I'll come from Kaarina's place."

Nevertheless, when the referent is [-human] we have two sets of lexical items: those that favour external cases can freely alternate, while those that favour internal cases only allow the 'luona'-structure. See the structures in (iii).

   (iii) *Finnish*
          a.   Odotan   tämän puun   luona /*Odotan   tällä   puu-lla
               Wait.PRS.1SG this.GEN tree.Gen at.ADE / wait.PRS.1SG this.ADE tree-ADE
               "I'll wait near this tree."
          b.   Olen   koiran luona / * Olen   koira-lla
               be.PRS.1SG dog.GEN at.ADE / be.PRS.1SG dog-ADE
               "I'm near the dog."
          c.   Olen   aseman   luona / *Olen   asema-lla.
               Be.PRS.1SG station.GEN at.ADE / be-PRS.1SG station-ADE
               "I'm at the station."

Kittilä & Ylikoski (2011, p. 43–44) report a somewhat 'complementary' state of affairs for the Uralic language Olonetsian (spoken in the Russian Republic of Karelia and adjacent areas), in which an analogous axial postposition item *luo* is only employed with [+human] locative grounds, whereas inanimate referents consistently employ case morphemes only.

to disappear whenever an axial adposition is present. The fact that this does not occur suggests that *-l* and *-s* may lexicalize something else.

4.3.2.2   *Previous accounts: Asbury (2008)*

Asbury (2008) posits that spatial cases represent an outer layer (which she labels as P) of the extended projection (Grimshaw, 1990a) of the noun phrase. She does not directly address the -l and -s morphemes, assuming that -ltA, -stA, and so on are interpreted as a single unit. In other words, she does not propose that -l and -s host their own projection. This could pose an issue if we assume that meaningful items must project their own phrase (and -l/-s conceptualize exterior/interior in Finnish). However, the main problem with her account seems to be that she assumes the inner layer of the structure (i.e., genitive/partitive) is occupied by determiner-like morphemes. Drawing from Kayne (1994) on English "of," she suggests that the Finnish genitive/partitive is a morpheme expressing definiteness (D). In (29), we provide a representation of her structure.

(29)

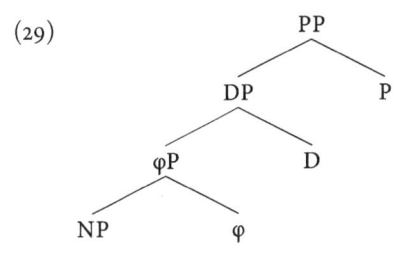

According to our own perspective, there is clear evidence that the morpheme *-n* is not a D item in Finnish. Just consider the 'quirky' contexts in (30), (31) and (32) where the meaning associated with the genitive inflection *-n* is ergative-like (cf. Woolford, 2006).[39] No Definiteness effects may be ascribed to the appearance of the genitive in such positions. Hence, we see no reason to link the genitive to D (analogous observations could be made for the partitive, which encodes aspect-like imperfective content, cf. Kiparsky, 2001; Kracht, 2002).

(30)   *Finnish*
Sinun   kannattaa   yrittää
You.GEN is worth.PRS.3SG try.INF
"It's worth for you to try."   [experiencer]

---

39. The standard characterization of the genitive as a structural case in Finnish (cf. Vainikka, 1989; Kiparsky 2001) may be questioned on the basis of the same empirical evidence. Nevertheless, the issue is orthogonal to the topics introduced in this work and will not be addressed any further in what follows.

(31) a. Karin   on   lähdettävä
          Kari.GEN is.PRS.3SG go.PTCL.PRS.PST
          "Kari has to go."   [necessity construction]

      b. *Finnish*
          Sinun   olisi   hyvä soittaa huomenna
          you.GEN is.PRS.3SG good call.INF tomorrow
          "It would be good if you would call tomorrow."   [necessity construction]

(32) *Finnish*
      Kakku on   äidin   leipoma
      cake is.PRS.3SG mom.GEN baked.PTCL.AGENT.
      "The cake was baked by the mom."   [agentive participle]

Rather, as pointed out by Fábregas (2007a), the relation between the Ground and the AxP is a part-whole/possessive one, namely a relation in which the Ground is the possessor of (an Axis) and the AxP is the possessum (of the Ground).

Further empirical evidence that a characterization in terms of definiteness of the genitive morpheme is inadequate is the fact that the genitive can also appear on determiners in Colloquial Finnish (Matthew Reeve, p.c.), as in (33) (cf. Laalo, 2009).[40]

(33) *Finnish*
      sen   koiran
      the.GEN Dog.GEN
      "Of his dog."

4.3.2.3 *Previous accounts: Svenonius (2012)*

Svenonius (2012), building on his (2006) work introduced in Section 4.1, argues that adpositions are AxPs, the series *–l/-s* 'exterior/interior' lexicalize Place, while the spatial cases on top of them represent Path (cf. Section 4.2). The illative (which in any case, as we have already pointed out, is historically related to the *-s* series) would be a suppletive form, acting as a portmanteau for Path+Place.

In Svenonius's account, we see a kind of conceptual clash (cf. Pantcheva, 2011, who possibly, for this reason, analyses *-l / -s* as AxP). Take the inessive in (20), repeated below in (34) for ease of reference. How can *-sA* represent a Path? It seems here that both *-s* and *-sA* lexicalize Place (there is no conceptual hints of Path, neither Goal or Source).

---

40. In Finnish the demonstrative *se* is turning into a definite article (Laury, 1997; Alexiadou et al. 2007).

(34) *Finnish*
Tyttö on   kirjastossa
girl   is-PRS.3SG Library.INE
"The girl is in the library"

Thus, the model seems to predict a wrong cartography, namely two distinct positions for morphemes expressing close (or the same) semantics (similar arguments can be provided for the -*l* series).

4.3.3 Axial Parts and elementary predicates in Finnish

In Finnish, spatial cases serve to express a variety of non-spatial meanings, beginning with possession. This phenomenon can be understood as a cognitive inclination to convey non-local relationships using locative morphemes (Jackendoff, 1983; Freeze, 1992; Den Dikken, 1995, Kracht, 2002, among others). However, it could also suggest the opposite: that a possession/inclusion relationship could be extended into the spatial domain (Manzini & Franco 2016, Franco & Manzini, 2017a). As demonstrated in (35) and (36), both external and internal cases are utilized to denote possession, encompassing tangible physical possession. Possession *strictu sensu* is not the sole non-spatial relationship expressible by the spatial cases in Finnish (cf. Ylikoski, 2011). The 'instrumental' function of the adessive in (37) serves as an example.

(35) *Finnish*
Tytöllä   on   kirja
Girl.ADE be.PRS.3SG book
"The girl has a/the book."

(36) a. Hän on   flunsassa
         s/he be-PRS.3SG flu.INE
         "The girl has a/the flu."
     b. *Finnish*
         Talossa   on   iso ovi
         house.INE be.PRS.3SG big door
         "The house has a big door."

(37) *Finnish*
Piirsin   tämän   lyijykynällä
Draw.PRS.1SG This.GEN/ACC pencil.ADE
"I draw this with the pencil"

Furthermore, the adessive case that we have seen is employed for instrumentals in (37), can be also used to encode the *causee* in causative constructions, as illustrated in (38) (cf. Pylkkänen, 2008; Ylikoski, 2011). This is not surprising, considering what we have seen in Chapter 3 for applicatives.

(38) *Finnish*
Keisari   rakennutti   orjilla   temppellin
emperor-NOM make.build.PST.3SG slaves.ADE temple.GEN
"The emperor made the slaves build a temple."

Thus, a conceptualization in terms of PATH > PLACE and related hierarchy do not immediately explain the non-spatial occurrences of Finnish spatial cases.

Given the data we have presented so far, and given the problems outlined above for some contemporary approaches to the syntax of Finnish locatives, we try to advance an alternative proposal. Consider an example including an AxP, such as (39). We assume that the Ground-complement is the possessor of the AxP (i.e. expressing a genitive relation). Following our standard way of reasoning, we notate the Finnish genitive (and partitive) relating the possessor (Ground) and the possessum (AxP) as (⊆). Again, the conceptual core of the relation between Grounds and AxP is that of part-whole. A representation is in (40) for the sentence in (39).

(39) Auto   kadun   keskellä
car-NOM street.GEN centre.ADE
"The car in the middle of the street."

(40)

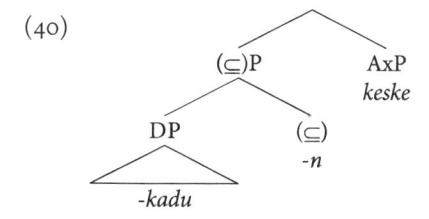

We assume that both –*l* ('exterior') and –*s* ('interior') express different flavours of the (⊆) relation (exterior vs. interior). The representation of the (growing) tree is, thus, as in (41).

(41)

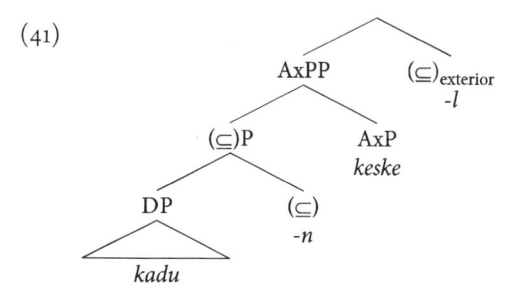

We hypothesize that the ($\subseteq$) part/relation, particularly contact-inclusion/exterior ($\subseteq$) in (41), projects and merges with the 'outer' inflection (-*lA, -tA*, etc.), provisionally denoted here as Place/Path, aligning closely with their respective content (state, motion either towards or from). This process yields the complete structure illustrated in (42), headed by the Figure DP (or potentially by an Event Figure, cf. Wood, 2015).[41] It's important to note that our model crucially avoids presupposing an ordered hierarchy Path > Place,[42] and it is arguable that, similarly to Romance languages, in Finnish, the fundamental locative/directional meanings of state-in,

---

41. Den Dikken & Dekany (2018) propose an in-depth analysis for the case system of Estonian, a cognate Finnic language. They argue that, in all eleven semantic cases of Estonian, the head of *x*NP takes genitive case (agreeing in case with any adjectival modifiers). However, in the seven spatial cases, case agreement also involves the semantic case particle, while in the remaining four cases, case agreement is limited to genitive. According to Den Dikken & Dekany, this arises from the fact that in the seven spatial cases, the semantic case particle represents a covert P, forming a morphological complex with the genitive case particle. Conversely, in the last four (non-spatial) cases, the semantic case particle acts independently as a realization of P, outside *x*NP.Across the seven spatial cases, the P-heads are silent, selecting a noun phrase headed by the abstract noun "Place," which hosts the case morphology for P. However, the abstract noun "Place" alone cannot support this morphology; in the post-syntactic stage, the case suffix is reassigned to the possessor of "Place," marked with genitive case. Consequently, the overt possessor noun phrase is doubly marked with case, resulting in the characteristic pattern of case stacking (Suffixaufnahme, cf. Chapter 6). The four cases traditionally listed last in Estonian's fourteen cases (terminative, essive, abessive, and comitative) are also adpositional and more directly linked to their respective Ps compared to the seven spatial cases. While the Ps in the latter are silent and represented by case morphology in their complements, the last four cases are direct manifestations of their respective Ps. We will try to see if the Estonian case system is compatible with the analysis proposed here in further research on the topic.

42. As we have seen in the previous Section, an influent stream of literature within the Cartographic framework takes spatial PP constituents to be structurally rich and articulated (Koopman, 2000; den Dikken, 2010; Svenonius, 2006, 2010; Cinque, 2010a), providing wide cross-linguistic evidence for the claim that there exists a Place head for stative meanings and a Path head for directed motion. Pantcheva (2011), within the Nanosyntactic framework, further decomposes the Path layer into three distinct functional projections: Goal, Source, and Route, which are hierarchically ordered. We refrain from employing cartographic encoding of meaning due to various reasons, including concerns regarding its lack of restrictiveness, as recently discussed by Chomsky et al. (2019) in terms of the learnability and evolvability of hierarchies (cf. Franco et al. 2021 for full discussion). For instance, assuming the hierarchy Loc > Goal > Source, Pantcheva (2010, 2011) rules out syncretisms between Location and Source to the exclusion of Goal. Indeed Nanosyntax (Caha, 2009; Starke, 2017) prohibits syncretisms of two nodes across a distinct intervening node (the *ABA constraint). However, despite the rarity of such patterns, they appear to be possible in natural languages, as demonstrated by Creissels (2006), with examples from Dinka and other North East African languages. In general, cartographic hierarchies have a tendency to undergenerate.

motion-to, and motion-from are differentiated based on the attachment level of a case (or prepositional) morpheme within a multitiered verbal structure, either at the level of the Resultative Phrase or higher, at the level of the Cause Layer, as we have seen in Section 4.2. Consequently, the involved obliques do not inherently contribute specific, fixed spatial meanings; rather, locatives represent specializations of a general relator, reflecting part-whole content. We will delve further into this point in the subsequent sections.

(42)

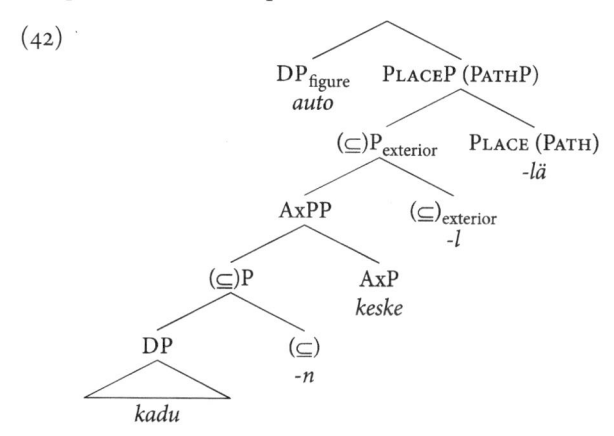

Just note that the same configuration is preserved when the suffixes *-s-sA, -l-lA* and so on, appear on nouns not denoting locations, as in *tytö-l-lä* (girl-adessive) seen in Example (35) above, for which we provide a representation in (43).

(43)

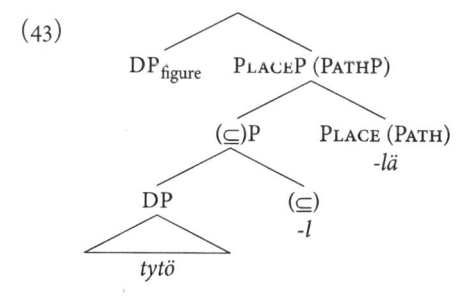

4.3.4   Evidence from linguistic variation within the Uralic family

There is a strict parallelism between the syntactic configuration/relation involving Axial Part and Ground and the proper Part-Whole relation, universally. Natural languages consistently employ the same strategy to lexically encode a Part-Whole and an Axial Part-Ground relation.

Uralic data support the proposal presented above, as shown in (44) and (45), for Skolt Saami and Nenets, respectively.

(44) to'b ǩie'đj   vue'lnn leäi   jõn pä'htträi'ǧǧ [koozz   sää'm
there Stone.GEN under   be.PST.3SG big rock.hole   [REL.SG.ILL Saami.PL
liâ   piijjâm   kåå'dd   vuei'vid   čue'rveezvui'm]
be.PST.3SG put.PST.PTCP reindeer.SG.GEN head.PL.ACC antler.PL.COM.3PL]
"There under the stone was a big hole in the rock, where the Saami used to put
the heads of reindeer, with their antlers."   *Skolt Saami* (Feist, 2010, p.351)

(45) a.   wen'ako-h xawoda lebtə-q   [part–whole]
dog-GEN   ears.3SG hang-3PL
"Dog's ears are hanging"
b.   yəx-h   war-h   n'in'a pidər yəŋku-n [figure–ground]
river-GEN bank-GEN are   you   not
"You are not on the river bank"   *Nenets* (Nikolaeva, 2014, p.59, 251)

In Table 1, we report the result of our survey on Uralic languages showing the main devices by which Uralic languages encode the two relations (sometimes two different strategies may show up, cf. Finnish genitives alternating with partitives in encoding the relation between AxP and Ground). Notably, proper part–whole and AxP-Ground relations are expressed consistently by the same device.

Table 1. Encoding part–whole and Axial Part relations in Uralic

Uralic varieties	Part–whole	AxPart-Ground
Eastern Khanty (Filchenko, 2007)	POSSESSIVE INFL.	POSSESSIVE INFL.
Enets (Kunnap, 1999)	GENITIVE	GENITIVE
Erzya Mordvin (van Pareren, 2013)	GENITIVE	GENITIVE
Estonian (Viitso, 1998)	GENITIVE	GENITIVE
Finnish (Lna Dal Pozzo, p.c.)	GENITIVE	GENITIVE
Hungarian (Kenesei et al., 1998)	POSSESSIVE INFL.	POSSESSIVE INFL.
Kamassian (Simoncsics, 1998)	GENITIVE	GENITIVE
Komi (Avril, 2006)	JUXTAPOSITION	JUXTAPOSITION
Moksha Mordvin (Pareren, 2012)	GENITIVE	GENITIVE
Nganasan (Chumakina, 2011)	GENITIVE	GENITIVE
Ostyak (Nikolaeva, 1999)	POSSESSIVE INFL.	POSSESSIVE INFL.
Skolt Saami (Feist, 2010)	GENITIVE	GENITIVE
Tundra Nenets (Nikolaeva, 2014)	GENITIVE	GENITIVE
Udmurt (Winckler, 2001)	JUXTAPOSITION	JUXTAPOSITION
Vogul (Riese, 2001)	JUXTAPOSITION	JUXTAPOSITION
Votic (Ariste, 1997)	GENITIVE	GENITIVE

We take the ($\subseteq$) part/relation to be very wide-ranging, potentially encompassing partitives, inalienable and alienable possession, light verbs, and also the notion of location, which is in competition with it as the true primitive underlying possession (Freeze, 1992; Den Dikken, 1995 *vs.* Levinson, 2011, Franco & Manzini, 2017b). In other words, as suggested in Section 4.2, we assume that in natural languages, a locative may be construed as a specialization of the part-whole relation,[43] roughly, as in (46):

(46) "x included by y, y location."

Therefore, we can propose that the Finnish series *-s* and *-l* are a locative specialization of this zonal inclusion ($\subseteq$). We may consider *-s* to be *containment* and *-l* to be *contact/vicinity*. In any event, both morphemes contribute to the lexicalization of a ($\subseteq$) node. Similar considerations can be advanced for more familiar languages, for instance Italian (Romance) *a* vs. *in*. Consider the pair in (47). (47a) means that the sea defines a vicinity including me (the Italian dative preposition *a* hence matches the *l* series of Finnish); on the contrary, (47b) says that I am properly contained by the sea.[44]

(47) *Italian*
    (a)   Sono al mare
          "I'm at the sea."
    (b)   Sono in mare
          "I'm in the sea"

The structure proposed in (40)–(42) for the AxP strongly implies that AxP in Finnish are real relational nouns. The fact that Finnish adpositions are case

---

43. As already pointed out, Manzini & Savoia (2011b), Manzini & Franco (2016) argue in favour of the primitive nature of the part–whole relation on the basis of considerations regarding the morphological shape of Indo-European languages. Thus, inflections alone suffice for the lexicalization of the more elementary possession/part–whole relation in languages where even the simplest of locative relations require the lexicalization of (complex) prepositions. In discussing the syncretic lexicalizations of dative and locative in Albanian, Manzini and Savoia construe locative as a specialization of the part–whole relation, where different locatives introduce different locative restrictions on inclusion. This is compatible with the expression of (certain types of) possession as locations, for instance alienable possession in Palestinian Arabic, according to Boneh & Sichel (2010).

44. In Italian, the preposition "a" serves as both a dative relator and expresses "to", whereas "in", like its English equivalent, solely conveys a locative meaning. From this, one could infer that the default locative constraint pertains to the proximity of a specified entity, with the interpretation assigned to "a" being contextually determined by default. Conversely, we might posit that a locative constraint is explicitly encoded in the lexical entry of "in", which further encompasses the notion of proper containment (cf. Franco & Lorusso, 2019; Franco et al., 2021).

inflected may suffice to determine this status, as case normally attaches to nouns. In many languages, AxPs have been shown to be indistinguishable from RelN (failing Svenonius' discriminating tests).[45] Johns and Thurgood (2011) provide evidence in this regard from Inuktitut and Uzbeki (cf. also Franco 2016 on the diachrony of the Italian items *presso/pressi* 'into/near').

Below we provide some further evidence from Uralic, focusing on Udmurt as recently described by Arkhangelskiy & Usacheva (2015). In Udmurt, axial postpositions are case inflected, just as in Finnish. They can pluralize, depending on the plurality of either the Ground (48) or the Figure (49).

(48) *Udmurt*
      Škafjos   puš-jos-en   kopo uka-śk-e.
      cupboard-PL inside-PL-LOC dust gather-PRS-3SG
      "Dust is gathering inside cupboards."

(49) *Udmurt*
      Milam d´erevna koter-jos-en   lud´-jos
      we.GEN village   around-PL-LOC field-PL
      "All fields around our village."

Inflected adpositions in Udmurt can appear in argumental position, namely inflected by core cases.

(50) *Udmurt*
      Škaf   puš-se   miśk-ono.
      cupboard inside-POSS.3SG(ACC) wash-DEB
      "The inside of the cupboard have to be washed."

Finally, possessive marking in Udmurt is possible on the dependent or on the head (Nichols 1986). Inflected adpositions pattern with ordinary nouns, as shown in (51)–(52).

---

45. As we have already pointed out, Svenonius (2006) argues against the notion that AxParts are identical to their homophonous RelNouns. He bases his claim on the observation that AxParts, unlike homophonous RelNouns, can stand without articles, bear no plural or gender morphology, do not take modifiers, and can be specified by a measure phrase. Still, some cross-linguistic evidence provided is not very robust. For instance, Svenonius provides a single example of an AxPart in Kîîtharaka (Bantu) which does not have a noun class prefix, namely "karibu" ('near'). All the other AxPs in that language behave like standard Relational nouns. Furthermore, Svenonius stipulates that determiners and quantifiers appearing with AxPs are all idiosyncratic.

(51) a. Mə   korka kośag-a-m   šu-iśk-i-z   zərgələ
          I.GEN house window-ILL-POSS.1SG hit-DETR-PST-3SG sparrow

      b. *Udmurt*
          Mə   korka-je-len   kośag-a-z   šu-iśk-i-z
          I.GEN house-POSS.1SG-GEN window-ILL-POSS.3SG hit-DETR-PST-3SG
          zərgələ
          sparrow
          "A sparrow bumped into the window of my house."

(52) *Udmurt*
      So təb-i-z   korka-je   dor.e / korka Dor-am   uža-nə
      he go.up-PST-3SG house.POSS.1SG Near.ILL house near-ILL-POSS.1SG work-INF
      "He went up to my house to work."

4.4   Interim discussion

To summarize the discussion so far, we impute an interpretive content to the
item which links Axial Parts and Grounds, which Svenonius (2006) descriptively
characterizes as K (case). This content is predicative (not the *D-like* content of
Asbury, 2008), and it can be realized by prepositions (Italian, English), or by
nominal inflections (Uralic). The inflectional realization of the ($\subseteq$) predicate
is conventionally called case. In present terms, case is definable at most as the
crossing of the more elementary notions of atomic predicate and inflectional
realization. As originally argued in Fillmore (1968), we see no other differences
between (oblique) cases and adpositions (see Manzini & Franco, 2016, Franco
& Manzini, 2017a for extended discussion and further arguments against *post-
syntactic* approaches to obliques).

  Every account of natural language must address the proximity of dative /geni-
tive/instrumental and locative specifications, corresponding to frequent syncretic
lexicalizations: e.g. the instrumental/adessive in Finnish; the ergative/
oblique=inessive in Caucasian languages (Comrie & Polinsky, 1998), the geni-
tive=inessive of Ossetic (an Iranian variety in contact with Caucasian languages,
Kulikov, 2009). Possession is often identified with a location in the literature,
in particular Freeze (1992), Lyons (1967). We reverse this perspective imputing
a broad part-whole content to locatives. As we have suggested above, a locative
may be construed as a specialization of the part-whole, inclusion relation, roughly
'x included by y, y location' (cf. Section 4.3.4) and motion to *vs.* motion from
readings depend on the shape of the events (cf. Section 4.2). The ($\subseteq$) content
may correspond to several inflectional cases or adpositions. According to Manzini
and Savoia (2011b), the languages where dative is lexically different from genitive

(including English *of* and *to*, Italian *di* "of" and *a* "to", etc.) display contextual sensitivity in the realization of the (⊆) category, which is externalized as dative "to" when attached to sentential projections, while it is externalized as genitive "of" when it is attached to nominal categories. Interestingly, the relation between AxPs and Grounds is instantiated in Italian by both *a* (e.g. *sotto al fiume*, "below to-the river") and *di* (*sotto di te*, "below of you"). This is related to a sensitivity to the animacy hierarchy (*di* is the obligatory choice here with pronouns, see fn. 36; cf. also Fábregas, 2015a, b). When the relator is not spelled out (e.g. *sotto il fiume*, below the river) we assume here that we are dealing with a silent category, following Kayne (2004a, b, 2007 and subsequent works; but see Tortora 2005, Folli, 2008; Garzonio & Rossi, 2016 for principled explanations). As we have seen in our typological survey, Uralic presents similar lexical variation in the realization of (⊆) (partitive, genitive, internal/external inclusion).

Svenonius (2003, 2007; cf. Franco, 2016; Wood, 2015) assumes that the Figure has properties reminiscent of external arguments, while the Ground has properties reminiscent of internal arguments. According to Svenonius (2003, 2007) figures are introduced by a functional head *p*, in a way that is analogous to the introduction of external arguments by *v*, along the lines of Hale & Keyser (1993), Chomsky (1995), See the trees in (53). Here we do not explicitly take a position on this point, despite endorsing approaches that make a strict parallel between P and V (cf. also van Riemsdijk, 1978; Emonds, 1985; Demirdache & Uribe-Etxebarria, 2000). In particular, we find quite appealing the recent proposal put forth by Wood & Marantz (2018), who assume that those heads introducing extra participants in the syntax (e.g. high/low applicatives, p/P, voice) can be reduced to one single argument introducer (that they label *little i*), whose morphological shape happens to be sensitive to the syntactic context in which it occurs.

(53) a.

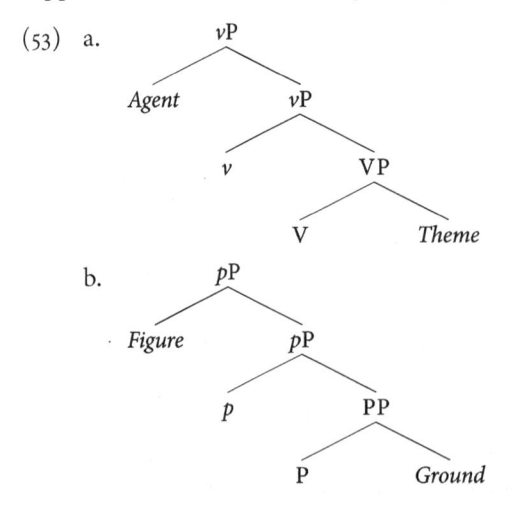

b.

Actually, what is most relevant for present purposes is that there seems to be nothing special with space in syntax (following Levinson, 2011). In our view, simple adpositions/case markers are interpreted as a locative only in so far as they denote *locatively constrained* inclusion (⊆). A locative *inclusion* arises from the locative nature of the element embedded by the lexical items involved (cf. the difference between 'I sent the letter to Peter' and 'I sent the letter to Rome') or from the locative nature of the verb the relator attaches to, or other. The locative interpretation just depends on their context of embedding.

We propose here a refinement of the model in (53). We assume that what are traditionally labelled as 'complex prepositions' in Italian and elsewhere are best characterized as involving an AxP, in the sense of Svenonius (2006, see also Cinque, 2010a). We propose that the projection of such elements is the 'external argument' of the lower P projection responsible of introducing a Ground complement (in Italian normally, the genitive *di* or the dative *a*, in English commonly the genitive *of*, etc.). The relation between AxPart and the complement of the genitive predicate is a kind of 'part-whole' relationship (cf. Fábregas 2007a), notated here as (⊆), following Manzini & Franco (2016), Franco et al. (2017), among others. This is precisely the same relation Manzini & Franco (2016) assume is entertained by the two internal arguments of a ditransitive structure, which can be conceived to be a possessum (Theme) – possessor (Goal) relation. In a Figure/Ground configuration *à la* Talmy the Ground-complement of (⊆) is the possessor of the Axis (Axial Part P) taken to evaluate the location of the Figure, standardly introduced by means of the pP node. An illustration of the model we propose is represented in (54b) for Example (54a).

(54) a.   The plates on top of the table
      b.

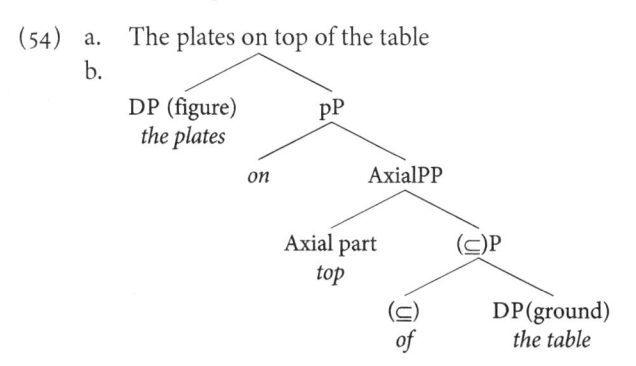

Axial Part has been taken to be a semi-lexical or properly functional category (cf. Svenonius 2006; Franco, 2016), but in many languages they retain full nominal properties, as we have shown above for Finnish/Uralic (cf. also John and Thurgood, 2011 for Inuktitut and Uzbeki, Ursini and Long, 2018 on Chinese, among others). Hence it is quite reasonable that Axial Parts and Grounds may stand in a possessum-possessor configuration (between a 'possessor' entity and one or more of its parts).

In brief, we assign interpretive significance to the element connecting Axial Parts and Grounds, as described by Svenonius (2006) in terms of K (case). Also, this content is predicative, and it can be realized by prepositions (Italian, English), or by nominal inflections (Uralic, Indo-Aryan, cf. Franco et al., 2017). Recall, the (⊆) content is primitive but it is not a case; it is an elementary predicate. The inflectional realization of the (⊆) predicate is just conventionally called *case* (cf. the discussion in the Introduction and the data and analysis provided in the previous Chapters). As far as the syntactic layer above the Axial Part is concerned, we can maintain the descriptive characterization p, in a way that is analogous to the introduction of external arguments by v. Nevertheless, taking into consideration the shape of the data we have reviewed for Finnish and the representations we have provided for them, the 'inclusion' layer appears to be 'reduplicated', pointing to the idea that the node above the AxP may have the same morpho-lexical status of the lower P/K, namely that of an elementary predicate (⊆) (by which arguably the Figure is 'included' in the AxP-Ground predication by the means of this upper (⊆) elementary predicate), leading to a revised structure as in (55) for the representation provided in (54b), where one may say that locative nouns-AxPs project, and a new inclusion relation is directly established between it (as a spatial *part* of the Ground) and the Figure.

(55)

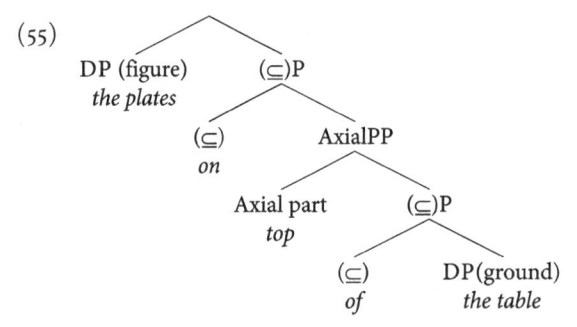

Actually, such a pattern, namely an AxP sandwiched between two (lexically) identical (⊆) predicates is cross-linguistically widespread. Just consider the examples from Catalan (56) (Romance), Pashto (Iranian) (57), Wandala (58) (Chadic, Afro-Asiatic), Mongsen Ao (Sino-Tibetan) (59). This is clearly consistent with Franco et al. (2021) idea that no specific spatial meaning is contributed by the adpositions/cases involved, which merely act as (⊆) predicates. Thus pP is just (⊆)P.

(56)   La rata va sortir **de** sota **de** la taula
        'the rat came out from under the table'   *Catalan* (Hualde, 1992)

(57) **də** mez-Ø   **də** pās-a   kitāb-una   zmā   ná
      of table-M.OBL of top-M.ABL book-PL.M.DIR 1SG.STR.POSS NEG
      day
      be.CONT.PRS.3SG.M
      'The books on top of the table are not mine'   *Pashto* (David, 2014)

(58) ká   kàt á-fk-á   ordinater
      2.SG be PRED-face-GEN computer
      'you are in front of computer'   *Wandala* (Frajzyngier, 2012)

(59) nuksənsaŋ-pàʔ **nə**   taŋ **nə** wa-lìkà?
      PN-M   ALL side ALL go-CONTEMP
      'When [the son-in-law] had gone to Noksensangba?'

          Mongsen Ao (Coupe, 2008)

Further evidence that we are on the right track in proposing a structure like the
one in (55) comes from Old Italian (cf. Franco, 2016; Ganfi & Piunno, 2017),
where – for instance – the item *fronte* (meaning *front*), employed as an AxP, can
be sandwiched between different lexicalizations of the (⊆) content. Consider the
examples in (60), taken from Ganfi & Piunno (2017).[46]

(60) a. *a fronte a*
          vidi **a** fronte alla   mia camera in un' altra   dimorare due donne
          I.saw P front P.DET my chamber in DET other.F dwell.INF two women
          "I saw in front of my chamber two women dwelling in another room"
                          Boccaccio, Filocolo, 1336–38, L. 4, cap. 23, pag. 389.13.
      b. *in fronte a*
          poi che 'l sol passa /   in fronte a Virgo
          after that the sun pass.PRS.3SG P front P Virgo
          "after the Sun passes in front of Virgo"
                          Fazio degli Uberti, Dittamondo, c. 1345–67 (tosc.), L. 1, cap. 1.18,
                                                                                    pag. 3.

---

46. Notice also that locative structures including an Axial Parts in (Old and Modern) Italian do
not employ different relators to disentangle between different meanings (namely stative Place
vs. dynamic Path), as shown in (i).

  (i) *Italian*
      a. sono di fronte alla ragazza *state-in* "I am in front of the girl."
      b. vado di fronte alla ragazza *motion-to* "I go in front of the girl."

c. *in fronte de*
le   belle   palazza [...] **in** fronte **de** Santo Cieizo
the.PL.F beautiful.PL.F building.PL.F P front P S.   C.
"The beautiful buildings in front of Santo Cieizo"
>   Bono Giamboni, Orosio, a. 1292 (fior.), L. 1, cap. 2, pag. 13.10.

Cf. Italian la ragazza **di** fronte al quadro "The girl in front of the picture"

The same happens with relational nouns/axial parts encoding temporal relations, as illustrated below in (61) with the body term *capo* (head), taken again from Ganfi & Piunno (2017). Note that, as in (60a), also in (61c) the items linking the AxP and the Ground and the Figure with the complex AxP+Ground can be lexicalized by the same element, providing further support to the model represented in (55). All the AxPs in examples in (61) mean the same: "*At the end of a period of time.*"

(61) a. *in capo di*
lo calende se   rencomenza[rà]   **en** capo **de** l' anno
the calendar CL.REFL commence.again.FUT.3SG P head P the year
"the calendar will commence again in a year"
>   Restoro d'Arezzo, 1282 (aret.), L. II, dist. 8, cap. 22, pag. 242.22.

b. *a capo di*
noi il   torneremo   a vedere **a** cchapo **d'** uno anno
we CL.3SG.ACC come.back.FUT.1PL to see.INF P head   P a   year
"We will come back to see him in a year"
>   Distr. Troia, XIII ex. (fior.), pag. 155.7.

c. *di capo di*
e   così sarà   **di** capo **del** detto tempo il Sole in principio di
and so be.FUT.3SG P head P   said time   the Sun P beginning P
Capricorno
Capricorn
"And thus the Sun will enter in Capricorn in the said time"
>   Ottimo, Par., a. 1334 (fior.), c. 27, pag. 602.2.

4.5   Oblique non-locative Axial Parts

The fact that Axial Parts are not confined to the syntax of locative/temporal complements is shown by the observation that they can be used to express relations which have nothing to do with spatial syntax. Consider the sentences in (62).

(62)   *Italian*
    a.   Ho captato il segnale radio **per mezzo de**lla nuova antenna
        "I picked up the radio signal with the new antenna"
    b.   Ho captato il segnale radio **con** la nuova antenna
        "I picked up the radio signal with the new antenna."

Here, "mezzo" in (62a) is a relational noun expressing an instrumental relation, as confirmed by the comparison with (62b). According to Franco & Manzini (2017a) and Franco & Lorusso (2020), based on microvariation facts in Romance, "per" expresses the same ($\supseteq$) relation as expressed with "con".[47] "Mezzo" is crucially an AxPart, as illustrated in (63), where it conveys a locative value.

(63)   *Italian*
    ho trovato una coccinella **in mezzo ai** fiori
    "I found a ladybug among the flowers."

We can provide the structures in (64) and (65), respectively, for (62a) and (63). The difference in interpretation is provided by the higher inclusion layer. In the locative use of the relational item "mezzo," the higher layer expresses a ($\subseteq$) relation (in our example, stating that 'the ladybug (as the figure) is included in the (middle of) the flowers'). Conversely, in its instrumental value, the higher layer lexicalized by "per" expresses a ($\supseteq$) relation, which, following insights from Franco & Manzini (2017b), takes as its internal argument the (core/middle) of the DP instrument, while its external argument is the VP event. In other words, in (62a), the ($\supseteq$) relation holds between 'the (middle of) the new antenna' and the event of

---

47. Franco & Manzini (2017b) ascribe to the Italian adposition *per* the same 'instrumental' ($\supseteq$) content expressed by the con ('with') morpheme, based (among others) on the evidence that *con* and *per* are both able to lexicalize causers, as in (i). Following their insight, it is possible to assume that the ($\supseteq$) relation between the *con/per* phrase and the VP event in (23) yields inclusion in an event/concomitance with it. In a sense, (23) is paraphrasable as something like: "The government raised taxes and the crisis was part of its acting to raise them." (cf. Franco & Manzini, 2017b, p. 8–9).

  (i)   Il   pericolo di conflitto aumentò con/per il   golpe.
     The danger of conflict increased with/for the coup
     'The danger of a confrontation increased with/for the coup.'

Actually, the same general relation (causation, in this case), may have more than one lexicalization in a given language. Though Italian *con* can express cause, there is no doubt that causation is also expressed, by a different preposition, namely *per*. The closest rendering of *per* in English is for, which expresses both purpose ('they do it for financial gain') and causation ('he died for the want of food'), as Italian *per* does. Franco & Lorusso extend this proposal showing that, as an aspectual marker, *per* relates two events through the same basic ($\supseteq$) operator that we have postulated here for *with* morphemes.

'capturing the TV signal', literally stating that this event includes 'an antenna'. In summary, either we say that we have two "mezzos" in Italian, or we must admit (based on Levinson, 2011; Franco and Manzini, 2017b) that there is no space for a specialized syntax of locatives, which are just rendered like other obliques in natural languages (cf. also the discussion on the construction *da parte di* 'by' in nominalization patterns in Chapter 6).

(64)

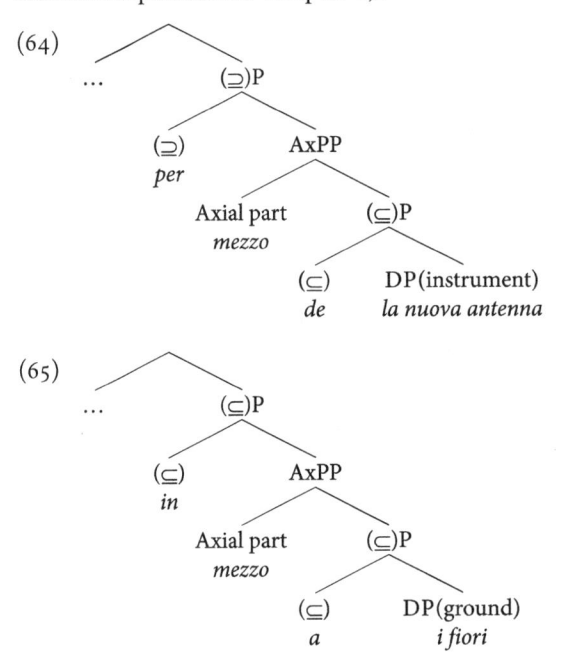

(65)

Further evidence supporting our ideas regarding the fact that so-called axial parts actually extend beyond locatives comes from body part terms, which are commonly used as relational nouns (Lehmann, 2018). Roy (2006) shows that in relation to inanimates, nouns that normally denote body parts lose their literal meaning when constructed in relation to an animate whole (e.g., "pied" for 'foot', "tête" for 'head', etc.) in French and instead acquire a spatial interpretation.[48]

In Italian, the body part "mano" (hand) in the phrase "per mano di" (cf. Veland, 2012) is typically used to encode causers, either with intransitive (66a) or

---

48. Also in the realm of applicatives, the use of body terms to encode spatial and non-spatial relations is widespread, as we already saw in Chapter 3. For example, Murrinhpatha (non-Pama-Nyungan, Australia) has a single applicative construction with the semantics of source/malefactive, encoded with an incorporated body part *-ma-* meaning 'hand' (Nordlinger, 2019), while Halkomelem (Central Salish) lexical suffix *-as* 'face' has been turned into a Dative Applicative suffix (cf. Gerdts & Hinkson, 2004).

transitive (66b) predicates, and demoted agents in passives (66c), as illustrated below (see also Palancar, 2002).

(66) a. La sua morte è avvenuta nella notte del 15 gennaio 1919 **per mano di** alcuni militari appartenenti ai Freikorps.
          "His death occurred on the night of January 15, 1919, due to some soldiers belonging to the Freikorps."
      b. Ha perso 7 a 6 al tiebreak **per mano de**lla sconosciuta brasiliana Dias.
          "She lost 7 to 6 in the tiebreak with the unknown Brazilian Dias."
      c. Non è possibile stabilire quanti cittadini di colore sono stati ammazzati **per mano de**lla polizia dall'entrata in vigore dello stato d'emergenza.
          "It is not possible to determine how many people of color have been killed by the police since the state of emergency came into effect.

Interestingly, as shown by Veland (2012), the string *per mano di* does not introduces animate referents only. Consider the examples in (67).

(67) a. dietro strane forme di pneumonia, di erpes, di candidosi, di sarcoma di Kaposi, in realtà si celava un unico male, che distruggeva il sistema immunitario di quei pazienti e li portava a morte **per mano di** infezioni opportuniste.
          "Behind strange forms of pneumonia, herpes, candidiasis, and Kaposi's sarcoma, there was actually a single disease, which destroyed the immune system of those patients and led them to death by opportunistic infections."
      b. Direttamente, grazie ad espedienti di cui non mancherà l'occasione, indirettamente **per mano d**'una «libera» decisione della DC.
          "Directly, thanks to expedients that will not lack opportunities, indirectly by a "free" decision of the DC."

Thus, we find a clear example of a body part term entering a non-spatial configuration and extending to inanimates. Note that the body part "mano" is never employed in locative configurations, based on our native knowledge of Italian. This is another indication that there is no special configuration for the grammar of locatives, and all obliques are encoded in the same manner, possibly resorting to a relational item (which in locatives acquires an axial configuration).

From the present viewpoint, we can propose the representation in (68) for all instances of "per mano di" depicted above, where the item introduced by "per mano di" is the causer/agent of the event, namely the DP causer/(demoted) agent is 'included by' the VP event via a relation (⊇). We will provide more details in the next section regarding the structure we assume for passives, based on Manzini et al. (2015), Manzini (2017), focusing on Persian, a language in which passives can only be encoded by means of a relational noun.

(68)

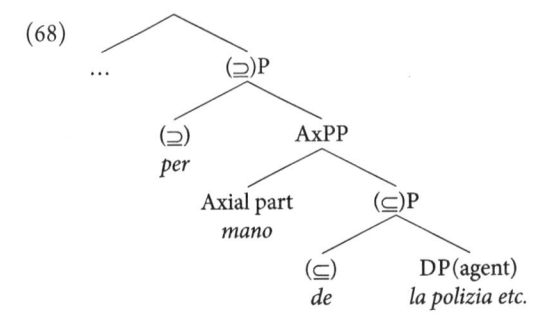

4.6   The case of Persian passives

Persian exhibits a subject-object-verb (SOV) word order and possesses a complex verbal inflectional system. An example of its active/passive alternation is depicted in (69).

(69)   a.   Shahin Shirin-ra   did.
           Shahin Shirin-DOM saw.3SG
           'Shahin saw Shirin.'

    b.   *Persian*
           Shirin (be) tævæsot-e   Shahin did-eh   šod.
           Shirin to   internediation-LNK Shahin seen.PTCP became.3SG
           'Shirin was seen by Shahin.'

(69b) exemplifies the periphrastic passive construction found in Modern Persian, contrasting with Old Persian which employed a morphological passive that is no longer in use. In structure (69b), an argument originating from an object position (thus lacking the ra object marker) is raised, followed by a past participle and the passive auxiliary "*šodæn*" ('to become'). Optionally, an agentive prepositional phrase (PP) may precede the verb (e.g., "tævæsote Shahin" meaning 'by Shahin'). While there is debate surrounding constructions like (69b), particularly concerning the nature of "*šodæn*" (see Karimi, 1997; Paul, 2004), we align with the perspective presented in Nemati (2013, cf. also Gavarro & Heshmati, 2014), which classifies (69b) as a genuine verbal passive.[49] Supporting arguments for this posi-

---

49. For instance, Moyne (1974) claimed that there is no passive in Persian and the 'so called' passive is in fact an inchoative construction. Actually, there are many languages that either do not have an agented passive or the agentless passive is their unmarked Passive (e.g. Limbu, Amharic, Latvian, Turkic and Kurdish, see Siewierska, 1984; Haig, 2008). Moyne believes that the 'so-called' passive in Persian is actually an inchoative construction to which a 'by-phrase' (i.e. Agent-phrase) is conjoined, and should the 'by-phrase' be omitted we will see the real

tion include (a) the demotion of the subject, (b) the elevation of the object to subject position, and (c) the morphological transformation of the verb, transitioning from an active form to a past participle, along with the incorporation of "šodæn", inflected for person and tense.

To the best of our knowledge, the investigation into the prepositional phrase encoding the agent in the context of Persian passive constructions has not received extensive attention, with the exception of the quantitative analysis conducted by Bahrami-Khorshid & Golfam (2013). Persian native speakers employ the following compound prepositions to encode the agent. All of these can be considered Axial Parts/Relational Nouns, also given their lexical meaning. Interestingly, the body part for 'hand' (dæst) in (70b) is employed in Persian to encode demoted agents, similar to the use in Italian, as illustrated in the previous section. Note that the adposition *be* (to) is optional in the complex structure *(be) tævæssot-e*.

(70) *Persian*
    a. (be) tævæssot-e
        to   intermediation-Ez
    b. be dæst-e
        to hand-Ez
    c. æz   suy-e
        from/of direction/side-Ez
    d. æz   tæræf-e
        from/of direction/side-Ez
    e. be væsile-y-e
        to instrument-Ez

---

inchoative structure of the 'so called' passive (Moyne, 1974, p.251–255). He believes that the oblique phrase in Persian agented passive is not really an agent-phrase but rather an instrumental construction. According to him "[t]hese instrumental constructions do not clearly specify an agent for the action" (Moyne, 1974, p.251); so the action is perceived as happened spontaneously and does not involve any agency. Naderi (2010) shows that an example like (i) has as the only possible interpretation the one which takes Ali as the agent of košt-n 'to kill'. Moreover, it is not actually possible to encode a real instrument with the preposition 'be dast-e', as illustrated in (ii) (cf. also Bahrami-Khorshid & Golfam, 2013).

  (i) be dæst-e æli košt-e šod   Ø.
      to hand-Ez Ali killed become.PAST 3rd pers.SG
      'S/he was killed by Ali.'
  (ii) be dæst-e æli košt-e šod   Ø.
      to hand-Ez Ali killed become.PAST 3rd pers.SG
      'S/he was killed by Ali.'   *Persian*

Consider in (71) a passive agent introduced by means of the relational noun for *hand*. The example is taken from Bahrami-Khorshid & Golfam (2013).

(71)   *Persian*
       mæsaʔel-e   mæntæqe bæyæd **be dæst-e**   kešvær-hæ-y-e mæntæqe hæl
       problems-Ez region   must   to hand-Ez. country-PL-Ez region   solve
       šæv-æd
       become.PRS.3SG
       'The problems of the region must be solved by the countries of the region'.

In Persian, the dative preposition ($\subseteq$) is *be* (72a) (which we find on top of three complex strings in (70)), normally employed with goal (and motion-to cf. (72b)) arguments, while the instrumental and comitative ($\supseteq$) preposition is *ba* (72c,d).

(72)   *Persian*
       a.   sæfæ-ro   **be** mæn dad
            record-DOM to me   gave
            'S/he gave the record to me'.
       b.   bæcce-ha **be** mædrese ræft-ænd
            child-PL to school   went-3PL
            'The children went to school'.
       b.   pænjere-ro   **ba**   ajor šikæst
            window-DOM with brick broke
            'She broke the window with a brick'.
       c.   **ba**   Shirin ræft-æm tehran
            with Reza   went-1SG Tehran
            'I went to Tehran with Shirin'.

That we are right in assuming a ($\subseteq$) encoding for the dative *be* and a ($\supseteq$) encoding for *ba* is confirmed by the fact that they alternate in a wide range of triadic constructions of the type 'I provided the pictures to the museum/ I provided the museum with pictures', as illustrated in (73)–(75), taken from Franco & Manzini (2017b) (cf. also the discussion in the Introduction, where some of the examples below have been already presented).

(73)   *Persian*
       a.   Pesar sang-ro   **be** sag zad
            boy   stone-DOM to dog hit.PST.3SG
            'The boy hit the dog with the stone'
       b.   Pesar sag-ro   **ba**   sang zad
            boy   dog-DOM with stone hit.PST.3SG
            'The boy hit the dog with the stone'

(74) *Persian*
    a. Pomad-ro **be** dastash   malid
        cream-DOM to her/his.hand spread.PST.3SG
        'S/he spread the cream on her/his hand'
    b. Dastash-ro   **ba** pomade malid
        her/his.hand-DOM with cream   spread.PST.3SG
        'S/he spread her/his hand with the cream'

(75) *Persian*
    a. Chakkosh-ra **be** divar koobidam
        nail-DOM   to wall stick.PST.1SG
        'I stick the nail on the wall'
    b. Divar-ro **ba**   chakkosh koobidam
        wall-DOM with nail   stick.PST.1SG
        'I stick the nail on the wall'

In structure (76) for (73a), P($\subseteq$), instantiated by *be*, the dative preposition, takes as its internal argument its sister DP (*sag* 'dog') and as its external argument the sister to its projection (*sang* 'stone'). The reverse pattern represented in (77) for (73b) shows a P($\supseteq$) elementary predicate, morphologically realized as the instrumental/comitative *ba*, taking as its internal argument the possessum (*sang*) and as its subject the possessor (*sag*).[50]

(76)

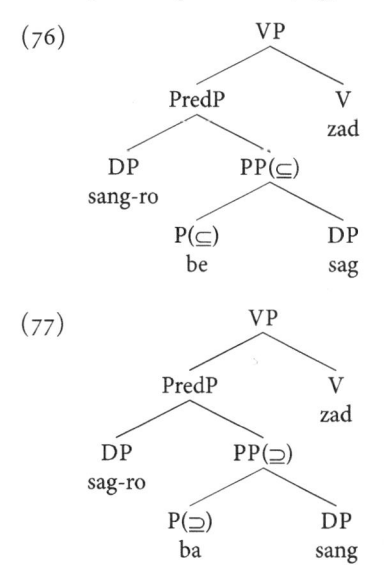

(77)

---

50. Despite the fact that Persian is a verb final language, the direct object appears in a higher position, preceding the indirect object. This property is shared by various languages (Hindi, German, Turkish, etc. Folli et al., 2005).

Interestingly the adposition *ba* can be used in Persian to introduce inanimate entities (e.g. natural forces) in passive structures, as illustrated in (78). On the contrary, animate agents in passives require an embedding under a complex structure involving a relational noun of the type in (70).

(78)   dær nagæhan **ba**   fešar-e   bad baz   šod
        door suddenly with force-Ez wind open become.PST.3SG
        'The door was suddenly opened by the force of wind'.
                                         Persian, (Bahrami-Khorshid & Golfam, 2013).

This difference in the pattern of lexicalization is not surprising, if we follow Alexiadou et al. (2015), who propose that (passive) agents and causers (i.e. natural forces) are licensed by two distinct functional heads, Voice and v (Schäfer, 2012; Harley, 2013; Legate, 2014), as illustrated in (79). Voice introduces the external argument and bears features relating to agentivity; prepositions related to agents and instruments are licensed by Voice. On the contrary *v* introduces a causal relation between a causing event and the resultant state denoted by its complement; prepositions related to causers are licensed by v. Agent/instrument PPs are found only with transitives and passives – but unaccusatives still co-occur with causer PPs.

(79)   [VoiceP (agent PP/instrument PP) [vP (causer PP) [Root(/ResultP)]]]

Nonetheless, Manzini (2017), Franco & Manzini (2017b) assume that (at least for Italian) there are no empirical data that force us to assume two distinct Merge position for causers vs. agents. Considering *da*-phrases in (80)–(81), we can (more economically) assume that they invariantly attach to the vP projection providing a lexicalization for the argument which 'owns' the causation event. Thus, for a passive structure as in (80), we can interpret it as 'there is a caused event of the house being built and Gianni is the owner (author) of this causation'. With causers, as in (81), we may assume that 'there is a caused event of me dying and the causation belongs to hunger'. The structure is basically the same. The adposition, lexicalizes an elementary inclusion predicate, notated with the ($\subseteq$) relation. The structures in (80b)–(81b) are coherent with the representation of the verb phrase (*v*-V) we have provided in the previous Chapters.

(80)   a.   la casa è costruita dal muratore
              "The house is built by the mason."
        b.   [vP CAUSE [VP costruita la casa] [($\subseteq$)P dal muratore]]

(81)   a.   muoio dalla fame
              "I'm dying of hunger."
        b.   [vP CAUSE [VP muoio (io)] [$\subseteq$P dalla fame]]

Franco and Manzini (2017b) assumes that causers are more likely to be interpreted as 'included by' the event they are connected to and use the relation ($\supseteq$) for structures involving them, as in (82), focussing on *per, con*.

(82) a. muoio *per* la fame
          "I'm dying of hunger."
      b. [vP CAUSE [VP muoio (io)] [$\supseteq$P per la fame]]

This would seem not to be problematic. The structure is the same and it is possible that, given the *weakness* of the inclusion relation, ($\subseteq$) and ($\supseteq$) represent distinct flavours of/perspectives on the event (possibly relevant at the Conceptual-Intentional interface). The structure in (82b) for instance could be paraphrased as 'there is a caused event of me dying and hunger is part of it'. Clearly, this reasoning can be applied to the Persian data introduced above in (78) involving the *ba* elementary predicate.

The adposition "be" in the upper layer of the complex strings in (70)–(71) encodes a ($\subseteq$) predicate, given its dative/allative nature. The same ($\subseteq$) value can be assumed, based on our discussion in Section 4.2, for the item "æz," (also topping off some structures in (70)), which in Persian encodes an ablative/source and, unsurprisingly, partitive values, as illustrated in (83).

(83) a. *Persian*
          Shirin færda   **æz** širaz mi-res-e
          Shirin tomorrow from Shiraz DUR-arrive-3SG
          'Shirin is arriving from Shiraz tomorrow.'
      b. do-ta **æz** bæcce-ha
          two-Cl from child-PL
          'Two of the children'

The (lower) relation between the AxP/RelN and the DP agent/causer is consistently marked by the *Ezafe* Morpheme, as shown in (70)–(71). In Persian, Ezafe [-e], derived from the term meaning 'addition', serves as a semantically *fuzzy* morpheme, signaling -among other things- possessive relations within the DP, as shown in (84).[51]

---

51. The Ezafe morpheme is phonologically affixed to the head Noun, influenced by the presence of right-branching complements or modifiers. When multiple modifiers or complements exist, Ezafe can be repeated, with each instance prompted by a right-branching modifier or complement. However, it remains phonologically attached to the preceding constituent. The Ezafe construction has been the topic of many researches in generative linguistic in recent years. Ezafe has been examined through various perspectives in the literature, for example it has been taken to be a genitive case-marker by Samiian (1983, 1994), Larson and Yamakido (2008), Larson and Samiian (2020), while Ghomeshi (1997) has proposed Ezafe as a phonolog-

(84) sag-e   Shirin
      Dog-ez Shirin
      'the dog of Shirin'

Pantcheva (2006) assume that all the (complex) prepositions taking the ezafe in Persian (Class 2 prepositions,[52] according to the taxonomy proposed in Lazard, 1957) must be considered as Axial Parts in the sense of Svenonius (2006), introduced in Section 4.1. What is relevant here is that clearly the Ezafe act as an elementary relator signaling a broad 'inclusee-inclusor' relation between a part and its whole (with a wide pragmatic enrichment at the Conceptual-Intentional Interface). Thus, we assume that in the non-spatial contexts reviewed in this section, the Ezafe acts as a relational marker. We do not see any structural specificity for a locative syntax when comparing the sentences in (85) and (86). Their respective structures are provided in (87) and (88).

(85) Shirin ræft **be posht-e**   xane
      Shirin went to behind-ez house
      'Shirin went behind the house

(86) Ali **be dæst-e**   Reza košte šod.
      Ali to hand-ez Reza killed become.PST.3.SG
      'Ali was killed by Reza'

---

ical linker for non-projecting head nouns to indicate phrasing within the nominal constituent. Franco et al. (2015b) analyzed the Ezafe as an agreement (Determiner-like) affix with different realizations in the noun phrase. The difficulty of a comprehensive definition of the Ezafe is due to the fact that this lexical item seems to indicate nothing specific about the precise semantic or syntactic nature of the relation holding between the modifier and the head noun, as illustrated in (i).

(i) PREDICATE   asman-e abi   'blue sky'
     POSSESSOR   ketab-e Hasan   'the book of Hasan'
     AGENT   kar-e mardom   'the work of people'
     PATIENT   qatl-e Hoseyn   'the murder of Hoseyn'
     GOAL   rah-e Tehran   'the road of/to Tehran'
     LOCATION TIME   mardom-e emruz   'people of today'
     SOURCE   ab-e cesme   'water of/from well'
     SUBSTANCE   gombad-e tala   'dome of gold'
     PART   do najar-e an-ha 'two (persons) of them'

                                      Persian (Windfuhr and Perry, 2009, p.473)

52. Karimi & Brame (1986), Ghomeshi (1997), and Larson and Yamakido (2008) assign to Class 2 prepositions in Persian the status of true nouns. Samiian (1994) and Pantcheva (2006) defend their non-nominal status.

(87) ...

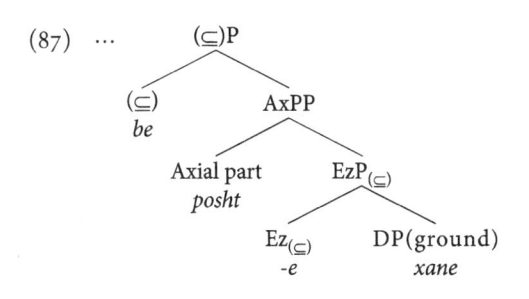

(88) ...

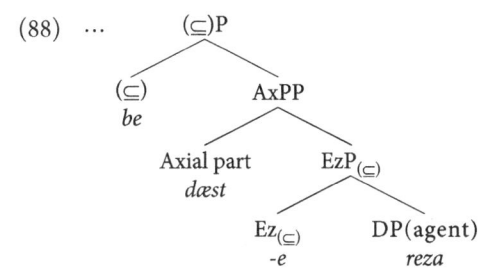

4.7   Conclusion

In conclusion, we have argued that AxPs/RelN are a category with a predicative relation to Grounds/Agents/Causers. This relation can be realized by prepositions or nominal inflections, and its specific interpretation depends on the context. We have shown that prepositions do not inherently encode spatial meanings, but function as general relators. The Finnish locative system presents a challenge to existing accounts, but can be explained by positing a double inclusion layer in the structure of spatial expressions. We have provided cross-linguistic evidence to support our analysis. Our findings have important implications for the understanding of spatial expressions and the role of prepositions. They also contribute to the broader debate on the nature of categories and the relationship between syntax and the lexicon.

CHAPTER 5

Existential sentences in Romance based Creoles

On the relational content of the *contextual domain*

In this Chapter we provide a comprehensive comparative overview of existentials sentences in Romance Creoles. Based on our empirical investigation, we also provide a theoretical analysis of existential constructions which mimic 'transitive' possession. Specifically, we assume that the pervasiveness of a predicative possession strategy for existentials in Creoles has reflexes in their syntax, for which a *possession configuration*, building on recent work of Manzini & Franco (2016), Franco & Manzini (2017a, b), will be draw. In essence, we argue that the 'contextual domain' of existentials (see Francez, 2007, 2009) can be encoded as the *possessor* of a (transitive) HAVE predicate including the pivot as its internal argument (cf. Manzini & Savoia, 2005), with the coda which is (optionally) introduced as an adjunct encoding a further possessor ('locative' *inclusor*) of the predicate (cf. McNally, 1992).

5.1 Introductory remarks

In this Chapter, we delve into existential sentences in Romance-based Creole languages with the aim of providing a comprehensive understanding of their structure. Our research is based on data collected from the Atlas of Pidgin and Creole Language Structures (APiCS: Michaelis et al., 2013) online database, particularly focusing on Features 64, 77, and 78. Existential sentences have been featured in many works within the field of creolistics, aimed at uncovering the structural properties shared among creoles, independently of their substrates and superstrates. As we have already shown in Chapter 2, Pidgin and Creole languages can serve as valuable empirical foundations for investigating Universal Grammar.

For instance, Bickerton (1981) enumerated a number of morpho-syntactic features present in many creoles, which can be related to an innate language bio-program deeply rooted in the human brain. Bickerton specifically assumes that all Creoles "have separate copulas for existential sentences (e.g., 'here get mountain'), which is the same as for the possessive (e.g., 'she get car')" (cf. also McWhorter, 2005, 2011). Markey (1982) claims that all Creole languages "*have one copula for existence and possession, but another one for location.*" Holm and Patrick (2007) show that 94.44% of their sample, which includes a large number of Creole languages, adopts a "have" = "there is" strategy for existentials, where existential sentences and predicate possession are encoded by means of the same verbal item. Consider, for instance, the examples in (1) and (2) from Krio, an English-based Creole spoken in Sierra Leone.

(1) dɛn **gɛt** bɔku pipul dɛm de   [Existential]
     3PL have a.lot.of people PL   there
     'There were a lot of people there', lit. 'They have a lot of people there'
                                    Krio (Finney, 2013, APiCS Structure dataset)

(2) wi **gɛt** fo   pikin   [Predicative Possession]
     1PL have four child
     'We have four children.'   *Krio* (Finney, 2013, APiCS Structure dataset)

In Krio, both predicative possession (2) and existential sentences (1) are expressed with the verb 'get', meaning 'have.' We find an expletive in (1) in the form of a 3rd person plural pronoun. This pattern clearly differs from English "there-sentence" with "be" (or "exist") as a main verb (see Moro, 2017).

McNally (2011, p. 1830) defines existential constructions as copular structures with specialized/non-canonical morpho-syntax, which describe (non-)existence or (un)presence in a given contextual domain. As shown in Bentley (2017, p. 347), the parts of an existential sentence are usually referred to with the terminology in (3).

(3) (PP = coda +) (expletive +) (proform +) copula + NP = pivot (+ PP = coda).

All the items in brackets in (3) are optional. Only the copula and the post-copular noun phrase (the pivot) obligatorily appear in an existential sentence. In the sentence in (1), the *pivot* is the NP *bɔku pipul* ('a lot of people'). An expletive is, for instance, the adverbial item *there* in English or the personal pronoun *dɛn* ('they') in Krio in (1). According to Moro (2017, p. 2) existential sentences including only the pivot are rare. More commonly, existential sentences involve the so-called "coda," that is, normally, it is present a prepositional (PP) phrase (or another XP) "specifying the domain of existence of the individual or set of individuals whose existence is predicated" (Moro 2017, p. 2), as for instance the PP *in the street* in (4).

(4) There are many dogs in the street.

The existential proform is a (possibly locative, cf. Bentley et al., 2015) clitic hosted by the copula, as illustrated in (5) for Italian, where the proform is lexicalized by the item *ci*, which shows up in many Romance varieties (Catalan *hi*, French *y*, Ligurian *i*, etc.).

(5) *Italian*
     Ci sono molti cani in strada
     'There are many dogs in the street.'

As shown in Bentley (2017, p.348) there are Romance varieties that lexicalize all the components illustrated in (3), as demonstrated by an example from Rocchetta Cairo (Ligurian) in (6).

(6) In sa   früt chì$_{\{coda\}}$ u$_{\{expletive\}}$ i$_{\{proform\}}$ è$_{\{copula\}}$ tante smenze$_{\{pivot\}}$
     in this fruit here   EXPL   PF   be.3SG many seeds
     'In this fruit there are many seeds.'   *Rocchetta Cairo (Ligurian)*

In this Chapter, we will provide a comprehensive overview of existentials sentences in Romance Creoles. Based on our empirical investigation we will provide a theoretical analysis of existential construction. We posit that the widespread use of a predicative possession strategy for existential sentences in Creoles is reflected in their syntax, prompting us to propose a 'possession/inclusion configuration' based on the theoretical literature referenced in previous chapters. Specifically, the rest of the chapter is structured as follows: in Section 5.2, we present the relevant data from the French, Spanish, and Portuguese Creoles featured in the APiCS online database while also briefly highlighting the similarities and differences of existential sentences in Romance Creoles compared to their lexifiers. Section 5.3 contains the theoretical core of the discussion, where we propose that the 'contextual domain' of existentials can be encoded as the possessor of a (transitive) HAVE predicate including the pivot as its internal argument (cf. Manzini & Savoia, 2005), with the coda, which is optionally introduced as an adjunct, encoding a further possessor (i.e., a 'locative' inclusor) of the predicate.

5.2 Existentials in Romance based Creoles: The data

Confirming the fact that the preferred strategy for encoding existential structure in Creoles is to use a HAVE predicate, as illustrated in (1)–(2) for Krio, the vast majority of Romance based varieties follow this pattern. Let's start from French Creoles. French do not license phonologically null subjects and requires an expletive subject for existentials ('il'), using an existential proform ('y') cliticized to a HAVE verb ('a', cf. *Jean a un chien* 'Jean has a dog'), as illustrated in (7).

(7) il y a des chiens dans le jardin
     'there are dogs in the garden'   *French*

In the vast majority of French based Creoles no expletive or proform is ever lex-icalized. As illustrated by the following examples, the existential HAVE predicate appears in first position, followed by the pivot ((a) examples). In these languages, predicative possession is 'canonically' expressed via SVO transitive sentences ((b) examples). Note that no relevant influence of the substrates can be assumed here, given that the same behaviour is found in Atlantic and Indo-Pacific Creoles. The verbal items recruited from the lexicon to encode existential and predicative pos-session are highlighted in bold in the examples.

(8)   a.   **Gen** manje sou tab   la.
           have food   on   table DEF
           'There is food on the table.'   *Haitian Creole* (DeGraff, 2007, p.103)

      b.   Mari **gen**   kouraj.
           Mary have courage
           'Mary has courage.'   *Haitian Creole* (DeGraff, 2007, p.115)

(9)   a.   **Ni**   manjè anlè tab-la.
           have food   on   table-DEF
           'There is food on the table.

                    Guadeloupean Creole (Colot & Ludwig 2013a, APiCS Structure
                                                                      dataset[53])

      b.   Mari **ni**   on kabrit.
           Mary have one goat
           'Mary has a goat.'

                    Guadeloupean Creole (Colot & Ludwig 2013a, APiCS Structure
                                                                         dataset)

(10) a.   **gen** manjé asou tab-a
           GEN food   on   table-DET
           'There is (some) food on the table.'
                             Guyanais (Pfänder, 2013, APiCS Structure dataset)

      b.   yé **gen**   roun liv/ liv-ya
           3PL have a   book/book-PL.DEF
           'They have a book/the books.'
                             Guyanais (Pfänder, 2013, APiCS Structure dataset)

(11) a.   **nana** enn armoir   dan la   kuizinn
           have INDF cupboard in   DEF kitchen
           'There is a cupboard in the kitchen' *Reunion Creole* (Barat et al., 1977, p. 81)

---

53. We have not inserted Martinican Creole among our examples, given that the data provided in the APiCS are practically the same as Guadeloupean Creole (cf. Colot & Ludwig, 2013b).

  b. son   papa **nana**   in   gran moustas.
      poss.3SG father have.PRS INDF big   moustache
      'His father has a big moustache.'   *Reunion Creole* (Barat et al., 1977, p 22)

(12) a. **ena**[54] manze lor latab
          Have food   on table
          'There is food on the table.'
                    Mauritian Creole (Baker & Kriegel 2013, APiCS Structure dataset)
      b. mo **ena** san   rupi
          1SG have hundred rupee
          'I have 100 rupees.'
                    Mauritian Creole (Baker & Kriegel 2013, APiCS Structure dataset)

The only French-based Creole that diverges from this pattern is Tayo, which is spoken by around 3000 speakers in Southern New Caledonia. Tayo does not have a verb dedicated to (transitively) encoding predicative possession. Tayo uses a 'locational predication' (see Creissels, 2014) to encode both existentials and possession, as illustrated in (13)–(14). Thus, it is true that we do not have a dedicated lexical item which is the counterpart of HAVE in this language; still, the expression of possession and existential meaning are not differentiated, like the other French Creoles illustrated so far.

(13) **na** ndipa ndesi latam   [existential]
      na bread LOC table
      'There is some bread on the table.'
                    Tayo (Ehrhart & Revis, 2013, APiCS Structure dataset)

(14) **na** a   ŋgra lafamij pu lja   [possession]
      na INDF.ART big   family P 3SG
      'He has a big family.'   *Tayo* (Ehrhart, 1993, p.173)

---

54. Note that Mauritian Creole has two different verbs for expressing possession: *ena* is a stative verb; *ganye* is non-stative. Baker & Kriegel (2013) highlight this difference (cf. also Syea, 2013, 2017). Consider the existential sentences in (i)–(ii):

  (i)   **ena** buku leksi lor pye-la
        have many litchis on tree-the
        'There are lots of litchis on the tree'
  (ii) **gany** buku leksi parti Ti-Rivyer
        have many litchis in   Ti-Rivyer
        'There are lots of litchis in the Ti-Rivyer area'*Mauritian Creole*

What (ii) means is that Ti-Rivyer is a suitable place to go if one wants to get litchis. This, actually, seems to confirm the strict link between existentials and possession. Indeed the same stative/non-stative distinction is at work in the possession domain as illustrated in (iii)–(iv).

  (iii) mo **ena** 100 rupi'I have 100 rupees (in my pocket)'
  (iv)   mo **gany** 100 rupi'I earn/get Rs 100 (for doing a particular task).'

Turning to Spanish-based Creoles, we observe again that the verb which encodes predicative possession is almost always the one recruited to convey an existential meaning. Spanish, on the contrary, uses two distinct lexical items for this purpose, respectively *haber* and *tener*, as illustrated in (15) and (16).[55]

(15) *Spanish*
      hay gatos en la calle   [existential]
      'There are cats in the street'

(16) *Spanish*
      José **tiene** un gato   [predicative possession]
      'José has a cat'

Spanish-based Creoles behave just like the French Creoles illustrated in (8)–(12). Again, no relevant influence of the substrates can be assumed in such cases, provided that the same kind of encoding for existentials and predicative possession is found in both Pacific and Atlantic Creoles.

(17) a. **Tyéne** komída na   mesa.
          have   food   LOC table
          'There is food on the table.'
          Zamboanga Chabacano[56] (Steinkrüger, 2013, APiCS Structure
                                                                   dataset)

      b. le   **tyéne** tres ermáno.
          s/he have three brother
          S/he has three brothers.
          Zamboanga Chabacano (Steinkrüger, 2013, APiCS Structure
                                                                   dataset)

(18) a. **tin** un   gai Portuges   aden.
          have INDF guy Portuguese inside
          'There's a Portuguese guy inside.'
          Papiamentu (Kouwenberg, 2013, APiCS Structure dataset)

      b. awor mi **tin** un   lista basta   largo
          Now 1SG have INDF list sufficiently long
          'Now I have quite a long list.'
          Papiamentu (Kouwenberg, 2013, APiCS Structure dataset)

---

55. Spanish employs a unique form of the predicate *haber* 'have' in the present indicative tense, namely *hay*, which stems the fusion of the third-person singular present tense of *haber* and the locative pronoun *y* (cf. Suñer, 1982; McNally, 2011).

56. According to the data available in the Atlas of Pidgin and Creole Language Structures, this pattern including a 'tener' verb, is attested also in Cavite and Ternate Chabacano, that are cognate languages spoken in the Philippines.

(19) a. **aten** mucho hende aí   plasa.
          Have much   people there plaza
          'There are lots of people in/at the plaza.'
          Palenquero (Schwegler, 2013, APiCS Structure dataset)

      b. Gutabo **aten** ese kusa aí   memo.
          Gustavo have that thing right there
          'Gustavo has this thing right (over) there.'
          Palenquero (Schwegler, 2013, APiCS Structure dataset)

The sole exception among Spanish based Creoles is represented by Media Lengua, which is a mixed language spoken in Ecuador. Media Lengua uses different predicates, respectively 'sit' for existentials (20) and 'hold/have' for predicative possession (21). The pivot in the existential sentence in (20), *manchani plata* 'a lot of money' seems to be the subject of the predication here: It is unmarked for case (contra the internal argument of the possessive verb, which is marked accusative, as in (21)) and triggers agreement on the verb.

(20) Isti olla-bi   manchani plata **sinta**-xu-n   [existential]
      this pot-LOC a.lot.of   silver sit-PROG-3SG
      'There is a lot of money in this pot.'   *Media Lengua* (Muysken, 1981, p.55)

(21) tres gato-s-ta kaza-bi   **tini**-ni
      three cat-PL-ACC house-LOC have-1SG
      'I have three cats in the house.'   *Media Lengua* (Muysken, 1981, p.63)

Finally, also many Portuguese based Creoles follow a HAVE pattern for existentials.[57] Once again, this strategy is at work in Atlantic and in Pacific creole, providing support for the idea of an innate language creation mechanism at work in such contexts, along the lines of Bickerton (1981; 1984). Consider the examples below, where, as before, the (a) examples show an existential construction and the (b) examples show a sentence expressing transitive possession.

---

57. No preforms or expletives are found in European and Brazilian Portuguese. Consider the examples in (i)–(ii), adapted from Bentley (2017, p.349–350).

  (i) Nesta fruta **há**   moitas sementes
       in.this fruit have.3SG many seeds
       'In this fruit there are many seeds.'   *European Portuguese*

  (ii) **tem**   muitos caroços nessa fruta.
       have.3SG many   seeds   in.this fruit
       'In this fruit there are many seeds.'
       Brazilian Portuguese

(22) a. **Ten** un radin   na menza.
　　　Have DET radio.little on table
　　　'There is a little radio on the table.'

　　b. N **ten** un radin.
　　　1SG have DET radio.little
　　　'I have a little radio.' *Cape Verdean Creole of São Vicente*[58] (Swolkien, 2012)

(23) a. (I) **teŋ** poŋ na mesa.
　　　3SG.SBJ have bread on table
　　　'There is bread on the table.'
　　　　　　　　Casamancese Creole (Biagui & Quint 2013, APiCS Structure dataset)

　　b. Joŋ **teŋ** kabalu.
　　　John have horse
　　　'John has a horse.'
　　　　　　　　Casamancese Creole (Biagui & Quint 2013, APiCS Structure dataset)

(24) a. (Ê) **tê**　tôvada.
　　　EXPL have storm
　　　'There is a storm.'　　　　　　*Principense* (Maurer, 2009, p. 58)

　　b. N **tê**　dôsu kaxi.
　　　1SG have two house
　　　'I have two houses.'　　　　　*Principense* (Maurer 2009: 104)

(25) a. Mete patio **té**　wan bityil ku　wan aza　kabadu.
　　　Inside yard have ART bird　with ART wing broken
　　　'There is a bird in the yard with a broken wing.'
　　　　　　　　　　　　　　Fa d'Ambô (Post, 1999, p. 63)

　　b. Eli **té**　wan lapizi.
　　　3SG have ART pencil
　　　'He has a pencil.'　　*Fa d'Ambô* (Post, 2013, APiCS Structure dataset)

(26) a. **tiŋ**　　ũ　makak i　ũ　crocodile.
　　　have-PST one monkey and one crocodile
　　　[Once upon a time], there was a monkey and a crocodile.
　　　　　　　　　　　Diu Indo-Portuguese (Cardoso, 2009, p. 167)

　　b. Nə Go yo **te**　　bastãt cousin i auntie.
　　　Loc Goa 1SG have.npst many cousin　and auntie
　　　'I have many cousins and aunties in Goa.'
　　　　　　　　　　　Diu Indo-Portuguese (Cardoso, 2009, p. 167)

---

58. An identity between existential and possession predicates is attested also in the Cape Verdean Creole of Brava and the Cape Verdean Creole of Santiago, as documented in APiCS feature 78.

(27) a. **Teng** kumeria na   mesa
          have food   LOC table
          'There is food on the table.'
          Papia Kristang (Baxter, 2013, APiCS Structure dataset)

      b. Maria **teng** ñgua baisikal
          Maria have one   bicycle
          'Maria has a bicycle.'*Papia Kristang* (Baxter, 2013, APiCS Structure dataset)

(28) a. Nu meo   di matu **teng** ung pos grandi.
          In middle of forest have a   well big
          'In the middle of the forest there was a big well.'
          Batavia Creole (Maurer, 2011, p. 67)

      b. Ile **teng** ung kabalu.
          He have a   horse
          'He had a horse.'   *Batavia Creole* (Maurer, 2011, p. 66)

There are also some exceptions among Portuguese based Creoles. For instance, in Korlai, which is a Creole language spoken by ca. 1,000 speakers in an isolated area around the Indian village of Korlai, possessives and existentials are construed with the copula, not with a transitive possession verb, which doesn't exist in that language, as shown in (29)–(30). Korlai displays a 'locational predication' pattern for possession and existentials similar to the one represented for the French based Creole Tayo, illustrated above in (13)–(14).

(29) Mi   pɛrt doy sajkəl **tɛ**
      1SG.POSS near two bicycle COP.PRS
      'I have two bicycles.'   *Korlai* (Clemens, 2013, APiCS Structure dataset)

(30) ũ ɔm **ti**
      A man COP.PST
      'There was a man.'   *Korlai* (Clemens, 2013, APiCS Structure dataset)

In some other Portuguese based Creoles the expression of possession and existential meaning actually overlap. For instance, in Santome there are various ways to morpho-syntactically encode existential meaning. Consider the following examples.

(31) Meza **tê**   kume.
      Table have food
      'There is food on the table.'
      Santome (Hagemeijer, 2013, APiCS Structure dataset)

(32)   Meza **sa ku**   kume.
       Table be with food
       'There is food on the table.'
       Santome (Hagemeijer, 2013, APiCS Structure dataset)

(33)   Ngandu, (ê) **tê**   ngê   ku na ka   kum'=ê fa.
       Shark   3SG have person REL neg IPFV eat=it   NEG
       'Shark, there are people that don't eat it.'
       Santome (Hagemeijer, 2013, APiCS Structure dataset)

(34)   Ngê   **sen** ni Putuga ku ka   dumu uva   ku   ope.
       person exist in Portugal REL IPFV pound grape with foot
       'There are people in Portugal that smash grapes with their feet.'
       Santome (Hagemeijer, 2013, APiCS Structure dataset)

(35)   Vêndê **tê**   sapê ũa data.
       Store have hat a lot
       'The store has a lot of hats.'
       Santome (Hagemeijer, 2013, APiCS Structure dataset)

In the sentences in (31) and (32) we find that the coda is the subject of the predication. The examples in (31) expresses existential meaning with a HAVE verb, which is also responsible for encoding transitive possession in Santome (cf. the example in (35)), while the example in (32) expresses the existential meaning with a 'be with' strategy, which is not uncommon cross-linguistically, as an alternative to transitive HAVE in encoding (abstract, temporary, etc.) possession (see Stolz, 2001; Stassen, 2009; Levinson, 2011; Myler, 2016, among others, cf. the discussion in the previous Chapters). The example in (33) shows an expletive personal pronoun as the subject of the HAVE predicate followed by the pivot *ngê* 'person'. In (34) the pivot appears to be the subject of the predicate *sen* ('be, exist').

Angolar displays an analogous variability in the encoding of existentials. This language has three constructions, which express both transitive possession and existential contexts, respectively *tê* 'have', *tha ki* 'be with' and *tha ku ê* 'be with it' as illustrated in (36)–(38). In all these ('possessive') examples, the pivot follows the verbal item.

(36)   Tepu nakulu kwanda tia   ta   **tê**   ũa ome.
       time old   high   land PST have one man
       'In the olden days, in the highlands, there was a man.'
       Angolar (Maurer, 1995, p.103)

(37)   Hô letu   kanua e   tambe **tha ki**   tano baburu
       then inside canoe DEM also   be with five baburu
       'So in the canoe there were also five baburu'   *Angolar* (Maurer, 1995, p.103)

(38) Aie **tha ku** (*ê*) kikiê.
 Now be with it kikiê.
 'Now there is fish.'   *Angolar* (Maurer, 1995, p. 67)

In Angolar, there is also a verb solely used for conveying an existential meaning,[59] the item *the* (possibly derived from the copula *tha*, cf. (37)–(38)). In such case, the pivot precedes the verb, matching the behaviour of the example from Santome in (34), where an EXIST/BE and not a HAVE verb is used.

(39) Aie kikiê **the**.
 Now fish there.is
 'Now there is fish.'   *Angolar* (Maurer, 1995, p. 67)

Finally, according to the data reported in the APiCS on line (feature 77), Guinea-Bissau Kriyol has two different verbs for expressing existentials and transitive possession, respectively *ten* ('exist'), and *tene* ('have'), as shown in (40)–(41). Actually, the two verbs appear to be lexically related. Thus, we assume that at most, the existential verb *ten* can be considered as a specialized allomorph for existential contexts of the HAVE predicate. Note that an optional expletive personal pronoun can show up as the subject of *ten*.

(40) (I) **ten** un minjer ki **tene** um fiju-femea.
 3SG exist one woman who have one child-female
 'There's a woman who has a daughter.'
                    Guinea-Bissau Kriyol (Intumbo et al., 2013, APiCS Structure dataset)

(41) Djon **tene** un bisikleta.
 John have one bike
 'John has a bike.'   *Guinea-Bissau Kriyol* (Peck, 1988, p. 36)

Regarding the morphosyntactic characteristics of existentials in the Romance-based Creole languages explored thus far compared to their lexifiers, it's noteworthy that Romance-based Creoles consistently avoid the use of a proform to encode existentials. This tendency could stem from the simplification process inherent in pidginization/creolization, which often results in the loss of inflectional morphology.[60] It is worth noting that French-based Creoles universally lack a (locative)

---

59. In his typological survey, Creissels (2014) show that the use of a predicate solely recruited for the expression of existential meaning is a strategy quite common among natural languages.

60. Actually it must be noted that inflections are not at all uncommon in pidgins. Bakker (2003) shows that pidgins can have richer inflection than creoles, though much of this could be due to the fact that many creoles are lexified by 'inflectionally rich' Romance languages (cf. e.g. Roberts & Bresnan, 2008). DeGraff (2001, p. 232, 2003) assumes that the presence of inflec-

proform in their grammar. In Ibero-Romance, the proform is either absent, as in Portuguese, or incorporated into present tense forms of the HABERE verb paradigm, as in European Spanish (see Bentley, 2017). Interestingly, Spanish-based Creoles consistently employ an existential verb derived from Spanish *tener*, which exclusively encodes transitive possession.[61] When it comes to expletive subjects, in Romance languages where phonologically null subjects are disallowed, there's typically an obligatory expletive pronoun in existentials, such as il *in* French (cf. Example (7)). Certain French-based Creoles exhibit an optional expletive subject (usually a 3rd person pronoun), as shown in (42)–(44). Therefore, the correlation between the allowance of phonologically null subjects and the obligatory presence of an expletive pronoun for existentials isn't consistently observed in Romance-based Creoles.

(42) (**i**) ni   onlo moun.
      3SG have much people
      'There are a lot of people.'
          Guadeloupean Creole (Colot & Ludwig 2013a, APiCS Structure dataset)

(43) (**i**) ni   anlo moun.
      3SG have much people
      There are a lot of people.   *Martinican Creole* (Ludwig, 1996, p. 338)

(44) (**ye**) gen de   kalite demi.
      3PL have two kind berry
      'There are two kinds of berries.'
          Louisiana Creole, Pointe Coupee (Klinger, 2003, p. 309)

Spanish-based Creoles typically do not employ an expletive pronoun. Conversely, many Portuguese-based Creoles spoken in Africa, akin to the French ones previously discussed, allow for the optional presence of an expletive, as illustrated by the examples in (45)–(47) (cf. APiCS online: Feature 64).

(45) (**i**)   teŋ arus ciw na Sindoŋ.
      3SG.SBJ have rice a.lot in Sindoŋ.
      'There is plenty of rice in Sindone.'
          Casamancese (Quint, 2013, APiCS Structure dataset)

---

tional morphology in Haitian Creole can be seen as evidence against the idea that creole genesis involves that sort of "break in transmission" commonly ascribed to pidginization.

61. In Romance languages *tenere* is attested as an existential predicate only in Brazilian Portuguese (cf. Bentley 2017, p. 352). All the Portuguese based Creoles illustrated in Section 2 use a *tenere* strategy for existential purposes, departing from their lexifier, which is – with good evidence – European Portuguese which uses an HABERE predicate.

(46) (Ê) tê   ningê nhon di pasa lala   fa.
      3SG have person no   of pass there NEG
      'There is nobody who passes by over there.'   *Principense* (Maurer, 2009, p.58)

(47) (Ê) tê   dja ku n   na ka   kume fa.
      3SG have day REL 1SG neg IPFV eat   NEG
      'There are days on which I don't eat.'
                                    Santome (Hagemeijer, 2013, APiCS Structure dataset)

Furthermore, in Romance languages, the pivot consistently appears post-verbally (cf. the example in (3)). In contrast, in Creoles, with predicates specifically expressing existence (and non-possession), the pivot precedes the verbal item, arguably occupying a subject position. For instance, consider the examples in (34) from Santome and in (39) from Angolar. Regarding the definiteness effect, it has been well-documented since Milsark (1974) that Romance languages do not demonstrate the same evidence for it as English, as definite noun phrases are freely permitted in existential sentences.[62] APiCS does not offer conclusive comparative evidence regarding this matter. However, it is noteworthy that it lacks examples featuring the pivot introduced by a definite determiner among Romance Creoles. Additionally, Syea (2013) explicitly posits a definiteness effect in the syntax of Mauritian Creole, as demonstrated in (48).

(48) *Ena loto la   kot labutik
       have car DEF near shop
       'There is the car near the shop'   *Mauritian Creole* (Syea, 2013, p.66)

We have observed that all the Romance languages examined in this study (French, Spanish, and Portuguese), as well as the Creoles based on them, utilize HAVE-like predicates to convey existential meanings.[63] However, it remains unclear whether the pivot in Romance languages functions as the syntactic subject or the object of the existential construction. Bentley (2017) demonstrates that in Spoken Brazilian Portuguese, the invariant copula *tem* co-occurs with nominative pronominal piv-

---

62. As reported in Bentley (2017: 357–358) however, in-depth analysis brings to light two kinds of evidence for the Definiteness Effect in Romance: (i) a definite post-verbal NP cannot be followed by the coda within the same prosodic unit (Leonetti's 2008 *Coda Constraint*); (ii) many Romance varieties distinguish between definite and indefinite post-verbal NPs in existential by means of verb selection and/or agreement pattern (see La Fauci & Loporcaro, 1993; Manzini & Savoia, 2005; Bentley, 2013, among others). Actually, Romance existentials with definite post-verbal NPS have been argued to be inverse locatives (Moro, 1997; Zamparelli, 2000, among others).

63. Note, however, that HAVE predicates for existentials are also widely attested for English and Dutch based creoles. Consider for instance the examples from *Krio* in (1)–(2).

ots, as seen in (49). Conversely, Manzini & Savoia (2005) and Cruschina (2015) illustrate that many southern Italo-Romance dialects with existential HAVE verbs select Differentially Object Marked (DOM) pivots, as shown in (50), indicating a clear object status for them.

(49) Tem   eu.
      hold.3SG 1SG.NOM
      'There's me.'   *Spoken Brazilian Portuguese*, Bentley (2017, p.353)

(50) Ave   a   mie.
      have.3SG DOM I
      'There's me.'   *Salentino Apulian*, Bentley (2017, p.353)

In Creole languages, we cannot discern the object versus subject status of the pivot of HAVE predicates based on agreement/case patterns, as the verbal predicate is typically uninflected, and the pivot remains unmarked for case. However, there are at least two clear indications suggesting their object status. First, as illustrated above, we find the presence of an optional subject pronoun in various Creoles. Second, whenever a different predicate is involved in an existential construction, the pivot – as previously noted – shifts to a pre-verbal position. Considering that Creole languages consistently follow SVO word order (cf. APiCS feature n. 1), this pattern strongly suggests their status as (logical) subjects.

5.3   Towards an analysis

The present section constitutes the theoretical core of the discussion. We will propose that the 'possessive' encoding of existential sentences in Creole languages can be easily explained if we assume that the 'contextual domain' of existentials is encoded as the (covert, implicit) possessor of a (transitive) HAVE predicate, with the pivot serving as its direct object (cf. Rigau, 1997; Manzini & Savoia, 2005). The coda, which is optionally introduced as an adjunct, encodes a further possessor (a 'locative' inclusor) of the predicate, following the insights of Franco & Manzini (2017b), Franco et al. (2021), as well as the discussion in the previous chapter. Before introducing our analysis in Section 5.3.2, we provide an overview of the theoretical background in Section 5.3.1.

5.3.1   Theoretical background on existentials

Existential sentences have been a prominent research topic in generative linguistics, at least since Milsark (1974). Two main proposals have been put forward concerning the syntax of existentials. The most well-received and widespread proposal is based on the assumption that a small clause structure in which the pivot is the subject and the coda is the predicate is involved (see e.g. Stowell, 1978; Chomsky, 1981; Safir, 1983; Freeze, 1992; Moro, 1997, among many others).[64] The second proposal takes existential sentences to be structures in which the pivot is hosted as the complement of the verbal predicate and the coda is an adjunct (see McNally, 1992; Francez, 2007, 2009; Villalba, 2013, among others).[65] The two competing proposals are illustrated, respectively, in (51) and (52).

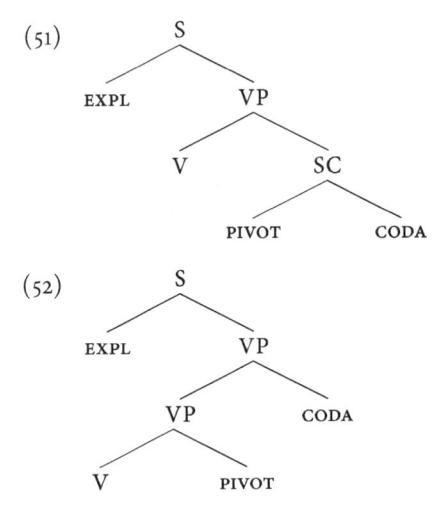

(51)

(52)

Here we follow the view advocated in (52), in order to account for the syntax of HAVE existentials in Romance based Creole languages. Specifically, we follow Francez (2007, 2009) in assuming that the *contextual domain* has a direct role in shaping existentials and in assuming that codas are VP adjuncts. Francez assumes that existentials have an implicit argument that can be thought of as a contextual variable. For instance, a sentence like 'John left' is understood as pertaining to a contextual interval – it is true relative to a given interval if this interval contains an event of 'John leaving'. Francez (2007, p. 54) argues that: "*the implicit argument [...] is a contextual domain, defined as a set (of individuals, times, locations, worlds, or possibly other types of entities) determined by context or by contextual modifiers.*"

---

64. Note that Williams (1983, 1984) (cf. also Higginbotham, 1985) developed a theory in which syntactic predication is defined independently of the presence of a clausal constituent. Williams argues that, syntactically, a predication is a relation holding between a maximal projection and some phrase external to that projection. Given that external arguments are by definition 'external' to the maximal unit of which they are subjects, according to Williams there can be no small clause constituent encoding a subject–predicate relation.

65. Another possibility would be to consider the coda as a further complement of the existential verb in a triadic structure, as suggested, for example by Keenan (1987).

Intuitively, the function of existentials [...] is to convey information about such contextual domains, and particularly to say what a domain or a set of domains contains or does not contain."

We argue that the contextual domain can be syntacticized in subject position, namely it can be rendered in the form of a (possibly covert) expletive item, which is the subject of a transitive HAVE predicate. In other words, the contextual domain is encoded as a 'possessor'. Thus, in our view, expletives are meaningful items.[66]

Note that the sensitivity to the 'contextual domain' of existential sentences has been often suggested in the semantic literature. For instance, Borschev & Partee (2001, p. 22) argue that: *"It is important that existence is always understood with respect to some LOCation. An implicit LOCation must be given by the context. This is usually "here" or "there", "now" or "then"". An answer to the existential question must explicate what it means to be "understood with respect to some LOCation."*

Francez (2007) provides a comparison of existentials with other syntactic domains involving implicit arguments, which reveals much about and their interaction with context. For instance, implicit arguments (of the kind relevant here) include "missing/covert" objects of transitive verbs. Fillmore (1986) identifies two types of readings for these kinds of objects: an existential quantification reading (53a) and a definite reading (53b) (cf. Francez 2007: 58).

(53) a. I ate. (= I ate something)
      b. I noticed. (= I noticed that)

Francez (2007, 2009) claims that contextual domains are actually analogous to the context sets usual in the semantic literature on contextual domain restriction (see Barwise & Cooper, 1981; Von Fintel, 1994; among other). Consider the example in (54) (adapted from Francez 2007).

(54) E. Coli endotoxin caused death in all animals within 16 to 29 hours.

The quantified expression *all animals* in (54) is interpreted as if some hidden constituent such as for instance *in the experiment, in the study* were involved in contextually restricting the NP *animals*. We can assume, following Francez (2007, p. 53), that the context set is constructed as a set of entities related to this discourse referent by some contextually salient relation: *"Generally, one can speak of the contextual domain of an entity, the context set determined through a salient discourse referent and relation."*

---

66. Perhaps, in the generative literature, the most interesting attempt to defend the view that expletives are meaningful items is the one advanced in Moro (1997). According to Moro, English *there* or the Italian proform *ci* are meaningful, being 'predicates predicated of the pivot', occurring in subject position due to a mechanism of predicate raising.

5.3.2   Our proposal for Romance based Creoles: The contextual domain (and the coda) as 'possessors'

We argue that the *contextual domain*, as defined above can be encoded in the form of the possessor of an existential event. This is the most widespread strategy in the case of Romance based Creoles, as we have illustrated in Section 5.2. Consider this basic intuition. The Italian sentences in (55) and (56) basically express the same existential meaning. The example in (56) mimics the behaviour of the vast majority of Romance Creoles, namely it uses a HAVE predicate to convey an existential meaning. This pattern is quite widespread in Spoken Italian, at least according to our native judgements.

(55)   C'**è** la nebbia a Milano
'There is fog in Milan'
Italian

(56)   C'**hanno** la nebbia a Milano
'There is fog in Milan'
Italian

Crucially, in (56) the HAVE predicate is inflected for 3rd person plural, suggesting the presence of a covert expletive pronoun, that we argue to be devoted to encode the contextual domain. Substantially, we claim that the event described by the VP predicate has the property of being 'witnessed', namely included in (or concomitant to) a relevant discourse universe, representing – in a sense – the set of individuals which can attend the described event. These individuals can be precisely rendered as the 'contextual domain' of the event. Actually, they are *present* to a given event and this is coherent with what Creissels (2014, p.2) says, namely that: "*What distinguishes existential clauses from plain locational clauses is a different perspectivization of figure-ground relationships whose most obvious manifestation is that, contrary to plain locational clauses, existential clauses are not adequate answers to questions about the location of an entity, but can be used to identify an entity present at a certain location.*" Evidence that we are on the right track, in assuming that expletives are meaningful and encode the contextual domain, comes from examples like the following.

(57)   A Ostia c'**hai** il sole mentre a Milano c'**hanno** la nebbia
'In Ostia, there is the sun, while in Milan there is the fog'
Italian

In the existential sentences in (57) the contextual domain that is perceived as more 'proximal' is encoded via a second person singular inflection on the HAVE verb (namely, encoding a covert 'participant' pronoun), while the contextual domain that is perceived as more 'distal' is rendered through a third person plural inflection.

Interestingly, this is not uncommon within Creole languages. As reported in Haspelmath (2013, APiCS, Features 64), for instance in Jamaican Creole, existential sentences are formed with *gat* (< English got) or *hav* (< English have) preceded by an indefinite pronoun, usually *yu* 'you' or *dem* 'they'. In some cases, even the 1st person plural *wi* 'we' can be used for existentials. According to what reported in the APiCS, which pronoun is selected depends on the speaker's attitude towards the entity which the context is about. Clearly, this fact militates against the view the expletive pronouns are meaningless.

Following Svenonius (2007), Bassaganyas-Bars (2015), and the discussion in the Introduction regarding the behavior of *hold* predicates in some Southern Italian dialects, we assume that HAVE predicates encode a basic relation (of 'inclusion'), that we notate as ($\supseteq$) (cf. Franco & Manzini 2017 on an analogous proposal concerning the adposition *with* and its application in the previous Chapters). Consider the representation in (58). This structure basically says that the *possessum* is the complement of ($\supseteq$)P and the *possessor* is its sister.

(58)

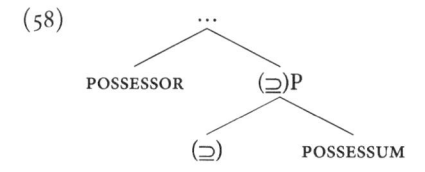

In the case of languages utilizing a possession schema for existential structures, such as the Romance-based Creoles illustrated in this study, we argue that the possessum is the pivot, and the possessor is its contextual domain. Clearly, we posit that the use of the same predicate to encode transitive possession and existential meaning is not coincidental. The contextual domain is precisely rendered, in such cases, with an expletive pronoun, representing the set of individuals which can possess/attend/witness/be present at the described event.

Regarding the codas, particularly when they are introduced by a (locative) prepositional phrase (PP), we posit that they serve as additional possessors of the pivot, incorporated into the syntactic structure through an adjunction operation. Consider again the sentence in (56). This sentence clearly implies that 'the coda includes the pivot,' indicating that 'Milan has fog.' Evidence supporting this characterization stems from the fact that an existential meaning can be expressed in Creole languages as shown in (59)–(60), which echoes (31)–(32) for ease of reference. Here, the coda (or more precisely, the argumental material embedded within the coda) is precisely introduced as the possessor of the pivot. In such instances, the contextual domain could be assumed, as demonstrated in the example in (54), to be introduced as a covert PP/adverbial adjunct that restricts the discourse universe.

(59) Meza tê   kume.   =(31)
      Table have food
      'There is food on the table.'

> Santome (Hagemeijer 2013: APiCS Structure dataset)

(60) Meza sa ku   kume.   =(32)
      Table be with food
      'There is food on the table.'

> Santome (Hagemeijer 2013: APiCS Structure dataset)

We follow Franco & Manzini (2017a, b), Franco & Lorusso (2019), Franco et al. (2021) and the discussion in Chapter 4 in assuming that locatives are interpreted as such only in so far as they denote locatively constrained 'inclusion'. Specifically, as we have already pointed out, locative is a specialization of an 'inclusion' relation, which arises for instance from the locative nature of the nominal element embedded under an adposition/oblique case, endowed with an elementary interpretive 'zonal inclusion' content interacting with the internal organization of the predicate/event (Belvin & Den Dikken 1997).

Locative *in*, *to*, etc. are nothing else than a specialization of the ($\subseteq$) relation (cf. Chapter 4), which is notably the 'inverse' of the relation expressed by the verb for HAVE (or by the adposition *with*, cf. Levinson, 2011), namely ($\supseteq$), as shown in (58). Thus, we argue that in the Romance based Creoles that we have considered above the coda (actually, the nominal constituent expressed *via* the coda) is a second possessor of the event including the pivot and whose external argument (first possessor) is the contextual domain. A representation is given in (61) for the Casamancese example in (23a).

(61)

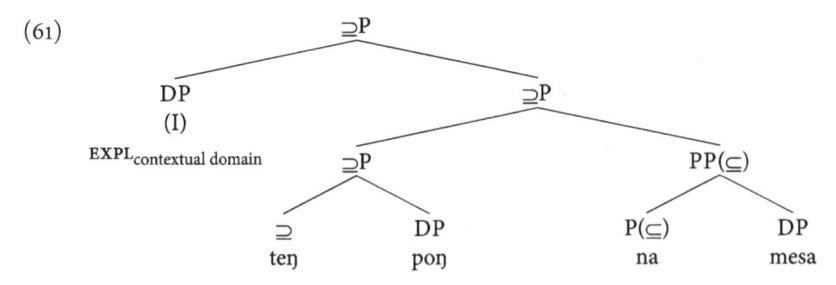

What (61) says is that those entities/individuals which represent the (implicit, covert) contextual domain (possibly expressed via an expletive pronoun) possess/include/witness 'the bread' & the state/event of 'having the bread' is also possessed/included by the item which is usually termed as the coda (the 'table' in the example). This is the prevalent configuration for existentials in Romance based Creoles, where transitive possession and existential meaning *overlap*.[67]

5.4   Conclusion

To sum up, in this work we have provided a comprehensive overview of existentials in Romance Creoles. Based on our empirical investigation, we have also provided an analysis of existential sentences, which mimic 'transitive' possession in the vast majority of Romance based Creole languages. Specifically, we have assumed that the pervasiveness of a predicative possession strategy for existentials in Creoles has reflexes in their syntax, for which a *possession configuration*, building on recent work of Manzini & Franco (2016), Franco & Manzini (2017), Franco and Lorusso (2019, 2020) has been advanced.

In essence, we have claimed that the 'contextual domain' of existentials (see Francez 2007, 2009) can be encoded as the *possessor* of a (transitive) HAVE predicate including the pivot as its direct object (cf. Manzini & Savoia 2005), with the coda which is (optionally) introduced as an adjunct, encoding a further possessor ('locative' *inclusor*) of the predicate (e.g. embedded under a PP constituent).

---

67. As for the other minority strategies employed by these Creoles to encode existentials, we have to say that Tayo (cf. Examples (13)–(14)) and Korlai (cf. Examples (29)–(30) use a locative strategy for expressing possession, namely possessors are encoded via a locative adjunct. Still, there is no difference with existentials, which are encoded according to the same pattern. In other cases, as in Media Lengua, Angolar or Santome the pivot may be expressed as what appears to be the subject of the existential predicate. We leave an account of such 'deviant' patterns for future research.

CHAPTER 6

The morphosyntax of Italian ethnic adjectives

In this study, we address ethnic adjectives in Italian, challenging the dichotomy between 'thematic' and 'classificatory' ethnic adjectives recently posited by Alexiadou & Stavrou (2011). Drawing upon the frameworks of Manzini & Savoia (2011a), Manzini & Franco (2016), Franco & Manzini (2017b), Savoia et al. (2017), and Franco et al. (2020), we present a unified characterization of Italian ethnic adjectives. We propose that the derivational morphemes shaping these adjectives serve as a derivational counterpart of the genitive adposition "di" (of) (along with other types of obliques), sharing a common predicational core and signature with them. Furthermore, we suggest that the framework proposed for ethnic adjectives can be broadly extended to relational adjectives in general.

6.1   Introductory remarks

In this chapter, we deal with ethnic adjectives in Italian, arguing against the dichotomy between 'thematic' and 'classificatory' ethnic adjectives, recently assumed by Alexiadou & Stavrou (2011). Building again on Manzini & Savoia (2011), Manzini & Franco (2016), Franco & Manzini (2017a,b), Savoia et al. (2017, 2018), Franco et al. (2020) among others, we provide a unified characterization of Italian ethnic adjectives and we take the derivational morphemes shaping this kind of items to be a derivational counterpart of the genitive adposition *di* (of) (and other kinds of obliques), sharing with the latter a common predicational core and a common signature. The proposal advanced for ethnic adjectives can be broadly extended to relational adjectives in general.

Ethnic adjectives of the type illustrated in (1) have attracted some interest in the recent theoretical literature.

(1)   a.   The **Persian** invasion of Greece
      b.   The **Persian** carpet

From the one hand, Alexiadou & Stavrou (2011) assumed that ethnic adjectives of the type represented in (1a) are 'nouns in disguise', having a nominal source visible at the level of interpretation, while items of the type in (1b) are proper 'classificatory' adjectives, which happen to be 'homophonous' to the thematic items employed in contexts where a deverbal noun is present, as for instance 'invasion' in (1a). From the other hand, Arsenijevic et al. (2014) (cf. Boleda et al., 2012) have proposed a unified treatment of ethnic adjectives, assuming that the two uses (thematic *vs.* classificatory) in (1a) and (1b) derive from a single lexical entry (a proper adjective). Indeed, they assume that a common semantic analysis involving an *Origin* relation accounts for both readings.

In this chapter, focussing on Italian ethnic adjectives, we will provide a unified characterization of this kind of items, enhancing the role of derivational morphology. Building on Borer (2003, 2014), we will assume that inflection and derivation can convey the same morpho-syntactic relation/content. We will extend this idea to stand-alone morphemes (i.e. adpositions). We take the derivational morphemes shaping Italian ethnic adjective to be a derivational counterpart of genitive/obliques adpositions, sharing with the latter a common (elementary) predicational core and a common signature. The Chapter is structured as follows. In Section 6.2 we will briefly illustrate in some more detail the competing proposals on ethnic adjectives advanced in the recent generative literature. In Section 6.3 we will empirically describe how Italian ethnic adjectives are shaped in the lexicon. Section 6.4 advances an analysis, that rejects Alexiadou & Stavrou's idea that thematic and classificatory ethnic adjectives have different class labels in our lexicon (reflecting different syntaxes), and assumes that the derivational suffixes recruited to introduce these nominal modifiers are elementary relational predicates, signalling a broad part-whole relation, based on a series of morpho-syntactic evidence.

6.2   Background on ethnic adjectives

Alexiadou & Stavrou, taking Distributed Morphology (Halle & Marantz, 1993; Marantz, 1997) as a framework, assume that the thematic ethnic adjectives of the type depicted in (1a) are nominal items, while classificatory ethnic adjectives, as in (1b), are real adjectives, which just happen to be homophonous to thematic ethnic adjectives. Since the present work is couched in a framework which takes the lexicon as the locus of externalization in the sense of Berwick and Chomsky (2011), pairing syntactico-semantic content with phonological content, we are aprioristically unsatisfied with a characterization of the items in (1a) and (1b) as merely homophonous.[68] Actually, as will see below, there are some empirical flaws in the

---

68. As in standard minimalism (Chomsky, 1995), we assume that syntax does not exist but as the product of the merger of lexical items. In what follows we consistently use the expression 'x lexicalizes y'. What we mean is that lexical item *x* lexicalizes concept *y*, by pairing *y* with a phonological form *z* (cf. Manzini & Savoia, 2007, 2011, cf. Boeckx, 2009).

approach of Alexiadou & Stravrou which theoretically substantiate a *sensu lato* lexicalist approach to the problem (Chomsky, 1995, cf. also Stump, 2001).

Alexiadou & Stravrou mainly focus on the syntax of thematic ethic adjectives, stipulating a different syntactic encoding of 'classificatory' ethnic items (for which they do not provide a detailed syntactic representation). Thematic items are claimed to carry "a nominal source visible at the interpretation level" (Alexiadou & Stravrou 2011, p.120, cf. also Fábregas, 2007b, Marchis Moreno, 2010, 2015), consistently bearing an agent theta-role assigned by a deverbal noun (*invasion* in (1a)) in a nominalization grid. The minimal pair in (2) serves as illustrating the issue with Italian examples.

(2)   *Italian*
     a.   L'invasione italiana dell'Albania
         'The Italian invasion of Albania'
     b.   L'invasione dell'Albania dell'/da parte dell'Italia.
         'The invasion of Albania of/by (from part of) Italy'

(2a) and (2b) essentially mean the same. The agent of the construction in (2b), namely Italy, is introduced by the genitive preposition *of* or by the complex prepositional string *da parte di* (lit. 'from part of'). That an agent is involved when introduced by such complex preposition phrase is ensured by the fact that the same strategy may be employed in Italian for introducing demoted agents, as illustrated in (3).

(3)   Il pacco bomba fu spedito da (parte di) un poliziotto infiltrato.
     'The parcel bomb has been sent by (from part of) an infiltrator'
     Italian

Thus, arguably, the adjective *italiana* in (2a) expresses the same agent theta role. For Alexiadou & Stavrou, the difference in the syntax between (2a) and (2b) is given broadly assuming the Case Filter (Chomsky, 1981), namely the principle by which every noun needs to bear case. The thematic ethnic adjective in (2b) is a deficient (caseless) noun, which becomes an adjective during the derivation. The syntactic derivation of Alexiadou and Stavrou (2011, p.136) is represented in (4b), for the Greek example in (4a).

(4) a.   germaniki epithesi
         German   attack
     b.

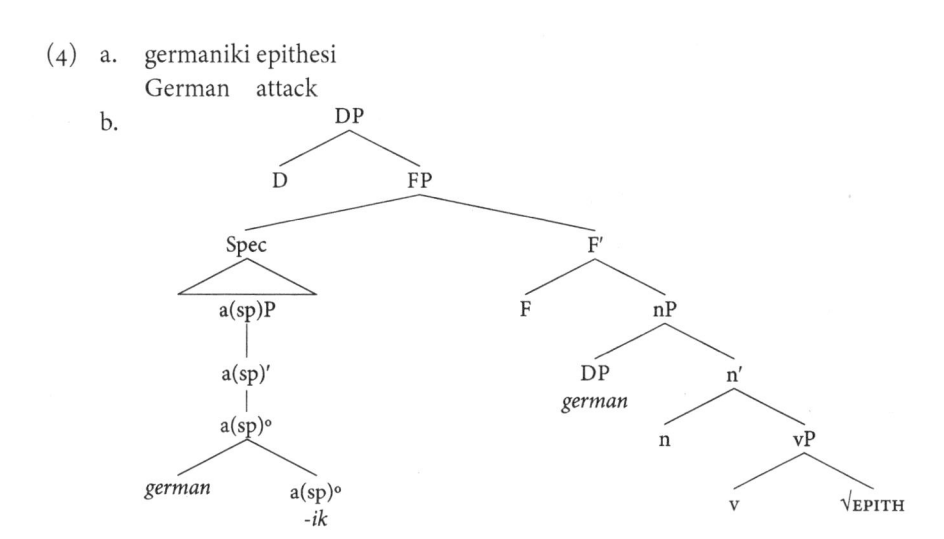

Alexiadou & Stavrou take the suffix *–ik* to be the overt exponent of a category that they label a/ASP, which is assumed to act as an adjectivizer, building an adjective out of a noun. Such suffix selects for a particular set of nouns and the spell-out of this combination is interpreted as an adjective. In (4b), *german-* starts out as a DP in the specifier of the noun phrase *epithesi* 'attack', represented in (4a) via the root EPITH (matching the syntax of the verb for 'attack'). In this position, the item *german-* is necessarily assigned the agent theta role by the underlying verb, in analogy to genitive DPs (cf. 2b), which are also assumed to be generated in this position (cf. Marchis Moreno, 2010). Since *german-* is not valued for case and since every noun needs to bear case, it is forced to move up and to adjoin as a head to a(sp) (the head of an adjectival projection which, in line with Cinque (1994, 2010); Alexiadou & Stavrou assume to be sandwiched between D and N in the functional skeleton of N). In this 'defective' position (see Fábregas, 2007b), *german-* is spelled out as an adjective.

According to Moreno Marchis (2010, 2015) thematic adjectives and genitive PPs, as for instance *of* in "the attack *of* the Germans" (cf. (4)) are base-generated in the same position, and this assures that the relation to the event nominal they modify is the same, namely they both express a 'possessor' of the deverbal nominal and receive the agent theta-role by that nominal. However, broadly in line with Fábregas (2007b), since genitive DPs do not lack case, they are spelled out as nominals, whereas thematic adjectives undergo a movement to a(sp)P, as proposed by Alexiadou & Stavrou.

As far as the alleged difference in terms of the class labels of thematic and classificatory ethnic adjectives is concerned, Alexiadou and Stavrou (2011, p.138) state that: "*the differences between EAs (i.e. thematic) and homophonous descriptive adjectives are accounted for under the assumption that the formation of the latter takes place prior to insertion in the syntactic structure. This amounts to saying that EAs and their homophonous counterparts interact with syntax at different points of the derivation. Moreover, while classificatory adjectives of provenance are formed prior to insertion in the syntactic structure, EAs are formed in the syntax."*

In order to highlight this assumption on the special status of thematic ethnic adjective, Alexiadou & Stravrou, present a series of tests which try to cast light on the basic difference they assume between thematic ethnic adjectives and their 'homophonous' classificatory counterparts. We will illustrate some of their tests below, providing examples that show that such a strict dichotomy does not seem to hold in Italian.

First, in line with many authors (e.g. Bartning, 1980; Levi, 1978; Bosque & Picallo, 1996; Fábregas, 2007b; Marchis Moreno 2010, 2015, among others) they assume that predicativity is a possible first tool to disentangle between thematic and classificatory ethnic adjectives. Indeed, they argue that Ethnic adjectives cannot be predicative, while classificatory adjectives can. Such difference should be highlighted by the examples in (5) for Italian.

(5) *Italian*
   a.   Il tappeto è persiano
        'The carpet is Persian'
   b.   (*)L'invasione è persiana
        'The invasion is Persian'

The example in (5b) has been 'starred' (in brackets) only to illustrate what Alexiadou & Stavrou argue for Greek and English, namely the fact that, according to their judgements, thematic ethnic adjectives cannot be used predicatively in such languages. Actually, according to our own judgements, in Italian it is not difficult to imagine contexts in which a 'thematic' ethnic adjective can be employed predicatively, as illustrated by the examples in (6) and (7).

(6) *Italian*
   a.   l'invenzione italiana del telefono
        'The Italian invention of the telephone'
   b.   l'invenzione del telefono è italiana
        'The invention of the telephone is Italian'
        cf. *Gli italiani hanno inventato il telefono* 'Italians invented the telephone'

(7) *Italian*
   a.   l'invasione americana dell'Iraq
        'The American Invasion of Iraq'
   b.   l'invasione dell'Iraq è stata americana
        'The Invasion of Iraq was American'
        cf. *Gli americani hanno invaso l'Iraq* 'Americans invaded Iraq'

Further consider that the assignment of an agent theta role, as assumed by Alexiadou & Stavrou, is not a good diagnostic to consistently disentangle thematic ethnic adjectives from other 'common' relational adjectives. Arsenijevic et al. (2014) already show that deverbal 'unaccusative' nominals are not incompatible with an ethnic adjective as shown in (8).[69]

(8) *Italian*
l'arrivo francese in Louisiana
'The French arrival in Louisiana'

Note however that Alexiadou et al. (2015) assume unaccusative verbs to be endowed with a *v* layer (and we have assumed that this perspective is on the right track in Chapter 4). Thus, more robust evidence can be provided showing that an internal argument (i.e. a patient-like) role for ethnic adjectives can be triggered also by 'transitive' deverbal nominals, as illustrated in the examples in (9) and (10). In (9a,b) a patient role for the adjective *africana* or *persiana* is ensured by the presence of a *bona fide* agent introduced by the complex prepositional string *da parte di* (cf. the example in (3)). In (10) the same interpretation can be rendered switching the adjective and the Agent, namely pragmatic cues do favour a patient interpretation for the adjective in (10a), and such example is nor ungrammatical neither marked according to our own judgement (and also basing on a small informal survey conducted among linguistically naïve Italian speakers).

(9) *Italian*
a. la colonizzazione africana da parte dei tedeschi è ancora un tasto dolente
lit. 'The African colonization by (from part of) Germans is still a sore point'
(*L'Espresso* 2011/3/23)
b. l'ammissione persiana al negoziato da parte delle potenze occidentali
'The Persian admission to the negotiation by (from part of) the Western Countries'

(10) *Italian*
a. la colonizzazione africana della Cina
'The African colonization by China'
b. la colonizzazione cinese dell'Africa
'The Chinese colonization of Africa'
Both interpreted as: 'China colonizes Africa'

---

69. As pointed out in Arsenijevic et al. (2014), it is crucial for Alexiadou & Stavrou's analysis that the nominal inside the adjective refers to an agent-role since it is always base-generated in a slot where agents are base-generated in.

Conversely, it is not difficult to trigger an agent interpretation for (non-ethnic) relational adjectives employed with some types of deverbal nominals. The item *invasion*, already employed above in (2), is a case in point, as illustrated in (11).

(11) l'invasione tecnologica della sfera intima
      'The technologic invasion of the intimate sphere'
      Interpreted as: 'Technology invades the intimate sphere'
      (C.J. Jung, *L'io e l'inconscio*, ed. Bollati Boringhieri 2011, trad. Arrigo de Vita)
      Italian

On the contrary, evidence that we are dealing with the same object when we consider thematic ethnic adjectives and classificatory ones is provided by a series of facts. For instance, both types of adjectives are not naturally gradable as illustrated in (12) (contra what assumed in Alexiadou and Stavrou, who say that thematic items only are not gradable, but in line with Arsenijevic et al. 2014, who say that both sub-types are marginally gradable), and both can appear only sandwiched between the noun and its complement/internal argument (cf. Cinque, 1994, p. 86, for the original observation of this constraint for 'thematic' items), as in (13).[70]

(12) *Italian*
      a. ?l'invasione molto americana
          'The very American invasion'
      b. ?Il tappeto molto persiano
          'The very Persian carpet'

(13) *Italian*
      a.   L'invasione italiana dell'Albania
      a'. *L'italiana invasione dell'Albania
           'The Italian invasion of Albania'
      b.   Il tappeto persiano di Gianni
      b'. *Il persiano tappeto di Gianni
           'The Persian carpet of Gianni'

Furthermore, Alexiadou & Stavrou (2011, p. 121–122) argue that thematic (adjectives) contra classificatory ones cannot be coordinated with 'normal' adjectives, but only with other thematic items, as shown in (14) with their Greek examples (cf. also Fábregas, 2007b).

---

70. Alexiadou & Stavrou (2011, p. 122) say that one property that thematic and classificatory ethnic adjectives share in Greek and Germanic is their adjacency to the noun they appear to modify, as illustrated in (i).

(i)   a.   the unexpected aggressive Italian invasion to Greece
      b.   these small round wooden Chinese tables

(14)   *Greek*
   a. *i {amesi, grigori, pithani} ke amerikaniki anamiksi
        the {immediate, quick, possible} and American intervention
   b. ?to oreo, zesto, malino ke egleziko palto tu
        the nice warm woolen and English overcoat.his

Actually, in Italian both kinds of adjectives appear to be quite marked, if not completely ungrammatical, when coordinated with non-ethnic items. Thus, we argue that no differences between classificatory and thematic items can be detected on the basis of this test.

(15)   *Italian*
   a. ??L'invasione americana e militare
        'the military and American invasion'
   b. ??Il tappeto persiano e nuovo
        'the new and Persian carpet'

In the light of the data presented above, we can conclude that there are no clear facts that might lead to hypothesize a substantial dichotomy between thematic ethnic adjectives and their classificatory counterparts.

A more appealing proposal is the one put forth in Arsenijevic et al. (2011), who propose a semantic account to the topic arguing that both types of adjectives are actually one and the same thing. They start their analysis from 'classificatory' adjectives, assuming that this type of ethnic adjectives combines with descriptions of kinds and work as intersective modifiers (cf. also Cinque, 2010b; Partee, 2007) of the kind description (as suggested by the classificatory label). Thus, they introduce a contextually-determined relation (*R*) between the kind described by the nominal property (*Pk*) and the nation associated with the ethnic adjectives (cf. Carlson, 1977). Their basic (adapted) representation for an example like *French wine* is in (16).

(16)   a. [wine]: λxk[wine(xk)]
   b. [French]: λPk λxk [Pk (xk) ∧ R(xk , France)]
   c. [[$_{NP}$French wine]]: λxk[wine(xk) ∧ R(xk, France)]

Arsenijevic et al. assume thematic adjectives to have an identical semantic representation. So, an example like *French discovery* (17) does not differ from something like *French wine* in (16). In (15) the eventive noun *discovery* is taken by Arsenijevic et al. (cf. also McNally & Boleda, 2004; Boleda et al., 2012) to describe an eventuality type (i.e. a sub-kind of kind).

(17)   [French discovery]: λyo∃xk[discovery(xk) ∧ R(xk, France) ∧ R(y, xk)]

A potential problem, acknowledged by the same Arsenijevic et al., for extending their proposal to thematic ethnic adjectives, as in (17), is that there is no immediate explanation of why the thematic items commonly can only target those subkinds of events in which a given nation (or, as an extension, individuals of a given nation) bears an agent theta role. For instance, nothing in (17) *"blocks France from being what is discovered"* (Arsenijevic et al 2011, p. 23). As a solution, they propose that the relation R in (16)–(17) generally expresses a relation of *Origin*. Indeed Arsenijevic et al. assume that *origins* can be ascribed to kinds – including eventuality kinds – and, essentially, agent participants in an eventuality can be taken to be the *Origin* of that eventuality (cf. also Manzini & Savoia, 2002).

Now, we have seen in (8)–(10) that thematic ethnic adjectives are not universally assigned the agent role, given that we may imagine sets of eventive nominals allowing a patient-like thematic ethnic adjective. Furthermore, as illustrated in (11) other relational adjectives can access the agent theta role in nominalization patterns. Thus, we will advance the hypothesis that a more general relation of 'belonging to (something)/part-whole/possession' is at work with ethnic adjectives, and relational adjectives in general.[71] This view is shared with Marchis Moreno (2010), who assumes that a common 'possession' relation is involved with ethnic adjective, as well as with other relation adjectives. Marchis Moreno, however, accepts the dichotomy between thematic and classificatory ethnic adjective proposed by Alexiadou & Stavrou.

In the next section, we will introduce Italian Ethnic adjectives in some more detail, focussing on the derivational morphemes employed to render this kind of adjectives in the Italian lexicon. Then, in Section 6.4 we will provide a unified syntactic analysis of (thematic and classificatory) ethnic adjectives. We will take the derivational morphemes shaping this kind of items to be a derivational counterpart of the genitive/oblique adpositions,[72] sharing with the latter a common predicational core. This common predicational core we think about precisely represents a *belonging to (something)*/part-whole/possession morpho-syntactic relation, as outlined in the previous Chapters. The proposal advanced for ethnic adjectives can be broadly extended to relational adjectives in general.

---

71. Note that the inclusion relation can convey a predicative act, in which it is either predicated on the possessum, as in *the car is the student's*, or on the possessor, as in *the student has a car*. The first is a predication of belonging. The second is an ascription of possession. The recognition of the subtle difference between the two constructions goes back to Benveniste (1966), where it is made in terms of 'appartenance' vs. 'possession', respectively. This distinction is practically the same made by Bickerton (1981, p. 245) in terms of "ownership" vs. "possession".

72. Consider also Franco (2015) for similar assumption concerning Italian adverbs in –*oni*.

6.3   Italian ethnic adjectives and how they are built: An overview

In Italian, many different suffixes are used to build ethnic adjectives (Rohlfs 1968, Crocco Galèas, 1991, p. 29–39, cf. also Rainer, 2004). Crocco Galèas (1991) lists up to 44 derivational suffixes active in the realm of ethnic adjectives. This proliferation of suffixes has to be ascribed to the fact that their distribution is influenced, and somewhat determined, by areal factors. For instance, the suffix –*asco* of *bergamasco* (from Bergamo), *comasco* (from Como), is almost only diffused in northern Italy (and southern France, e.g. *monegasco*, 'from Monaco') (see Rohlfs 1969, § 1120), while the suffix –*oto*, of *liparioto* (from Lipari), being of Greek origin (cf. Rainer 2004: 402ff, Rohlfs 1969, § 1139, Meyer Lübke, 1911), is diffused almost only in Southern Italy.

Interestingly, there are various Italian toponyms which have suppletive (sometimes conveying an aulic flavour) ethnic adjectives, together with their 'standard' derivational counterpart (Crocco Galèas, 1991, p. 238), as illustrated in (18).

(18)   *Italian*
    a.   Bolognese
    a′. Felsineo   (From Bologna)
    b.   Napoletano[73]
    b′. Partenopeo   (From Napoli)
    c.   Livornese
    c′. Labronico   (From Livorno)

It is interesting to notice that, if one assumes that thematic ethnic adjectives and their classificatory counterparts are only accidentally homophonous, along the lines of Alexiadou & Stavrou, it would be likely – in principle – to find specialized suppletive forms able to encode one of the two interpretations only. Actually, this is not the case, as illustrated in (19).

(19)   *Italian*
    a.   La pasticceria bolognese
    a′. La pasticceria **felsinea**

                                 (both: 'the Bolognese patisserie')

    b.   L'invasione bolognese
    b′. L'invasione **felsinea**

                                   (both: 'the Bolognese invasion')

---

73. Note that we do not consider here the shape of interfixes, as for instance –*et* in Napoletano, in the formation of ethnic adjectives. See Rainer (2004) for some notes about them.

Coming back to the derivational suffixes involved in the formation of ethnic adjectives, according to Crocco Galèas (1991, p. 29–39, 177) the entire set includes 44 variants, 35 of which are confined to unproductive toponyms from Trentino (that we will not take into consideration here). According to Crocco Galèas the most productive suffix is *-es* (forming around 68% of the adjectives derived from Italian toponyms), as illustrated in (20).

(20) *Italian*
    a. portoghese
        (from Portugal)
    b. bolognese
        (from Bologna)
    c. genovese
        (from Genova)
    d. lucchese
        (from Lucca)

The suffix *–ens* is taken to be (cf. e.g. Rainer 2004) a variant of *–es* (as in *Ostiense*, *Panamense*, etc.). The suffix *-es* and its variant *–ens* are not exclusively employed to form ethnic adjectives. As shown below, for instance the suffix *–es* can be employed to indicate the language of a given social subgroup or a given medium with a somewhat pejorative connotation,[74] as in (21), while both the suffix *–es* (cf. also Hohnerlein-Buchinger, 1996, for a description of many *–ese* adjectives employed in the sub-lexicon of Italian wine-makers) and the suffix *–ens* (from which *-es* is historically derived, cf. Rainer 2004, employed for the 1,26% of Italian toponyms) can be used to form various relational adjectives:

(21) *Italian*
    a. sindacalese
        mumbo jumbo of syndicalists
    b. politichese
        mumbo jumbo of politician
    c. burocratese
        mumbo jumbo of bureaucrats
    d. sinistrese
        mumbo jumbo of leftists

---

74. Note that, In Italian, the names of languages and dialects are always homophonous to ethnic adjectives (e.g. l'italiano, *Italian*, il francese, *French*, il portoghese, *Portuguese*, il napoletano, *Neapolitan*).

(22) *Italian*
    a. cortese
       kind/courtly
    b. borghese
       bourgeois/middle class
    c. circense
       circus (e.g. 'a circus show')
    d. forense
       forensic

The other two suffixes most commonly employed to encode ethnic adjectives in Italian, are *-in* (23) and *-an* (24) (employed respectively in the 7,8% and 7,6% of occurrences, according to the statistics provided in Crocco Galèas, 1991). All the other suffixes retrieved in Crocco Galèas's survey are not able to *adjectivize* more than the 1% of the toponyms in her sample. The interested reader is, in fact, referred to Crocco Galèas (1991) for a comprehensive discussion.[75]

(23) *Italian*
    a. fiorentino
       (from Florence)
    b. algerino
       (from Algeria)
    c. perugino
       (from Perugia)

(24) *Italian*
    a. italiano
       (from Italy)
    b. palermitano
       (from Palermo)
    c. grossetano
       (from Grosseto)

The suffix *–in* is employed in various contexts in Italian. As recently illustrated in Savoia et al. (2017), Franco et al. (2020), it can be used as an evaluative (i.e.

---

75. Scalise (1990, p.76) assumes that the derivational suffixes employed to form ethnic adjectives are unable to derive adverbs in *–mente*. Actually, as shown in Ricca (2004, p.526), once ethnic adjectives are associated to properties (and *clichés*) that can be attributed to the members (as a whole) of a given locality, such kind of derivation is widely attested, as illustrated in (i).

  (i) imprecano, ordinatamente, elveticamente, ma imprecano
     'They swear, neatly, Swissly, but they swear'
  (ii) avvezzo italianamente all'approssimazione
      'Italianly accustomed to the approximation'

diminutive) morpheme,[76] as in (25), and as a singulative morpheme (both from mass noun or verbal bases, cf. Ott, 2011, de Belder et al., 2014, among others, for a set of cross-linguistic facts linking diminutives to singulatives), as in (26).

(25) *Italian*
    a. lettino
       'small bed'
    b. macchinina
       'small/toy car'
    c. uccellino
       'little bird'

---

76. Note that the interplay between evaluative and ethnic morphology can be seen with many other suffixes. Consider for instance the can of –*ott* (i), -*on* (ii), or –*ell* (iii).

(i)   a.   aquila 'eagle' > aquilotto 'little eagle'; leper 'hare' > leprotto 'little hare'
      b.   Rovigo > rovigotto (from Rovigo); Choggia > chioggiotto (from Chioggia)

(ii) a.   orso 'bear' > orsone 'big bear' ; letto 'bed' > lettone 'bid bed'
      b.   Borgogna > borgnognone (from Borgogna) ; Montagna in Valtellina > montagnone (from Montagna in Valtellina)

(iii) a.   vino 'wine' > vinello 'light wine'; bambino 'child' > bambinello 'little child'
      b.   Centa San Nicolò > centarello (from Centa San Nicolò)

Further notice that the suffix –*esc*, sometimes employed to build ethnic adjectives, may have an evaluative (i.e. pejorative) connotation (Wandruszka, 2004, cf. Dardano 2008, p.102) when employed as opposed to a more typical derivational suffix in the formation of a relational adjectives (cf. (iv).

(iv) a.   Pantelleria > pantesco (from the island of Pantelleria); Barberia > barbaresco (from Barberia)
      b.   Produzione artigianale *vs.* Produzione artigianesca
          'handmade production' 'low-quality handmade production'
      b'. titolo baronale *vs.* titolo baronesco
          'baronial title' 'snobbish title'

Nevertheless, the suffix -*esc* is employed to form full sets of relational adjectives, without any evaluative flavours, as shown in (v):

(v) a.   cinquecento > cinquecentesco (e.g. 'palazzo cinquecentesco')
          'sixteenth century' 'of the of the sixteenth century' 'building of the sixteenth century'
      b.   polizia > poliziesco (e.g. indagine poliziesca)
          'police' 'police' 'police investigation'

(26)   *Italian*
   a.   zucchero 'sugar'
   a'.   zuccher**ino**
         'sugar cube'
   b.   piombo 'lead'
   b'.   piomb**ino**
         'sinker'
   c.   crema 'cream'
   c'.   crem**ino**
         'chocolate truffle'
   d.   accendere 'to light'
   d'.   accend**ino**
         'lighter'
   e.   imbiancare 'to paint'
   e'.   imbianch**ino**
         'painter'

Moreover, the suffix *–in* can be employed to form various relational adjectives unrelated to toponyms, as illustrated in (27).

(27)   *Italian*
   a.   vacca 'cow'
   a'.   vacc**ino** 'of a cow, *latte vaccino cow's milk*/'vaccine'
   b.   mare 'sea'
   b'.   mar**ino** 'marine'
   c.   sale 'salt'
   c'.   sal**ino** 'saline/salt'
   d.   corallo 'coral'
   d'.   corall**ino** 'coral'
   e.   cristallo 'crystal'
   e'.   cristall**ino** 'crystalline'

The suffix *-an* is again not only employed to form ethnic adjectives. It is one of the most common devices to form (relational) adjectives from an anthroponimic base (together with *–iano*, which can be taken to be an allomorph of *–ano*, cf. Rainer, 1996, Seidl, 2004),[77] as illustrated in (28); it can form agent nouns from collective

___

77. Note that this property is shared with the suffix *-in*, as illustrated in (i). Another widely employed suffix in de-anthoponimic contexts is *–esc-* (ii), also employed with toponyms (cf. Rainer 1996).

   (i)   Cervantes > Cervant**ino** (of/related to Cervantes) / Garibaldi > Garibald**ino** (of/ related to Garibaldi)
   (ii) Dante > Dant**esco** (of/related to Dante)/ Boccaccio > Boccacc**esco** (of/related to Boc- caccio)

nouns (in a fashion similar to the singulative behaviour on -*in* illustrated in (26)), as in (29), and, like the suffix -*in* is able to convey various kinds of relational adjectives (30).

(28) *Italian*
    a.   Copernico > Copernicano (of/related to Copernico)
    b.   Maometto > Maomettano (of/related to Maometto, muslim)
    c.   Francesco > Francescano (of/related to Francesco)

(29) *Italian*
    a.   mandria > mandriano
         'herd'   'herdsman'
    b.   milizia > miliziano
         'militia' 'militiaman'
    c.   popolo > popolano
         'people' 'commoner/member of the lower class'

(30) *Italian*
    a.   monte > montano (e.g. valico montano)
         mountain mountain/alpine   mountain crossing
    b.   pioggia > piovano (e.g. acqua piovana)
         rain rain   rain water
    c.   uomo > umano (e.g. corpo umano)
         man human   human body

Given this overview, we can conclude that there is a clear interplay between ethnic adjectives and other relational adjectives, and between ethnic adjectives and evaluatives (cf. fn. 76). In particular, there is no derivational suffix which is dedicated to the formation of ethnic adjectives only. From a morpho-lexical perspective this fact weakens the view of Arsenijevic et al. concerning a 'narrow' semantic *Origin* relation responsible of the peculiarities of the behaviour of ethnic adjectives. Once we assume that morphology is a window for syntax (and semantics), it is likely that the relation being established between an ethnic adjective and its head noun is broader, encompassing a *sensu lato* possessor-possessum/part-whole relation. In fact, the set of the suffixes responsible for the formation of ethnic adjectives is also responsible for the formation of 'typical' relational adjectives, singulatives, evaluatives, etc.

In the next section, we will assume that such suffixes play a role in the syntax, and we will characterize them as expressing a unified basic predicational core, comparable to that of the Italian genitive adposition *di* (of), and other oblique devices. On the basis of the data presented in the preceding sections, we reject the idea that ethnic adjective involved as agents (or patients) in nominalization patterns are different in any respect from the ethnic adjectives involved in expressing 'classificatory' property relations within a given noun phrase.

6.4   A morphosyntactic analysis of ethnic adjectives in Italian

6.4.1   The relational content of 'ethnic' suffixes

At this point, we have enough evidence to introduce our analysis. The morphemic analysis of Italian/Romance implies a first component which is a root √; following Marantz (1997), we may think of the root √ as category-less. Next to the root √ we find different kinds of morphemes, including derivational and inflectional ones (e.g. gender, number); inflectional morphemes generally follow derivational suffixes (cf. Franco et al., 2015a, Manzini & Savoia, 2017a, b).

We assume that the (derivational) suffixes reviewed so far syntactically express the same relational content (a very elementary *belonging to, part-whole* relation), notated as (⊆), that we have ascribed in the previous Chapters to inflectional case affixes, adpositions, applicatives and serial verbs, following Manzini & Savoia (2011b), Manzini & Franco (2016), Franco & Manzini (2017a, b), among others. The different flavours these suffixes happen to encode are a matter of pragmatic inference. Furthermore, following Borer (2003, 2014) and Savoia et al. (2017, 2018), Franco et al. (2020), we assume that the same lexical content can be expressed by inflectional and derivational morphemes, both intra-linguistically and cross-linguistically.

Specifically, in Romance languages, inflectional morphemes can introduce properties more standardly introduced by derivational tools, for example category change, size properties (e.g. *melo* 'apple tree'/*mela* 'apple'; *buco* 'hole'/*buca* 'pit', cf. Franco et al., 2015a). Conversely, derivational morphemes can introduce types of contents generally associated with inflection, as for instance gender specifications, which is also introduced in Italian by the derivational suffix *–ess* (e.g. operaio – operaia 'male/female labourer' *vs.* dottore – dottoressa 'male/female doctor'). The same is true when we introduce in the picture stand-alone morphemes such as adpositions, which generally express a *bona fide* relational content. The same content is expressible inflectionally (e.g. in languages with case paradigms), and derivationally, as we will show below. The gist of the present proposal is precisely that the Italian adposition *di* (of) in the nominal domain (as well as other adpositional items, such as *da*) expresses the same (⊆) syntactic primitive of the derivational morphemes involved in the formation of relational adjectives. Following Manzini and Savoia (2007, 2011), indeed, a key point of our analysis is that Merge takes morphemes as its input and single morphemes are visible to syntactic computation. Consider the examples in (31). Leaving aside from our discussion/representation the content expressed by the nominalizer morpheme *-sion* in (31b)[78] and class(ifier) layers (see Manzini & Savoia, 2017a, for an extensive discussion on the role of the node Class in the syntax) we may assume that both items in (31) can be actually represented as in (32a)–(32b), where we assume a fully interpretable ($\subseteq$) node, sandwiched between the root and an inflectional node (visible to agreement) in the morpho-syntax of ethnic adjective.

(31) *Italian*
    a. la ceramica persiana
        'The Persian ceramics'
    b. l'invasione persiana
        'The Persian invasion'

(32) a.

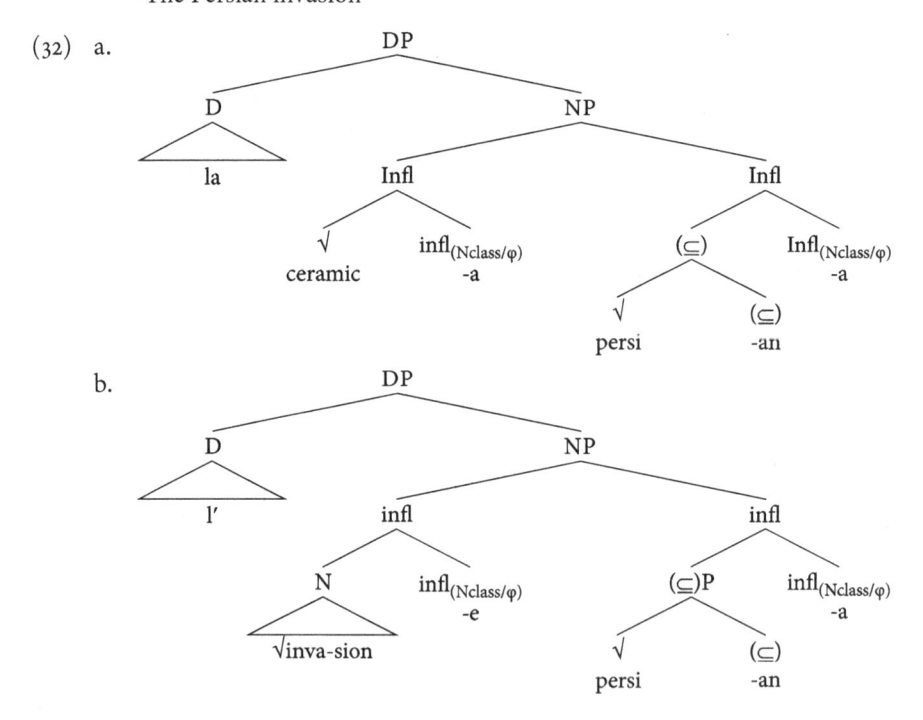

    b.

---

78. The different layers at work in the 'functional skeleton' of deverbal (i.e. event) nominals have been assigned different labels in the literature: *Event Phrase* (van Hout & Roeper, 1998) or different flavors of *AspP* (Borer 2003, 2014; Alexiadou et al. 2009). In such proposals, normally a correlation between event structure and argument structure is realized by taking arguments to be introduced by functional heads (one of which being also responsible of the introduction of the event variable).

Thus, we take both classificatory and thematic ethnic adjective to basically express a broad part-whole content, namely in (31) both the *ceramics* and the *invasion* belongs to/originate from Persia. Such content may be surely interpreted as an (semantic) *Origin* content along the lines of Arsenijevic et al., but the evidence provided in section 3, namely the use of the various suffix able to encode an ethnic adjectives as meaningful devices in many other contexts, lead us to think that such characterization is (morpho-syntactically) too narrow. Evidence that we are on the right track in our characterization of ethnic adjectives is provided by the fact that (31a) and (31b) are paraphrasable (without any significant shift in the meaning) as in (33a) and (33b), using an adposition, as a ($\subseteq$) device.

(33) *Italian*
    a. la ceramica della/dalla Persia
       'The ceramics of/from Persia'
    b. l'invasione della/dalla/da parte della Persia
       'The invasion by/from Persia'

Interestingly, in (33) the adposition *di* can alternate with the adposition *da* (and in (33b) with the complex adpositional string *da parte di*, lit. *from part of*, which can be assumed to be a non-spatial Axial Part as discussed in Chapter 4).[79] Following Franco et al. (2021), Manzini (2017) we can attribute to *di* and *da* headed phrases the same ($\subseteq$) signature/content. One piece of evidence that confirms that this assumption is on the right track comes from the fact that the adposition *da* in Italian can be pronominalized by the same clitic that pronominalizes genitive/partitive *di*, namely *ne*, as shown in (34), repeating the examples already introduced in Chapter 4.

(34) *Italian*
    a. **Ne**   esco   ora (dal parrucchiere/da casa)
       from.it I.get.out now (from the hairdresser/from home)
       'I get out now from there'
    b. **Ne**   vedo tre (di ragazzi)
       of.them I.see three of boys
       'I see three of them'

Further evidence that the same signature is at work with *di/da* morphemes is given by the genitive/ablative alternation in introducing (demoted) agents. For

---

79. Note that in some contexts, for instance with animate/human head nouns, the *da* morpheme appears to be more natural than *di*, as shown in (i).

  (i)   Una ragazza dal Brasile/?del Brasile
       'A girl from Brazil'

instance, there are Italian dialects, which introduce (demoted) agents by means of a genitive adposition, as illustrated in (35) and (36) for Cosentino (northern Calabria) and Mussomelese (south-western Sicily), respectively. Standard Italian (37) employs the *da* adposition for such purpose. Indeed, considering causative constructions, we can standardly distinguish between *faire-infinitif* ((a) examples, introduced by dative adpositions) and *faire-par* ((b) examples, introduced by genitive/ablative adpositions) constructions. There is lexical micro-variation (as in the canonical passive) in relation to the choice of preposition that introduces the (demoted) agent (DE+AB 'from, by' *vs.* DE 'of') (cf. Manzini & Savoia, 2005, for a comprehensive overview, and Ledgeway, 2020, from which the examples in (35)–(36) are taken).

(35) a. Maria fa   pulizzà u cessu a Cicciu   (faire-infinitif)
        Maria makes clean.INF the toilet to Cicciu
        'Maria makes Cicciu clean the toilet'
     b. Maria fa   pulizzà u cessu 'i Cicciu   (faire-par)
        Maria makes clean.INF the toilet of Cicciu
        'Maria has the toilet cleaned by Cicciu'   *Cosentino* (northern Calabria)

(36) a. Maria fa   puliziari i gabbinetti a Giuwanni   (faire-infinitif)
        Maria makes clean.INF the toilets   to Giovanni
        'Maria makes Giovanni clean the toilets'
     b. Maria si fa   puliziari i gabbinetti di Giuwanni (faire-par)
        Maria self makes clean.INF the toilets   of Giovanni
        Maria has the toilets cleaned (by Giovanni)'
                                       Mussomelese (south-western Sicily)

(37) *Italian*
     a. Maria fa pulire i gabinetti a Ciccio   (faire-infinitif)
        'Maria makes Ciccio clean the toilet'
     b. Maria fa pulire i gabinetti da Ciccio   (faire-par)
        'Maria makes Ciccio clean the toilet'

On the basis of the evidence illustrated above (cf. also the discussion in Section 4.2 on *da*), we can provide the representation in (38a) and (38a) respectively for (33a) and (33b).[80]

---

80. For the sake of the present discussion, we can take constructions such as 'l'invasione *da parte della* Persia' (cf. 33b) to instantiate a layered PP/($\subseteq$) domain, including an Axial Part node (Svenonius, 2006), with the complex adpositional string 'da parte di'. Actually, *parte* precisely means 'part'. Remember that, as shown in (3), the same adpositional string is commonly employed in Italian to introduce (demoted) agents in passive constructions. For a broader picture, see the data and analysis in Chapter 4.

(38)   a.

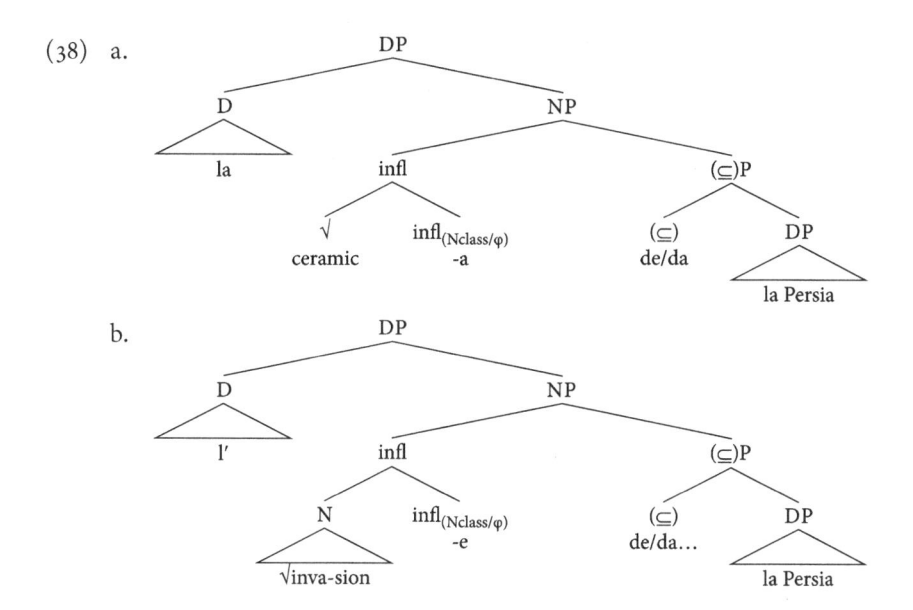

b.

6.4.2   Deverbal nominalization patterns

Once assuming that *di* and *da* have the same ($\subseteq$) content (as well as their derivational counterparts), it is quite easy to include in our model the 'puzzling' prevalent agent-like interpretation of 'thematic' ethnic adjectives in nominalizations. Consider the examples in (39)–(41).

(39) *Italian*
   a. l'esclusione italiana (dal G8) da parte delle grandi potenze
       'the Italian exclusion (from G8) by the great powers'
   a'. L'esclusione dell'/*dall'Italia (dal G8) da parte delle grandi potenze
       'the exclusion of Italy (from G8) by the great powers'
   a''. -> Le grandi potenze hanno escluso l'Italia (dal G8)
       'the great powers excluded Italy (from G8)'
   b. La conquista italiana dell'Etiopia
       'the Italian conquer of Ethiopia'
   b'. La conquista dell'Etiopia dell'/da parte dell'Italia
       'The conquer of Ethiopia by Italy'
   b''. -> L'Italia ha conquistato l'Etiopia
       'Italy conquered Ethiopia'

(40) *Italian*
   a. Il trasferimento tecnologico da parte delle università[81]
       'Technology transfer by universities'
   a'. Il trasferimento della/*dalla tecnologia delle/da parte delle università
       'the transfer of Technology by universities'
   a". -> Le università hanno trasferito (la) tecnologia
       'Universities has transferred technology'
   b. l' innovazione tecnologica del processo produttivo
       'the technological innovation of the productive process'
   b'. l' innovazione del/*dal processo produttivo della/da parte della tecnologia
       'the innovation of the productive process by technology'
   b". -> la tecnologia ha innovato il processo produttivo
       'Technology has innovated the productive process'

(41) *Italian*
   a. La ricezione dantesca da parte del popolo[82]
       'Dantes' reception by the people'
   a'. La ricezione di Dante/*da Dante del/da parte del popolo
       'the reception of Dante by the people'
   a". -> Il popolo ha ricevuto Dante
       'The people received Dante'
   b. La manipolazione dantesca della lingua
       'Dante's manipulation of the language'
   b'. La manipolazione della lingua di Dante/da parte di Dante.
       'the manipulation of the language by Dante'
   b". -> Dante ha manipolato la lingua
       'Dante has manipulated the language'

As shown in the examples above, in deverbal nominalization patterns (cf. Grimshaw. 1990b; Alexiadou, 2001; Harley, 2009, among others), ethnic adjectives pattern with 'normal' relational adjectives[83] in being able to encode both a patient-like ((a) examples) and an agent-like ((b) examples) role (cf. also the discussion

---

81. The example is taken from the book *Market orientation nelle imprese ad elevato contenuto tecnologico* – by Tindara Abbate (Franco Angeli), retrieved from Google Books.

82. The example is taken from the book *Recte sapere. Studi in onore di Dalla Torre* – ed. by Geraldina Boni et al. (Giappichelli), retrieved from Google Books.

83. Note that the suffix *–ic* employed in a 'standard' relational adjective like *tecnologico* (or *alcolico*, 'alcoholic' *angelico*, 'angelic', etc.) is employed also with some ethnic adjectives, as for instance labronico (from Livorno) or asiatico (from Asia). Note that, actually, a DP phrase like *bevanda alcolica* 'alcoholic drink' seems to instantiate a reverse part-whole relation ($\supseteq$), meaning 'a drink containing/possessing alcohol' (cf. Fábregas, 2007b, for a unified treatment of the predications involving relational adjectives, and Franco & Manzini, 2017b, for a comprehensive treatment of 'inverse' part-whole relations in DP and at the clause level). See Section 6.4.4.

surrounding Examples (8)–(11) in Section 6.2). We have introduced deanthroponymic adjectives (41) in the picture because despite being strictly correlated to/derived from (prototypically agentive) human entities, they are freely compatible with a patient-like interpretation. Thus, the prevalent interpretation of (thematic) ethnic adjectives as agent participant in an event is possibly triggered by our knowledge of the world, namely as already suggested in Arsenijevic et al. (2011), the reference to a given geographical locality can be easily extended to the inhabitants of that locality.[84] The human feature, as in the case of deanthroponymic adjectives, is relevant from a pragmatic viewpoint to trigger an agent-like interpretation of the adjective. Crucially, such interpretation is pragmatically favoured, but not syntactically determined, as shown above.

What the examples in (39)–(41) interestingly show (cf. a′ examples) is that the *da* morpheme, to which we have imputed the same (⊆) content of the *di* adposition is unable to introduce an internal argument in a nominalization structure. As far as the external arguments of nominalization constructions are concerned, they can be freely introduced by *di* and the *da parte di* string, and they do not pose particular issues to us: it is not difficult to impute to them, as well as for their derivational counterparts, a (⊆) content. Following Manzini et al. (2015) they can be taken to be as ergative-like participants. A well-established stream of literature (cf. e.g. Johns, 1992, 2013, among others) connects genitive and 'possession' structures with 'ergative' structures in general. Montaut (2004, p.39) quotes Benveniste's (1966, 176–186) conclusion that "the Old Persian ergative structure [...] is intrinsically possessive in its meaning, and is analogical with the periphrastic perfects in Latin (*mihi id factum*, me-DAT this done)". In other words, the external (ergative) argument is treated not so much as a causer/agent in an event as the possessor of a property. Following this basic insight, we will assume an ergative-like characterization of the external (genitive) argument in nominalizations. Within the generative literature, Alexiadou (2001, p.172–173) assumes that *"nominalizations and ergative patterns [...] are reflections of the same structure: one that involves a single theme argument that appears as sister of the lexical root, and an adjunct type of phrase that introduces the agent"*.

Thus, we can assume that there is a possession/part-whole (i.e. a (⊆)) 'adjunction' relation between the event described in a nominalization construction and the 'originator' of such event. For instance, we may conceive

---

84. Note that the nouns denoting the inhabitants of a given locality are constantly expressed in Italian by means of the same suffixes which express the relational/ethnic adjective for that toponym, as in (i)

(i)   a.   Gli italiani/i francesi/I fiorentini/i panteschi
          'The inhabitants of Italy/France/Florence/the Island of Pantelleria'

(39b)–(39b′) in the following terms: 'Ethiopia has been conquered and Italians 'possess' (or *cause*, cf. Manzini, 2017, Bellucci, 2017, and the discussion in Chapter 3) that event, namely the event 'conquer of Ethiopia' is part of the whole activities Italians are involved in.

In principle, ascribing the same (⊆) to the internal argument of a nominalization construction could be more problematic. Indeed, as we have already pointed out, it is impossible to alternate *di* and *da* in such contexts. Furthermore, many authors have assumed that the genitive item appearing in such position is a structural device deprived of any interpretive content (see e.g. Siloni, 1997; Alexiadou, 2001). Actually, this is by far the most popular analysis in approaching *of* phrases within the DP – starting with Chomsky's (1981) rule of of-Insertion. 'Of' would act as a syntactic repair, allowing for case assignment to the object of an N, which would otherwise be caseless. One family of proposals takes the repair to be a matter of PF. For instance, Richards (2010) proposes that *of*-Insertion avoids a potential N-N local identity, working as a morphosyntactic counterpart of the phonological OCP. Another family of proposals takes of to parallel the copula (Hoekstra, 1999; den Dikken, 2006).

Nevertheless, it seems to us that theories relying on a non-contentive construal of *of-like* items face empirical problems (cf. Franco & Manzini, 2017b for a full array of arguments). Saying that *of* repairs lack of case or is a means for identity avoidance is not applicable, for instance, to those verbal contexts which have arguments introduced by genitive adpositions (cf. Haspelmath & Michaelis, 2008), as shown in (42).

(42)   *Italian*
    Il sangue ha rifornito le cellule **di** ossigeno
    'the blood supplied oxygen to the cells'
    lit. 'The blood has supplied the cells of oxygen.'

As for the 'copular' proposal, in (42) we would have to find a predication of which *of* is the copula. Clearly, there is neither a direct nor an inverse copular relation between 'the oxygen' and 'the cells' in (42). We conclude that (universally) genitives must be endowed with a predicative content, however elementary.

Furthermore, regarding nominalization patterns, as shown in Franco (2018), the prediction that a genitive is involved as a structural device, reshaping the internal argument of a verb into a genitive 'di' (of) is not always borne out, if we consider those cases where a dative 'a' (to) PP or a benefactive/cause 'per' (for) PP surface to encode the internal argument of a deverbal nominal, as shown in (43)–(44).

(43) *Italian*
La punizione **a/??di** Maria **di/da** parte di Gianni
'Gianni's punishment to Mary'

(44) *Italian*
La predilezione **per** la /**??della** musica brasiliana di/da parte di Gianni
'The veneration for Brazilian music by Gianni'

Given the data above, it is easy to follow Manzini & Savoia (2011b), Manzini & Franco (2016) in proposing a unified construal of the genitive/dative in terms of the predicative relation (⊆). Indeed, assuming that dative is an inherent case for most authors nowadays (cf. Woolford, 1997, 2006), it is difficult to see how it (or a 'lexical' benefactive/cause, cf. (44)) could alternate with a 'structural' genitive in nominalizations. The ban of *da* with internal arguments may be ascribed to a contextual sensitivity in the pattern of lexicalization of the (⊆) relation. Actually, in Italian the lexical item *di* 'of' generally specializes for nominal embedding and *a* 'to' for sentential embedding. Nevertheless, they still encode the same (⊆) primitive. *Da* does not lexicalize (⊆) with the patient-like arguments of deverbal nominals (cf. also Rugna & Franco 2022).

Thus, a representation of (39b) and (39b'), could be respectively as in (45a) and (45b-b', cf. Chapter 4, where Axial Parts are the focus of our discussion). The interpretation of the structure that we propose here is that the external argument 'Italian/Italy' is introduced as including (possessing/locating) the event/property represented by the NP 'conquer of Ethiopia' (where in turn the eventive nominal 'conquer' is, *lato sensu*, the possessum of Ethiopia).

(45) a.

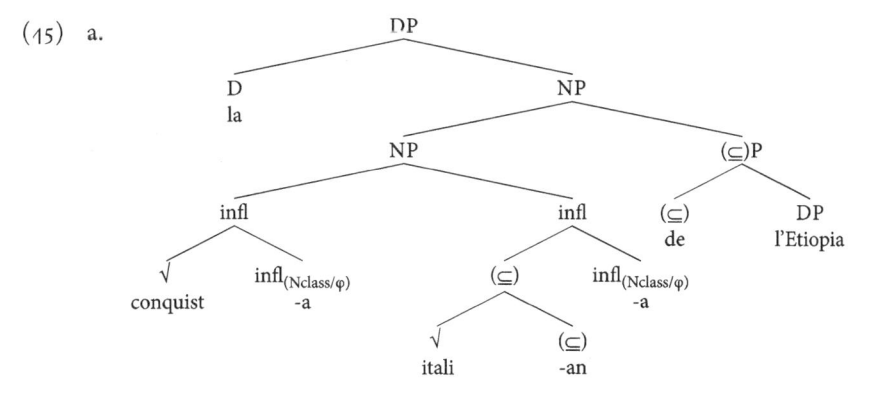

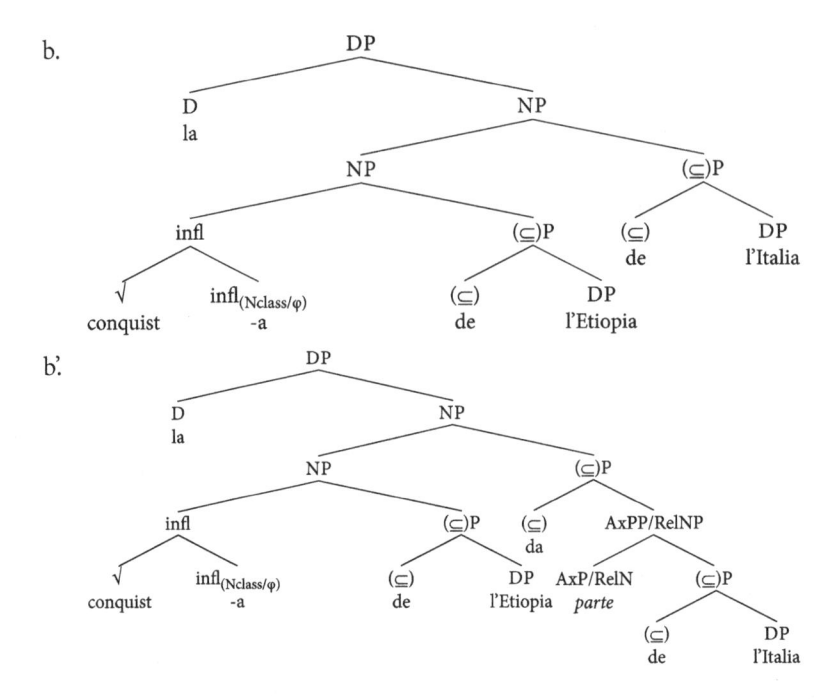

Given the representation provided above, we argue that the same ($\subseteq$) predicate establishes a relation with the head, either when relational adjectives (ethnic, deanthroponymic, whatever...) or adpositional complements/adjuncts are involved. This is true both in 'classificatory' context and in thematic ones.

Our model accounts for the fact that the suffixes recruited for the derivation of ethnic adjectives can be involved in many other relational settings. Furthermore, the characterization of such suffixes as ($\subseteq$) is in line with the 'singulative'/individualizing' properties of many of the suffixes reviewed here. For instance, the interpretation of *-in* as endowed with a singulative/individualizing property (cf. (26) above)[85] agrees with the occurrences of *-in-* in nouns referring to town inhabitant constantly homophonous with ethnic adjectives, as in *fiorent-*

---

85. Note that both etymologically/diachronically (cf. e.g. Grandi, 2001) and formally (cf. Savoia et al., 2017, 2018, Franco et al., 2020) we may establish a link between singulatives/individualizers and evaluative morphology (cf. Section 6.3 for the interplay between ethnic and evaluative affixes, cf. Chapter 7). For instance, as shown in Jurafsky (1996), the word for 'child' (i.e a small individual of a group) is the most common base for the grammaticalization of diminutives in the languages of the world. This process begins when such words are employed as a type of classificatory element to refer to young animate individuals and then are extended to inanimate entities, targeting small sizes with countable items and small quantities with uncountable items, and being employed also to turn mass items into count nouns (Heine & Kuteva 2002, p.65–66; Di Garbo, 2014).

in-o 'of Florence, Florentine', *regg-in-o* 'of Reggio Calabria', etc. Clearly an inhabitant of a town is (broadly speaking) 'part' of that town. The same way of reasoning can be extended without difficulties, for example, to the suffix *–an* (e.g. a *miliatian* is part of a militia, cf. (29)).

6.4.3 A note on Agree (and the connection with Suffixaufnahme)

As far as the agreement relation established between the ethnic/relational adjective and the head noun is concerned, we follow Manzini & Savoia (2007, 2011, 2017a, b) in assuming that matching (agreement) of genders between head nouns and relational adjectives means that the respective inflections (infl) can individuate the same argument (slot). In the minimalist framework (Chomsky, 2000, 2001a, b), agreement processes are standardly associated with the rule of Agree – which however is conceived so as to account for one-to-one agreement in the sentential domain. Here, we keep the assumption that Agree also applies within DPs. However, we avoid attributing interpretable/uninterpretable, valued/unvalued status to any of the categories inside DP (cf. Manzini et al., 2019; Manzini & Franco, 2019). We assume that given two elements in a c-command configuration, the higher is the Probe and the lower the Goal. Everything else proceeds as in the standard definition of Agree, by Minimal Search and Match of the relevant features (cf. Manzini et al., 2019). We assume that what impels Agree to apply is the necessity of creating equivalence classes of phi-feature bundles denoting a single referent (the equivalent of uninterpretable feature deletion).[86] In Italian, Agree applies between the adjective and the noun, as well as with the determiners and quantifiers of the DP.

The assumption that the derivational morphemes of ethnic adjectives are endowed with a ($\subseteq$) content, makes the structures represented above quite similar to Suffixaufnahme constructions, by which a genitive/oblique item agrees with (i.e. is inflected by) the phi-features/case morphology of its head noun (cf. Plank, 1995 for a descriptive/typological overview and Manzini et al., 2019 for a formal characterization). Consider the Punjabi (Indo-Aryan) example in (46) and the Lardil (Pama-Nyungan, Australian, cf. Richards, 2013) example in (47).

(46) *Punjabi*
      darwaddʒ-e   d-i   tʃabb-i
      door-MSG.OBL GEN-FSG key-FSG
      'the key of the door'

---

86. In other words, Agree establishes that two sets of phi-features in fact reduce to two occurrences of the same set (cf. Manzini & Savoia, 2007).

(47)   *Lardil*
marun-ngan-ku maarn-ku
boy-GEN-INSTR spear-INSTR
'with the boy's spear.'

In Punjabi a genitive modifying a noun bears its own (oblique) phi-features inflection (-*e* in (46)), followed by the postposition *d*- and then by a phi-features inflection (-*i* in the example) agreeing with the modified noun. Namely, in Punjabi the outer inflectional slot of the genitive postposition, that we take here to instantiate a (⊆) predicate, registers agreement with the head noun. This inflection provides a partial saturation of (the external argument of) the (⊆) predication inside the (⊆)P projection. Case/agreement stacking precisely corresponds to the presence of complete or partial copies of the arguments satisfying the relator within its phrasal projection (we refer to Manzini et al., 2019 for full discussion). As for Punjabi, in Lardil (47) we take it that so-called genitive case introduces an (⊆) elementary predicate. We assume Agree to be responsible for the presence of a partial copy of the possessum, namely the external argument of the (⊆) elementary predicate, within the genitive phrase (⊆)P. In (47), the inflectional properties that copy under Agree are oblique case ones, which we can be notated as Instr(umental). Consider the representation for the Punjabi (46) and the Lardil (47) examples, respectively in (48) and (49). As with ethnic/relational adjectives, the inflectional node sister of (⊆) is visible to Agreement and matches the head noun in phi-features (and, eventually, case features). We can thus hypothesize a *continuum* between the two phenomena/constructions (cf. e.g. Nikolaeva & Spencer, 2013; Spencer & Nikolaeva, 2017).

(48)

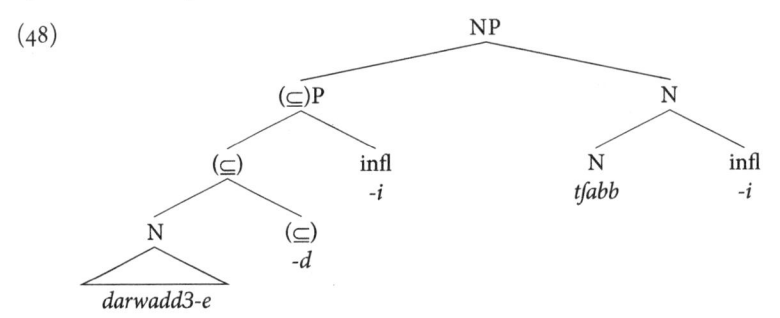

(49)

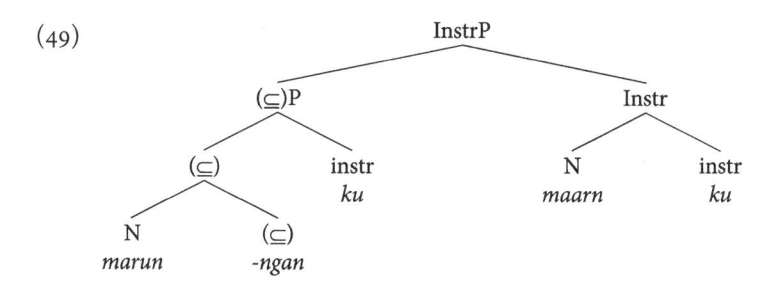

We are aware that some other issues, for instance affix rivalry, adjunct (free) vs. adjective (fixed) order within the DP,[87] the interaction of class node/features with the derivational tools building ethnic adjectives, etc. can be taken into consideration. We defer these additional theoretical issues to future research.

6.4.4   The representation of qualifying possessive adjectives

We have argued so far that the derivational suffixes in ethnic (and relational) adjectives syntactically express a relational content (an elementary belonging to, part-whole relation) that has the (⊆) signature. The different flavors these suffixes are able to encode are a matter of pragmatic inference at the Conceptual intentional Interface, something beyond our core syntactic module. Crucially, based on Borer (2003, 2014) and Savoia et al. (2017, 2018), we have assumed that the same lexical content can be expressed by inflectional and derivational morphemes,

---

87. Just a brief note of the difference in word order between PPs (free) and adjectives (constrained). Consider the examples in (i)–(iii).

(i) a. La colonizzazione dell'Africa della Cina
     b. La colonizzazione della Cina dell'Africa
         'The colonization of Africa by China'

(ii) a. La colonizzazione cinese dell'Africa
     b. ?*la colonizzazione dell'Africa cinese
         'The Chinese colonization of Africa'

(iii) a. il tappeto di Gianni del Turkmenistan/ Il tappeto del Turkmenistan di Gianni
          'Gianni's carpet from Turkmenistan'
      b. il tappeto turcomanno di Gianni/*Il tappeto di Gianni turcomanno
          'Gianni's Turkoman carpet'

The word order restriction, namely the obligatory adjacency of the adjective clearly applies to both 'thematic' and 'classificatory' items, showing once again that there are no significant syntactic gaps between them. We assume that the agreement relation, namely the matching of features between the adjective and the head noun must be local, and the presence of an adposition in between behaves as a barrier (a phase), disrupting the Agree relation (cf. Gallego 2010, Lorusso & Franco, 2017). Moreover, as shown also by the examples in (10), we can take that the scope of the (⊇)P predicates is influences by pragmatic cues only, hence the 'free' order in the adjunction of adpositional (⊇)P.

both cross-linguistically and intra-linguistically. In sum, the core of the present proposal is that the Italian preposition *di* (of) in the noun phrase (as well as other prepositions like *da*, cf. Franco et al., 2021; Rugna & Franco, 2022) expresses the same (⊆) relational primitive of the derivational items that are recruited in the formation of relational adjectives. Indeed, based on Manzini & Savoia (2007, 2011a), we have argued that the operation Merge takes morphemes as its input and single morphemes (within words) are visible to the syntactic computation.

Setting aside any discussion regarding the content expressed by the class(ifier) layers for the moment (i.e., number and gender values which we notate here as Infl and express the Class values in Franco et al. 2015a; Manzini & Savoia 2017a, b, 2018: see Chapter 7 for relevant discussion), we have seen above that both items in (50) can be represented as in (51a) and (51b), where we argue for a fully interpretable (⊆) node sandwiched between the root and the inflectional layer (visible to agreement) in the syntactic derivation of so-called relational adjectives.

(50) *Italian*
   a. acqua marina
       water sea(adj.)
   b. acqua di mare
       water of sea
       both 'sea water'

(51) a. [NP acqua [[√ mar] [-in (⊆) [infl -a]]]]
      b. [NP acqua [PP [P di (⊆) [NP mare]]]]

This representation is consistent with recent proposals, as the one put forth in Fábregas (2020, p.64), who assumes, for Spanish, that: "*a relational adjective derived from a noun is the spell out of a truncated prepositional structure headed by KP, the head that in the prepositional domain marks an argument with inherent case and expresses an underspecified relation with another entity. In contrast to other cases, here the complement of K is an NP denoting a kind, not a DP denoting an individual.*" The same Fábregas acknowledges that the relation instantiated by the case-like morpheme is semantically underspecified. We precisely argue that the 'inclusion' relation introduced by the (⊆) morpheme has an interpretation which is derived by pragmatic enhancement at the Conceptual-Intentional interface.

We assume that also in the realm of adjectival derivation the relation is *included* (⊆) as illustrated in the section above can be mirrored by an *includes* (⊇) relation (see Franco and Lorusso 2022). Actually, we argue that the latter relation is expressed by so called qualifying possessive denominal adjectives in Italian, which are encoded by various suffixes. As for relational adjectives, we assume that these suffixes are all allomorphs sharing the (⊇) signature as their basic content. Following the descriptive survey of Wandruszka (2004), we provide the following examples of qualifying possessive adjectives in (52).

(52) *Italian*
  a. terreno acquoso
      'watery soil'
  b. animale cornuto
      'horned animal'
  c. appartamento finestrato
      'windowed apartment'
  d. bevanda alcolica
      'alcoholic beverage'
  e. zio milionario
      'millionaire uncle'
  f. roccia silicea
      'siliceous rock'

According to Wandruszka (2004), qualifying possessive adjectives can be subdivided into two different classes, from a semantic viewpoint. The first class denotes only possession while the second one denotes possession plus an (often pejorative/augmentative) evaluation component, usually relating to the size of the possessed entity, as for instance in *uomo nasuto* '(ugly) man with a big nose'. We argue that this evaluative reading is again derived by an enhancement process, triggered by pragmatics at the Conceptual-Intentional interface and it not mapped by syntax (cf. Savoia et al., 2017; Franco et al., 2020). Indeed, according to the recent survey of Fábregas (2020, p.119–120), there are many different types of concepts that can be associated with possessive adjectives. In this underspecified sense, assuming that possession is better characterized (even in this domain) as (zonal) 'inclusion' in the sense of Belvin (1996) and Belvin & den Dikken (1997), the range of nouns that can act as bases of so-called qualifying possessive adjectives is quite large; Fábregas lists the following sub-classes: body parts (as in *uomo nas-ut-o* above), items of clothing (as in *giudice tog-at-o*, judge wearing a toga), substances (as in *terreno fang-os-o*, muddy ground), structural parts within the internal constitution of an object (as in *piede lob-at-o*, lobed foot), physical entities that can accompany, modify or decorate a given entity (as in *cielo stell-at-o*, starry sky), mental states (ad in *uomo paur-os-o*, fearful man), moral qualities (*donna coraggi-os-a*, brave woman), and diseases (*ragazzo allerg-ic-o*, allergic boy).

We assume that qualifying possessive adjectives as having the very same internal structure of relational adjectives, following Franco & Lorusso (2022). Namely, we argue that, for possessive adjectival items, we are dealing with the same structure as the one in (51a). The sole difference is that the direction of the relation is reversed, including (⊇) content. Consider the examples in (53) and the representation we provide in (54).

(53) a. terreno acquoso
          soil   water(adj.)
      b. *Italian*
          terreno con acqua
          soil   with water
          both 'watery soil'

(54) a. [NP terreno [[√ acqu] [-os (⊇) [infl -o]]]]
      b. [NP terreno [PP [P con (⊇) [NP acqua]]]]

In a word, in our theoretical framework, we assume that syntax stems from the lexicon and basically that "what you see is what you get". This model allows accounting for both relational and qualifying adjectives in the very same morphosyntactic fashion. Basically, we agree with Rainer (2013), who assumes that the definition of 'relation' is not enough to differentiate relational adjectives from possessive adjectives, given that 'possession', as well as 'similarity' and 'causation' (not considered here) are among the possible interpretations of 'relation'.

On the contrary, Fábregas (2020) argued that the syntactic structure of a qualifying adjective differs from that of relational adjectives in the presence of a P head above K, as represented in (55).

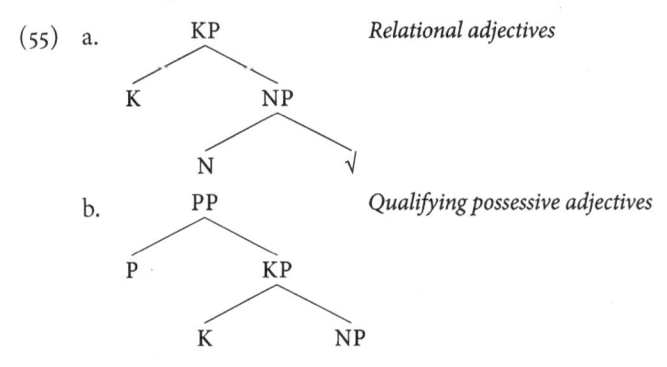

(55) a.   KP   *Relational adjectives*

      b.   PP   *Qualifying possessive adjectives*

This implies that for Fábregas (2020, p. 65), the qualifying adjective has 'more structure' than the relational adjective. This solution allows Fábregas to explain why relational adjectives differ from qualifying possessive adjectives with respect to some syntactic tests, which we consider in some detail below, providing evidence in favor of our proposal.

First, the possessive affix *-os* is employed to form *bona fide* relational adjectives in a number of contexts as illustrated in (56):

(56) *Italian*
 a. sangue arterioso
     blood   arterial
     'arterial blood'
 b. poesia amorosa
     poetry love(adj.)
     'love poetry'
 c. sistema nervoso
     system nervous
     'nervous system'

In all these cases, it is likely that we have an inclusion relation ($\subseteq$), standardly signaling relational adjectives, expressed by the suffix -*os*, which is usually recruited from the lexicon to encode a ($\supseteq$) value. In the examples in (56), we assume the possibility to encode the two flavors of the 'inclusion' relation in the same base position within the morpho-syntactic skeleton for the -*os*- morpheme, as illustrated with the pair in (57) and (58). This is a more economical solution with respect to the one adopted in Fábregas (2020), where the author assumed the possibility for the suffix -*os*- in Spanish to be the Spell Out of different nodes, based on the representation in (55), namely K for the example in (57) and the string P-K, via a phrasal spell-out mechanism, in the example in (58).

(57) a. sangue arterioso 'arterial blood'
      b. [NP sangue [[$\sqrt{}$ arteri] [-os ($\subseteq$) [infl -o]]]]

(58) a. giorno nevoso 'snowy day'
      b. [NP giorno [[$\sqrt{}$ nev] [-os ($\supseteq$) [infl -o]]]]

We argue that the application of a phrasal spell-out mechanism, in these contexts, is not empirically adequate due to the fact that the morpho-lexical shape of relational and qualifying possessive suffixes is quite interlinked, and it does not seem to be some idiosyncratic property of the -*os*- affix that allows it to spell out ($\subseteq$) or ($\supseteq$) values. Indeed, the same possibility is attested for other suffixes, which again are recruited from the lexicon to encode, under the right pragmatic conditions, both flavours of the inclusion relation, as shown in the pairs in (59). This provides evidence that it difficult to assume a clear-cut distinction based on the lexical shape of the affixes, between relational and possessive qualifying adjectives, which, arguably, if lexicon precedes syntax, have the same structural features. Thus, an alternative based on phrasal spell-out appears to be too strong, because it predicts that all the suffixes in (59) potentially instantiate the value K or the string P-K, based on an *ad hoc* mechanism stressing syntactic competence (cf. Chomsky 1995).

(59) *Italian*

    a.   zio (⊇) milionario/ concorso (⊆) universitario
          uncle milionaire competition university(adj.)
          'milionaire uncle/university competition'

    b.   bevanda (⊇) alcolica/ discorso (⊆) filosofico
          drink   alcoholic discourse   philosophical
          'alcoholic drink/philosophical discourse'

    c.   roccia (⊇) silicea/ catalogo (⊆) cartaceo
          rock   siliceous catalog   paper(adj.)
          'siliceous rock/paper catalog'

    d.   uomo (⊇) maniacale/ processo (⊆) culturale
          man   maniacal   process   cultural
          'maniacal man/cultural process'

Second, our proposal can account for the fact that, as widely recognized in the literature, relational adjectives normally do not allow degree modification while qualifying possessive adjectives do. Consider the data in (60), where an adjective marked with a (⊇) relator (60a) can take scale modifiers (as *molto*, very), while an adjective formed with a (⊆) relator is incompatible with this kind of modification.

(60) a.   un terreno molto fangoso
         a ground very   muddy
         'a very muddy ground'

    b.   *un incontro molto calcistico
         a   match   very   football(adj.)
         'a very football match'

Fábregas (2020, p.115), who, as we have seen, assumes a different syntax for qualifying and relational adjectives, argues that a Scale/Degree P is present only within the morphosyntactic skeleton of qualifying possessive items. Specifically, he assumes that the different behaviour of relational and qualifying possessive adjectives has to be ascribed to the fact that only the latter allow the "*presence of a ScaleP: if a scale is a set of ordered values, degree modification must necessarily build over that set of ordered values, and when the scale is absent there is no possibility of adding degree. The presence of ScaleP presupposes the presence of PP, in such a way that without PP there is no ScaleP. [...] PP is a lexical projection that assigns a conceptual dimension to the relation expressed by K.*"

Actually, we argue that the absence of degree modification with relational adjectives can be explained mereologically, namely, it does not depend on syntax and it has to be related to the conceptual properties expressed by the inclusion relation (⊆), selected within the morphosyntactic layer forming the adjectival items. We assume that something that is perceived as a 'whole', like the denominal adjectives formed with the inclusion relation (⊆), cannot be modified by degree values, given that it precisely modifies an entity (the head noun) which is taken to be a part of that whole (derivationally encoded). It will be conceptually anomalous/deviant to assume a scale of values for an entity which represents a whole, as long as the whole retains the same parts depicted by the head nouns (see also Adger, 2013). Still, this is not a problem pertaining to syntax, given that we can find pragmatic contexts in which also so-called relational adjectives can easily accept degree modification, as illustrated by the example in (61), retrieved via a Google search.

(61) *Italian*
      Quindici-zero. Riferimento poco tennistico   e   molto calcistico   allo
      Fifteen-zero. reference   little. Tennis(adj) and very   football(adj) to.the
      score di Josip Ilicic.
      score of Josip Ilicic.
      'Fifteen-zero. A reference which is scarcely related to tennis and mostly related to football in Josip Ilicic's score'

On the contrary, something that is taken to be a 'part' of a whole is readily subject to degree modification from a conceptual viewpoint. A part can be bigger or smaller when compared with other parts of a whole; namely, we can instantiate parthood relations based on scale values for them. This is why adjectives formed with the inclusion relation (⊇) usually allow degree modification.

Related to this point, it is the fact that relational adjectives in coordination can modify one single plural head noun, while this is impossible for qualifying adjectives (cf. Marchis Moreno, 2018). Consider the examples in (62).

(62) *Italian*
      a. gli ambasciatori americano   e   cinese
          the ambassadors. American.SG and Chinese.SG
          'The American and Chinese ambassadors'
      b. *i   terreni acquoso   e   fangoso
          the.PL soils   watery.SG. and muddy.SG.
      b'. i   terreni acquosi   e   fangosi
          the.PL soils   watery.PL and muddy.PL
          'watery and muddy soils'

Wholes-encoding suffixes (⊆) select complete (individual) entities, as in (62a). In the example, USA is taken as an (individual) whole and China is taken as another (singular) whole. It is clear that the sum of two individual wholes expresses a plurality of entities (of individuals, kinds, etc.). This is the reason why a plural noun phrase can show up in these contexts. At the same time, from our reasoning, it follows that it is conceptually infelicitous for the parts of a plurality of wholes as in (20b-b'), encoded derivationally via a (⊇) device, to be taken as singular items: the parts of a plurality of wholes are (at least distributively) plural in turn.

Given the data provided above, we can conclude that there are no clear hints that may lead one to assume a meaningful syntactic dichotomy between relational adjectives (⊆) and qualifying possessive adjectives (⊇), proving the idea that both of them are merged in the same layer.

6.5   Conclusion

In summary, this chapter has delved into the morpho-syntax of Italian ethnic adjectives, challenging the dichotomy between 'thematic' and 'classificatory' ethnic adjectives recently proposed by Alexiadou & Stavrou (2011). Drawing upon the works of Manzini & Savoia (2011), Manzini & Franco (2016), Franco & Manzini (2017), and Savoia et al. (2018), we have presented a unified characterization of ethnic adjectives. We have posited that the derivational morphemes shaping these adjectives serve as a derivational counterpart of the genitive adposition "di" (of) (and the 'ablative' adposition "da" 'from'), sharing a common predicational (⊆) core and signature with them. Moreover, the proposal advanced for ethnic adjectives has been widely extended to encompass relational adjectives in general and qualifying possessive adjectives.

CHAPTER 7

The morphosyntactic interaction of kinship terms with evaluative morphemes in Italian

In this final chapter, we address the interaction between evaluative morphology and kinship terms introduced by possessives in Italian, showing that the application of evaluative affixes influences the syntactic context in which kinship terms can be employed: they cannot be introduced by a bare determiner when evaluative morphemes attach to the lexical root. We argue that this empirical observation has some clear consequences from a theoretical viewpoint: the fact that derivational morphemes, such as evaluatives, alter the syntactic environment in which a noun is couched supports the theory of grammar advanced in Manzini and Savoia (2007, 2011), who assume that Merge takes morphemes as its input and single morphemes are fully visible to the syntactic computation.

7.1   The empirical facts and some theoretical background

In Italian, there exists an intriguing asymmetry regarding the distribution of determiners and possessives when a kinship term is chosen from the lexicon. With canonical kinship terms, we often encounter sentences where the determiner is (optionally) absent, as shown in (1a). This represents a distinct characteristic of kinship terms, as most nominal items (including both common nouns and proper names) must be accompanied by a determiner item in a corresponding syntactic position, as demonstrated in (1b). The application of evaluative morphology to kinship terms (highlighted in bold below) leads to noteworthy outcomes, as the determiner item becomes mandatory, as exemplified in the instances presented in (1c).

(1) *Italian*
   a. (La) mia sorella/ (la) mia zia/ (la) mia nipote è andata al mare
       'My sister/aunt/nephew(grandson) went to the sea'
   b. *(Il) mio amico/*(il) mio Gianni/*(il) mio cane è andato al mare
       'my friend/my Gianni/my dog went to the sea'
   c. *(La) mia sorel**lina**/*(la) mia z**ietta**/ *(la) mia nipot**ina** è andata al mare
       'My younger sister/auntie /little nephew(grandson) went to the sea'

This observation is far from being novel. Longobardi (1994, 1996), Giusti (2015), Cardinaletti & Giusti (2018), among others, have already noted the asymmetry between (1a) and (1c). However, to the best of my knowledge, there have been no attempts in the theoretical literature to formally explain the obligatory presence of determiner items in DP headed by kinship terms once evaluative morphemes are attached to these nominal items. The aim of this Chapter is precisely to address this gap by providing a formal explanation for these phenomena.

Longobardi (1994, and subsequent literature) has demonstrated that certain classes of singular nouns in Italian can undergo leftward movement, initiating an N-to-D chain, shifting from their base position to the one typically occupied by determiners, crossing potentially intervening lexical items (e.g., possessive items). This phenomenon holds true, for instance, for many proper names and the noun "casa" (home). In (2)–(3), it becomes apparent that the determiner is absent only when the nominal item moves leftward.

(2) a. L'antica Roma fu la città più importante del Mediterraneo.
         'the ancient Rome was the most important city of the Mediterranean'
     b. Roma antica fu la città più importante del Mediterraneo.
         'Rome ancient was the most important city of the Mediterranean'
     c. *Antica Roma fu la città più importante del Mediterraneo.
         ancientRome was the most important city of the Mediterranean
                              Italian (Longobardi, 2005, p 9–10)

(3) *Italian*
     a. La mia casa è bella
         the my home is beautiful
         'My house is beautiful'
     b. casa mia è bella
         home my is beautiful
     c. *mia casa è bella
         my home is beautiful

Interestingly, a subset of kinship terms behaves similarly to proper names and the noun "casa," allowing N-to-D movement, as illustrated in (4) (cf. Longobardi, 1994, 1996). However, as shown in (1), they can appear, at least for some kinship terms, without a determiner even in their base position, as in (4a)).[88]

---

88. We can ask ourselves how it is possible to account for the (micro)parametric variation attested in Romance (cf. Masi, 2020). For instance, in Spanish, with possessive modification, determiners are not available independently of the presence of evaluative morphemes (e.g. *(*la)* *mi hermana*, my sister, *(*el) mi gato*, my cat, *(*la) mi hermanita*, my little sister, *(*el) mi gatito*, my kitty). For the sake of the present discussion, we may assume that Spanish possessives (like their English counterparts) are directly merged in D, blocking any other lexical item in such position.

(4)   *Italian*
    a.   mio nonno è andato al mare
       My grandpa went to the sea
    b.   nonno mio è andato al mare
       my grandpa went to the sea
    c.   il mio nonno è andato al mare
       my grandpa went to the sea

Longobardi (1996) proposes an analysis for the entire set of kinship expressions in Italian, such as "mia sorella" ('my sister') in (1a), which are also likely to trigger N-raising, along with additional syntactic operations. He argues for a direct link between proper names and kinship terms, essentially suggesting that determiners are "expletive" when they appear with items prone to N-to-D movement. In subsequent papers, Longobardi connects the movement of a noun to a phonetically empty D with the obligatory co-occurrence of an overt or understood genitive argument (see Longobardi, 2005, 2008), assuming that such entities rigidly refer to particular individuals from a semantic viewpoint. Recently, Giusti (2015, cf. also Cardinaletti & Giusti, 2018) argues that kinship terms modified by possessive items are essentially analogous to proper names, as they are semantically interpreted as rigid designators (Kripke, 1980). For this reason, both nominal classes lack definite determiners in Italian.[89]

Giusti (2015), Cardinaletti & Giusti (2018) specifically propose that rigid designators project reduced syntactic nominal structures to address the issue of silent Ds with kinship terms (and proper names). They assume that while common nouns project three different layers (the lexical NP, the modification field including a set of functional projections FP, and the referential layer DP), rigid designators only project two layers, namely the lexical NP and the referential DP. According to Cardinaletti & Giusti (2018, p. 141), the possessive adjective which signals the possessor of the designator is theta-interpreted and referentially interpreted in a SpecNP position, which is immediately lower than D, given the absence of a functional layer sandwiched between D and N. In (5), we outline

---

89. A strong connection between kinship terms and proper names is evident based on typological considerations. For instance, Dahl & Koptjevskaja-Tamm (2001) propose a hierarchical structure suggesting that if any other kin terms are treated similarly to proper names, then those denoting ascending relations, especially direct ones such as 'father' and 'mother,' will also be treated as proper names. Pham (2011) argues that Vietnamese kinship terms exhibit a distribution pattern similar to that of proper names regarding the presence of determiner items. Stolz et al. (2017) demonstrate in Faroese the emergence of a unique clitic marker (*sa*) exclusively attached to personal names and kinship possessors, while possession involving common nouns or place names is conventionally expressed through a prepositional phrase in the language (cf. also Schlücker & Ackermann, 2017).

their model. In (5a), the kinship term appears with a silent D. In (5b), the proper name moves to D, following the standard analysis of Longobardi (1994). The parallelism between the two classes of nominal items is supported by the fact, already highlighted in (4b), that a subset of kinship terms can raise to D, as in (5c).[90]

(5)   a.   [$_{DP}$ Ø [$_{NP}$ mia sorella]]
         "my sister"
     b.   [$_{DP}$ Maria [$_{NP}$ mia ~~Maria~~]]
         "my Maria"
     c.   [$_{DP}$ mamma [$_{NP}$ mia ~~mamma~~]]
         "my mother"

We posit that an analysis of this kind is fundamentally sound, despite its inability to fully eliminate the expletive nature of determiners in contexts where proper names remain in their base position (cf. (*il) mio Gianni in (1b)). Nonetheless, we must seek an explanation for why kinship terms cannot function as 'rigid designators' when they carry evaluative morphology. Specifically, we need to understand why evaluated kinship terms cannot appear without determiners, as demonstrated in (1c) above. Indeed, from a semantic perspective, discerning the difference between them is not immediately evident: both 'evaluated' and 'bare' kinship terms appear to rigidly denote individuals.

In the subsequent discussion, we aim to present a morphosyntactic analysis capable of elucidating why the application of evaluative affixes impacts the syntactic environment in which kinship terms are utilized. Section 7.2 will outline the analysis of evaluative morphemes proposed in Savoia et al. 2017 (see also Franco et al., 2020). Section 7.3 will apply such theoretical framework to the morphosyntax of kinship terms bearing evaluative morphemes. Section 7.4 will address potential counterexamples and other pertinent issues relevant to our analysis.

---

90. Another parallel between proper names and kinship terms in Italian, as highlighted in Giusti (2015), is that they can appear without a determiner only when they are to singular. Consider the examples in (i):

(i)   a.   *(i) miei fratelli
         the my   brothers
     b.   *(i) Rossi'the Rossi family'

7.2   The morphosyntax of evaluatives: (Class)ifying predicates

Following Franco et al. (2015a), Manzini & Savoia (2017a, b), for Italian/Romance, we assume a nominal morphosyntax in which the first component is a category-less root $\sqrt{}$ (cf. Marantz, 1997, 2007). Next to the root $\sqrt{}$ we find different types of morphemes, including derivational and inflectional ones. Inflectional morphemes generally follow derivational suffixes. The root is interpreted as a predicate, which has one open argument place (the R-role, cf. Williams, 1994), which is ultimately bound by a determiner or quantifier operator (see Higginbotham, 1985). Gender and number specifications – labelled as Class – apply to the argument x open at the predicate. We assume that they work as predicates themselves, restricting the content of the argumental variable, eventually topped off by a determiner/quantifier.[91]

Manzini & Savoia argue that the inflectional vowel of Italian occupies an Infl(ection) position embedding the root $\sqrt{}$ and the Class nodes, which encode gender ([feminine], [masculine], etc.) or number specifications ([singular], [plural], etc.). The content of the plural is represented as the relation part-whole [⊆], specifying that the *denotatum* of the predicate can be partitioned into subsets (cf. Manzini & Savoia, 2011 and subsequent literature). An illustration of their model is represented in (6) for the nominal items *ragazz-o/i* 'boy/boys', *ragazz-a/e* 'girl/girls'.

(6)   [[[*ragazz* $\sqrt{}$] [⊆] [fem]/[masc] $_{Class}$] [⊆] $_{Infl}$ -*a* -*e* -*i* -*o*]

Furthermore, as already pointed out, following Borer (2003, 2014) and Savoia et al. (2017), we take it that the same lexical content can be expressed by inflectional and derivational morphemes (as well as stand-alone lexical items, as we have seen in the previous Chapter). For instance, in Romance, inflectional morphemes are able to introduce properties which usually are introduced by derivational tools, for example category change, size properties (e.g. *melo* 'apple tree'/*mela* 'apple'; *buco* 'hole'/*buca* 'pit', cf. Franco et al., 2015a, 2020; Manzini, 2020). *Vice versa*, derivational morphemes can introduce kinds of contents generally associated with inflection, as for instance gender specifications, which can be also introduced in Italian by the derivational suffix -*ess* (e.g. *maestr-o-maestr-a* 'male/female teacher' vs. *avvocat-o*, *avvocat-ess-a* 'male/ female Lawyer', cf. Chapter 6).

---

91. In their framework, all lexical material is associated with interpretable contents; this proposal is not substantially different from the conception of *Agree* in Chomsky (2001a, b), expressing an identity relation between features under locality (Minimal Search).

Following Savoia et al. (2017), Franco et al. (2020) we take evaluatives to usually express size properties or the grading of individuals/events/features with reference to physical or culturally-determined properties and can be understood as predicates that contribute to restricting the argumental variable of a nominal root. We provide, for ease of reference, a basic structure for evaluatives in (7) for the lexical item *orso* 'bear'. The evaluative merges with the predicative nominal base combined with the (gender) Class specification. In the representation in (7), the complex noun inherits the class gender from the root (a masculine evaluative form is realized in our example). The inflectional node ensures that the structure is visible for Agree.

(7) *Italian*
   a.   orsino/orsone
        'small bear/big bear'
   b.

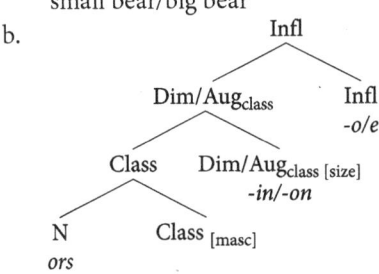

Diminutives/Augmentatives are to be construed as classifiers (i.e. DimClass/Aug-Class). Crucially, many recent works in the literature have highlighted the singulative nature of many instances of evaluative morphology. In particular, Savoia et al., following Wiltschko (2006), Ott (2011) Déchaine et al. (2014), among others, have assumed that the diminutive suffixes in Italian corresponds to something as 'a small/ little individual' to which the properties introduced by the root apply.

Given this singulative effect, diminutives are commonly able to change mass nouns and verbal predicates into count nouns (cf. also Mathieu, 2012; Franco et al., 2020 and the discussion in Chapter 6), as illustrated in (8) for Italian.

(8) *Italian*
   a.   cera > cerino.   [mass-individual]
        wax   wax match
   b.   imbiancare > imbianchino   [deverbal]
        'paint'   painter

A 'bare' singulative effect is not properly obtained with augmentative/pejorative morphemes, as shown in Savoia et al. (2017), Franco et al. (2020), given that derived forms with the augmentative *-on-* differ from the derived nouns formed by *-in-*, as in (8), in that *-on-* normally specifies an excessive/ habitual property

(Grandi, 2003). Consider the examples in (9), where *-one* applies to verbal, mass and adjectival bases (cf. Franco, 2015).

(9) *Italian*
    a. mangiare > mangione,   [deverbal]
        'eat'   'big eater'
    b. ciccia > ciccione   [mass>individual]
        'flesh' 'fat man'
    c. buffo > buffone   [deadjectival]
        'funny' 'fool'

The deverbal diminutive in (9a) do not introduce a quantified interpretation of the event and in fact do not usually entail size interpretation. Still, as shown above, inserting either a diminutive or an augmentative on the verbal/adjectival root generates an individual interpretation, more precisely it specifies properties associated with an individual referent.

According to Savoia et al., the individuating effect of Diminutives/Augmentatives is connected to the availability of a low position of such elements which act as classifiers, and Merge directly with the nominal, adjectival or verbal root. Specifically, the singulative effect is obtained by diminutive and augmentatives suffix both combining with events, qualities and mass roots, given that such predicates can be represented as *aggregates* of undifferentiated components or a continuum (Chierchia, 2010): a temporal continuum of the event, the continuum of parts of a substance, etc. We assume that verbal or adjectival roots are devoid of gender, which is selected by the evaluative 'class' morpheme itself. Consider the representation in (10), in which we present Savoia et al.'s model for 'individuating' evaluatives. We specifically target the adjectival base in (9c).

(10)

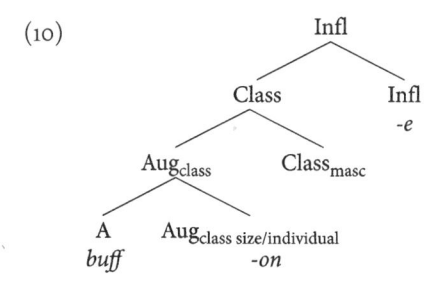

To sum up, canonical evaluative suffixes introduce predicates/ properties that contribute to restricting the argument of the nominal root. A second state of affairs emerges when the evaluative combines with verbal, mass or adjectival roots; in these contexts, they directly modify the properties of the root. Thus, we have two possible results: an intersective reading in which the evaluative behaves like a (size) adjective in a conjunction relation with the noun; a reading in which the evaluative introduces a size quantification and perform an individuating mechanism on the root. The evaluative classifier itself, in the latter case, selects for class gender (cf the representation in (10)). Thus, in keeping with Savoia et al. (2017), we argue that diminutive/augmentative morphemes applied to kinship terms express size / measure (Class) properties with reference to the lexical root, as in the examples in (11).

(11)   *Italian*
  sorell-**in**-a   / fratell-**on**-e
  sister-DIM-INFL   brother-AUG-INFL
  'small/ younger sister' 'big/ older brother'

As we have seen above, evaluatives on nominal items can be understood as (Class)ifying predicates that contribute to restricting the argumental variable of the root $\sqrt{}$, like gender and number layers (see also Percus, 2011). Actually, it is possible to extend the analysis of adjectives in Parsons (1979) to evaluatives. For Parsons (1979, p.157), adjectives in attributive positions are "*operators on the predicate contributed by the noun ... these operators can be further analysed in terms of conjunction with a predicate', whereby 'red box' can be translated as 'x is red and a box*".

Given this, it is possible to follow Cinque (2010b) in pursuing the idea that evaluative morphology is essentially *intersective*, namely it invariantly corresponds to the restrictive and intersective (or subsective) interpretation of adjectives,[92] giving rise to the interpretation in (12).

(12) *sorellina* x[(sister)x & (little)x], *fratellone* x [(brother)x & (big)x]

Syntactically, we argue that an evaluative interpretation arises from a structure in which the evaluative morphemes embed the Class node and the root, as illustrated in (13) for diminutives and augmentatives.[93] The evaluative Class item

---

92. This interpretation is supported by the fact that diminutive morphemes can be attached to postnominal adjectives but not in pre-nominal ones in Italian, as illustrated in (i) (see Savoia et al., 2017).

(i) a. *una grand-in-a casa/una casa grand-in-a
    a big-dim house/a house big-dim
  b. *una bell-in-a ragazza/una ragazza bell-in-a
    a cute-dim girl /a girl cute-dim

Following Cinque (2010b), pre-nominal adjectives have a non-restrictive reading (cf. also Partee, 2007), while post-nominal adjectives have an intersective meaning because they restrict the denotation of the head noun with the introduction of further specifications on its range of reference.

merges with the root √ combined with other Class specification (e.g. gender properties) below the inflectional/agreement layer Infl.[94] We assume a nominal structure in which inflectional and derivational morphemes enable a morpho-syntactic skeleton which provides different semantic (Class) interpretations.

(13) a.

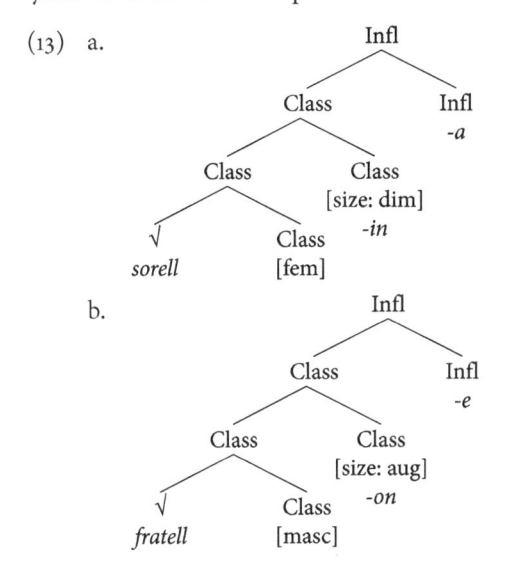

b.

7.3   The interaction of kinship terms with evaluative morphemes: An analysis

With the theoretical framework established, this section aims at providing an explanation for the inability of determiner-less kinship terms modified by pos-sessives to co-exist with evaluative morphology. Longobardi (2005) observed that

---

93. In (9) Dim/Aug are introduced as [Dim]Class/[Aug]Class, and so on in the case of the other evaluative class nodes, as for instance pejorative (e.g. *sorell-acci-a*, bad sister) and endear-ing (e.g. *zi-ett-a*, auntie) morphemes. For the ordering and mutual exclusions between evalua-tive suffixes, not strictly relevant for the present discussion, see the analyses in Cinque (2015) and in Savoia et al. (2017).

94. Other recent proposals in the generative framework aim to relate the nature and mor-phemic status of evaluatives to the discussion on the internal structure of the noun, also in a cross-linguistic perspective, see, among others, Wiltschko (2006), Ott (2011), de Belder et al. (2014), Cinque (2007, 2015), Franco et al. (2020). For instance, Wiltschko (2006) assumes that diminutive suffixes are 'light nouns', and specifically that they correspond to numeral classifiers. Ott (2011) proposes a detailed structure where the diminutives are analysed as 'numeral classi-fiers'. Both authors converge in identifying the diminutive suffix with a lexicalization of a nom-inal layer independent of the root.

the rigid denotation of an individual entity, morphosyntactically speaking, is a derivational attribute rather than a lexical one. In other words, the capacity for 'rigid designation' cannot be inferred solely from the lexical features of a nominal noun; it is determined through the syntactic module in a derivational manner. Consequently, proper names (along with other rigid designators) are permitted to occupy an empty determiner position only within specific syntactic contexts. Longobardi illustrates this by demonstrating that in contexts where proper names are treated akin to common nouns, pronouns (i.e., standard determiner-like items) are grammatically unacceptable, as exemplified in restrictive relative modifications in (14) (see also Matushansky 2009):

(14)   a.   Il (simpatico) Gianni che conoscevo non esiste più.
             'The (nice) Gianni that I used to know no longer exists.'
       b.   *Gianni (simpatico) che conoscevo non esiste più.
             'Gianni (nice) that I used to know no longer exists.'
       c.   *Il (simpatico) lui che conoscevo non esiste più.
             'The (nice) he that I used to know no longer exists.'
       d.   *Lui (simpatico) che conoscevo non esiste più
             'He (nice) that I used to know no longer exists.'
             Italian (from Longobardi, 2005, p. 16)

Crucially, when kinship terms are modified by intersective/subsective adjectives, they cannot appear determiner-less, as in (15) where the adjective *imbranata* 'clumsy' modifies the kinship term for sister.

(15)   *(la) mia sorella imbranata ha cambiato strada
        the my sister clumsy   has changed road
       'my clumsy sister changed direction'

In the terms of Cardinaletti & Giusti (2018), if modifiers enter the derivation, the kinship term is no more a rigid designator and works as the head noun of a (standard) syntactic structure in which the functional field is projected. In such (canonical) structure the possessor moves from SpecNP to SpecPossP, as illustrated in (16).

(16) $[_{DP}$ la $[_{PossP}$ mia $[_{FP}$ sorella $[_{FP}$ $[_{AP}$ imbranata $]$ ... $[_{NP}$ ~~mia sorella~~$]]]]]$
        the   my   sister   clumsy
       'my clumsy sister'

Thus, both Longobardi and Cardinaletti & Giusti assert that selecting a lexical item as a rigid designator becomes impossible when it undergoes subsective, intersective, or restrictive modification. However, while Cardinaletti & Giusti posit that rigid designation constitutes a lexical property of nominal items, Longobardi contends that rigid designation emerges derivationally within specific syntactic environments.

As demonstrated in the preceding section, Savoia et al. (2017) argue that evaluative morphemes can be treated as classifying morphemes that impose a [Size] restriction on the lexical root. This constitutes a morphological operation that, nevertheless, manifests at the syntactic level. Indeed, diminutives and augmentatives, as illustrated in (11)–(12), appear to function similarly to intersective adjectives, as shown in (17). This effectively precludes the possibility of kinship terms acting as rigid designators that permit an empty D position, potentially filled through N-to-D movement.

(17) *Italian*
   a. la   mia sorellina   ≈ la   mia sorella piccola
       the my sister.DIM   the my sister little
       'my little sister/my younger sister'
   b. il   mio fratellone   ≈ il   mio fratello grande
       the my brother.AUG   the my brother big
       'my big brother/my older brother'

This pattern extends to all other types of evaluatives in Italian. Pejoratives serve as a case in point, as they appear to support Longobardi's assertion that 'rigid designation' is compositionally shaped by the morphosyntactic derivation (cf. also Baggio & Cairncross, 2020 for a recent cartographic proposal, endorsing this perspective) and cannot be predicted solely based on the lexical features of a given nominal item. Take, for instance, the Italian pejorative suffix *-astr-* when applied to kinship terms, as illustrated in the examples in (18). These lexical items, from a semantic standpoint, seem to function as rigid denotators, as they specify particular specimens within the class of kinship terms. In (18), they can denote a daughter/son of one's step-parent through a marriage other than with one's own father or mother. In these contexts, it is not possible to ascribe a [size] interpretation to these evaluative morphemes, and they are *prima facie* linked to a *denotatum* that is fully stored in the lexicon (i.e., a fossilized form).

(18) *Italian*
   a. sorell-**astr**-a
       step-sister, half-sister
   b. fratell-**astr**-o
       step-brother, half-brother

Actually, such items are fully ungrammatical without a definite determiner in the possessor construction we have outlined so far, as illustrated in (19), just like the examples we have provided for kinship terms bearing diminutive or augmentative affixes.

(19) *Italian*
      *(la) mia sorellastra /   *(il) mio fratellastro
      The my step/half sister / The my step/half brother

Thus, it seems that the morpheme *-astr* is still active from a morphosyntactic viewpoint, given that it behaves just like the other evaluatives introduced in the discussion so far. The Italian suffix *-astr* derives from the Latin morpheme *-aster*, which encodes resemblance/similarity (cf. Thomas, 1940; Rohlfs, 1968). The evaluative (pejorative) meaning of this suffix, according to Merlini Barbaresi (2004), comes from the fact that the nominal items bearing this morpheme are all characterized by qualities which are *similar* to those of the respective bases, but less precise, less perfect.[95] Consider for instance the examples in (20a) where the lexical items have a clear pejorative flavour and the items in (20b) in which they encode an approximate (i.e. less intense, less clear, etc.) version of the lexical base.

(20) *Italian*
      a. poet-astr-o > poeta, filosof-astr-o   > filosofo
          bad poet   poet bad philosopher   philosopher
      b. ross-astr-o > rosso sord-astr-o > sordo
          reddish   red slightly deaf   deaf

We argue that the [approximate] value of the items in (20b) is shared by the kinship terms bearing the *-astr* suffix.[96] Thus, it is possible to propose, for these nominal elements, an intersective/subsective semantics like the one represented in (21) and a morphosyntax like the one illustrated in (22).

(21) *Sorellastra* λ x[(sister)x & (approximate)x],
      fratellastro λ x [(brother)x & (approximate)x]

---

95. Serianni (1988, p.550) points out that the suffix *-astr* can also convey an endearing or playful meaning, as with items like *topastro* 'little funny rat', *giovinastro* 'youngster'.

96. We can propose a similar 'approximate' value for the the (scarcely productive) evaluative suffix *-ign*, also employed with kinship terms, as in (i), which disallow an empty D as in (ii). The approximate (i.e less intense) value of this suffix is found with items like the one in (iii).

   (i)   patr-ign-o, matr-ign-a
          'stepfather' 'stepmother'
   (ii)   *(la) mia matrigna /   *(il) mio patrigno
          The my stepmother / The my stepfather
   (iii) aspr-ign-o *from* aspro
          slightly sour   sour

(22)

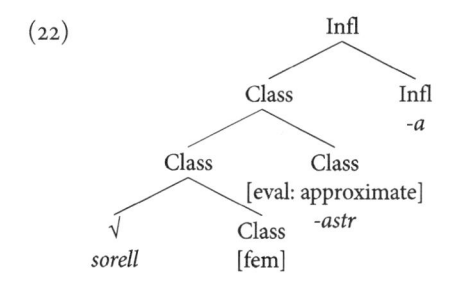

We argue that not only the outer node (Infl) of the nominal structure is recruited for the syntactic computation (e.g. for Agree operations), but also the Class layers of the nominal skeleton acting as predicates which restrict the referential properties of the root. In this precise context, they turn kinship terms, which are a set of nominal items sharing many features with proper names, into common nouns by applying a functional restriction on their reference. This, in turn, blocks the availability of an empty D position for kinship items. The fact that derivational morphemes of this kind alter the syntactic environment in which a noun is couched support the theory of grammar advanced by Manzini & Savoia (2007, 2011), who precisely assume that merge takes morphemes as its input and single morphemes are visible to syntactic computation (in the terms of Cardinaletti & Giusti, 2018, Class morphemes feed the functional field sandwiched between N and D, blocking rigid designation).

7.4   Further issues on possessives, kinship terms and evaluatives

In the preceding section, we outlined the primary focus of our analysis, which explored the interaction between evaluative morphology and kinship terms introduced by possessives in Italian. We demonstrated how the application of evaluative affixes influences the syntactic context in which kinship terms can be used, thereby conditioning the availability of an unpronounced definite D. Now, we turn our attention to certain aspects that may pose potential challenges to our arguments.

Firstly, we have posited that morphological elements (such as evaluatives) and syntactic modifiers (such as adjectives) hinder rigid denotation for kinship terms, following the framework of Cardinaletti & Giusti (2018). However, there exists a potential counterexample involving the comparative (suppletive) forms of adjectives in Italian, specifically "minore" (smaller, younger) and "maggiore" (bigger, older). Consider the examples provided in (23).

(23) *Italian*
   a.   Mia sorella minore è andata al parco
      'My younger sister went to the park'
   b.   Mio fratello maggiore è andato al parco
      'My older brother went to the park'

In (23), we observe that the kinship terms in the possessive construction are accompanied by a modifier yet still permit an empty D, contrary to what might be anticipated. We contend that expressions like "sorella minore" and "fratello maggiore" in (23) are treated akin to lexical compounds and are not subject to syntactic reordering. This is why they are regarded as lexical members of the kinship term category and can function as rigid designators. This idea is supported by the fact that these constructions cannot be altered by intervening intensifiers or other lexical elements, as demonstrated in (24).

(24) *Italian*
   a.   *un fratello molto minore (cf. e.g. un percorso molto minore)
      a   brother much younger   'a much shorter path'
   b.   *una sorella ben   maggiore (cf. e.g. una fatica ben maggiore)
      a   sister much older   'a far greater effort'

Furthermore, the items *minore* and *maggiore* are commonly recruited in Italian to form various other lexical compounds/multiword expressions, as shown in (25).

(25) *Italian*
   Orsa maggiore, panda minore, Si maggiore ...
   Ursa mayor   red   panda B major

A further note concerns the paradigm of possessives in front of kinship terms in Italian. Consider the data in (26).

(26) *Italian*

	SG		PL	
1st	mio padre	'my father'	nostro padre	'our father'
2nd	tuo padre	'your father'	vostro padre	'your father'
3rd	suo padre	'his/her father'	??(il) loro padre	'their father'

According to our native judgement, the third person plural possessive "loro" precludes the possibility of a bare determiner in the possessor-kinship term structure. The distinctive characteristics of the pronoun "loro" have garnered significant attention in the literature, tracing back to the research of Cardinaletti (1998) and Cardinaletti & Starke (1999), which delved into a nuanced typological analysis of strong versus weak pronouns in Italian. Here, we adhere to the framework proposed by Manzini (2014, see also Manzini & Savoia, 2014; Baldi & Savoia, 2019,

2021), which posits that "loro" encompasses an inflectional oblique morpheme, denoted as "-oro," representing the possession relation [⊆]. In genitive contexts, this morpheme takes the pronominal/definiteness base "l-" as its internal argument to which it attaches, along with the head noun as its external argument.

Specifically, Manzini (2014) shows that, in genitive contexts, *loro* can have the same distribution of full third person singular full pronouns *lui* (he), *lei* (she), as the object of the preposition *di* (27a), while the prenominal genitive position (27b) is available only for *loro* but not for *lui, lei*. In this latter case, *loro* patterns with the possessive pronouns *sua* (her). Note that in this case, *sua* agrees with the noun (*casa*), where *loro* is invariable (cf. *il loro cavallo* 'their horse'/*la loro cavalla* 'their mare').

(27) *Italian*
　　a.　La casa　di lui/di lei/di loro/*di suo/*di sua
　　　　The home of him/of her/of them/of his/of her
　　　　'Their/his/her home'
　　b.　La loro/sua/*suo/*lui/*lei casa
　　　　the their/her/his/him/her home
　　　　'Their/his/her home'

Manzini's idea (2014, p.179) is that *loro* is optionally oblique, as in (28). The *loro* that alternates with *lui/lei* is only plural; while the *loro* that does not alternate with *lui/lei* is both plural and oblique.

(28) *loro*: D, plural, (oblique)

Manzini (2014, p.179) further assumes that "*for oblique endings like -oro, since relational content within the nominal domain is associated with Q categories (cf. generalized quantifier theory), we label them as Q(⊆), though nothing hinges on the choice of Q.*" In terms of this notation and ascribing to the *l-* in *loro* the lexicalization of D, it is possible to provide the two representations in (29), replicating the ones provided in Manzini (2014, p.180), for the examples in (27). Note that P in (29a) has the canonical (⊆) 'inclusion' value we have assumed so far, lexicalized by a P.

(29) a.　*loro*: D, plural.

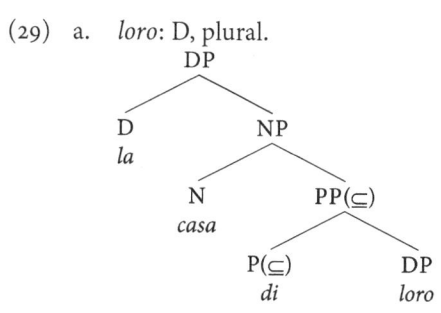

b. *loro:* D, plural, oblique

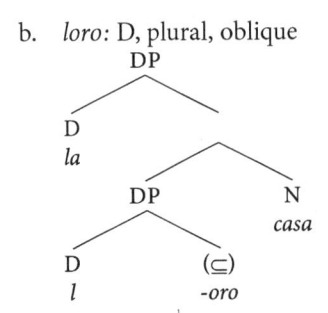

Thus, as shown above, genitive *loro* yields the inverse order of possessor and possessee: the possessor to the right requires an adposition; the possessor to the left implies oblique case properties. It is clearly possible to assume that prenominal *l-oro* with kinship terms behaves the same. Consider the representation in (30).

(30)

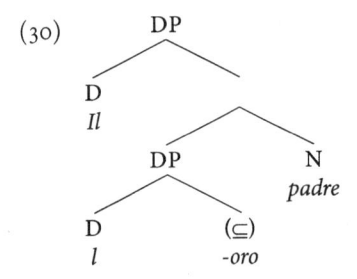

The open question is why *loro* in (30) seems to block an unpronounced D. The other possessive items, introducing the participants in the speech act (1st/2nd person, *mio/nostro, tuo/vostro*) or the singular reference to a discourse anaphoric argument (3rd singular person *suo*) do not require the presence of a definite determiner, possibly because their interpretive content is able to exhaustively externalize the referential domain of DP.

Our idea is that the definiteness *l-* base (the same base found in Italian definite determiners, e.g. *il*, the.m.SG, *la*, the.f.SG, etc.) encoded only in the (possessive) pronoun *loro* triggers the spell-out of a higher D item topping off the structure, given the argumental nature of the lower D item in *loro*. Such lower argumental D requires an (overt) higher D fixing its referential properties (cf. Lekakou & Szendrői, 2012; Franco et al., 2015b). It is possible, in other words, that the lower D values the argument slot of [⊆], awaiting further quantificational closure (operated by the higher D). This is only a tentative interpretation and we leave this matter for future works.

7.5   Conclusion

In this Chapter, we have addressed the interaction between evaluative morphology with kinship terms introduced by possessives in Italian, showing that the application of evaluative affixes influences the syntactic context in which kinship terms can be employed. We have argued that this empirical observation has some interesting consequences from a theoretical viewpoint: the fact that derivational morphemes, such as evaluatives, alter the syntactic environment in which a noun is couched support the theory of grammar advanced by Manzini & Savoia (2007, 2011), who assume that Merge takes morphemes as its input and single morphemes are visible to syntactic computation. Specifically, we have argued that it is possible to treat evaluative morphemes as classifying morphemes that operate a [Size/Approximation, etc.] restriction of the lexical root. This is a morphological restriction, which is however visible at the level of syntax. Indeed, diminutives and augmentatives seem to work just like intersective/subsective adjectives activating a functional skeleton sandwiched between the determiner and the noun. This blocks the possibility for kinship terms in possessive contexts to act as rigid designators allowing an empty D position, potentially filled via N to D movement.

CHAPTER 8

Conclusions

In essence, our findings suggest a unified conceptual framework for understanding the role of oblique cases, adpositions, serial verbs, applicatives, as well as derivational tools, shedding new light on their interpretive significance. Our analysis has highlighted, through a series of case studies, the pervasive role of the 'inclusion' relator across various linguistic contexts.

We have shown how natural languages lexically encode the relators/predicates that introduce a relation between two arguments or between an argument and the event/result predicate. This perspective attributes interpretive properties to the various obliques explored in our research, contrasting with views that consider them devoid of interpretive content (cf. Chomsky, 1981; Richards, 2010 on English *of*). Our proposal is consistent with the analysis of possession/have predicates in Belvin & Den Dikken (1997, p.170), who state: *"entities have various zones associated with them, such that an object or eventuality may be included in a zone associated with an entity without being physically contained in that entity [...] The type of zones which may be associated with an entity will vary with the entity"*.

We have assumed that functional categories externalize properties and relations that are not fundamentally different from those realized by the substantive lexicon. They are merely more elementary, typically partitioning the conceptual universe into broader classes than the exponents of traditional lexical categories (i.e., nouns, verbs, adjectives, cf. Baker, 2003). We have adopted a perspective in which the lexicon precedes syntax and projects it, aligning with the minimalist postulate of *Inclusiveness* (Chomsky, 1995; Manzini & Savoia, 2011a, 2018). Consequently, understanding how the items projected from the lexicon interact with one another under syntactic Merge (effectively projecting syntactic structures) becomes paramount.

Our main focus has been on the junction of externalization processes and the syntactic processor. We have investigated (cross-categorial) syncretism, considering paradigms as having no theoretical status and using "syncretism" to basically refer to homophony outside of paradigms. Our goal has been to outline an inventory of primitives shaping morpho-syntactic derivations.

In short, we have illustrated a formal approach to cross-categorial variation in argument marking, attempting to outline a unified morpho-syntactic template in which so-called 'cases' do not configure a specialized linguistic lexicon of functional features/categories. On the contrary, they help us outline an underlying ontology of natural languages, from which they derive some of the most elementary relations. Such primitive relations can be expressed by different lexical means (case, adpositions, light verbs, etc.). Moreover, the model we have outlined predicts that paradigms do not exist within the competence of speaker-hearers; in other words, linguistic data are organized in a non-paradigmatic fashion – just like generative syntax never quite achieves a match to traditional constructions such as *passive* or *ergative*, etc. Primitives are too finely grained, and the combinatorial possibilities afforded by Universal Grammar are too numerous to perfectly align with descriptive (macro)classes.

Bibliography

Aboh, E.O. (2009). Clause structure and verb series. *Linguistic Inquiry*, 40(1), 1–33.

Adger, D. (2013). *A Syntax of Substance*. Cambridge, MA, MIT Press.

Aikhenvald, A.Y. (2006). Serial Verb Constructions in a Typological Perspective. In A.Y. Aikhenvald & R.M.W. Dixon (Eds.), *Serial verb constructions: a cross-linguistic typology* (pp. 1–87). Oxford, Oxford University Press.

Aikhenvald, A.Y. (2008). Versatile cases. *Journal of Linguistics*, 44, 565–603.

Aissen, J. (2003). Differential Object Marking: Iconicity vs. economy. *Natural Language and Linguistic Theory*, 21(3), 435–483.

Alexiadou, A. (2001). *Functional structure in nominals*. Amsterdam, John Benjamins.

Alexiadou, A., Haegeman, L., & Stavrou, M. (2007). *Noun Phrase in the Generative Perspective*. Berlin, Mouton De Gruyter.

Alexiadou, A., Anagnostopoulou, E. & Schäfer, F. (2009). PP licensing in nominalizations. In A. Schardl, M. Walkow, & M. Abdurrahman (Eds.), *Proceedings of NELS* 38 (pp. 39–52). Ottawa, GLSA.

Alexiadou, A., & Stavrou M. (2011). Ethnic adjectives as pseudo-adjectives. *Studia Linguistica*, 65, 1–30.

Alexiadou, A., Anagnostopoulou, E. & Schäfer, F. (2015). *External arguments in transitivity alternations*. Oxford, Oxford University Press.

Aristar, A.A. (1996). The relationship between dative and locative: Kuryłowicz's argument from a typological perspective. *Diachronica*, XIII(2): 207–224.

Ariste, P. (1997). *A grammar of the Votic language*. Bloomington and The Hague, Indiana University Press and Mouton.

Arkhangelskiy T., & Usacheva, M. (2015). Syntactic and Morphosyntactic Properties of Postpositional Phrases in Beserman Udmurt as Part-of-Speech Criteria. *SKY Journal of Linguistics*, 28, 103–137.

Arsenijevic, B., Boleda, G., Gehrke, B., & McNally, L. (2014). Ethnic adjectives are proper adjectives. In R. Baglini, T. Grinsell, J. Keane, A. Roth Singerman, & J. Thomas (Eds.), *CLS-46-I the main session: 46th annual meeting of the Chicago Linguistic Society* (pp. 17–30). Chicago, IL, Chicago Linguistic Society.

Asbury, A. (2008). The Morphosyntax of Case and Adpositions. PhD dissertation, Universiteit Utrecht.

Avril, Y. (2006). *Parlons Komi*. Paris, L'Harmattan.

Bach, E. (1986). The algebra of events. *Linguistics and Philosophy*, 9, 5–16.

Baerman, M., Brown, D. & Corbett, G. (2005). *The syntax-morphology interface: A study of syncretism*. Cambridge, Cambridge University Press.

Baggio, P. & Caircross, A. (2020). The syntax of Puss in Boots and Sleeping Beauty. Proper names between productivity and atomicity, *Proceedings of ConSOLE* XXVIII.

Bahrami-Khorshid, S., & Golfam, A. (2013). Encoding the Agent in Persian Passive Construction: A Cognitive Approach. *International Journal of Humanities*, 20(4), 79–97.

Baker, M. (1988). *Incorporation: A theory of grammatical function changing*. Chicago, IL, University of Chicago Press.

Baker, M. (1989). Object sharing and projection in serial verb constructions. *Linguistic Inquiry*, 20(4), 513–553.

Baker, M. (1991). On the Relation of Serialization to Verb Extensions. In C. Lefebvre (Ed.), *Serial verbs: Grammatical, comparative and cognitive approaches* (pp. 79–102). Amsterdam, John Benjamins.

Baker, M. (1992). Thematic conditions on syntactic structures: Evidence from locative applicatives. In I. M. Roca (Ed.), *Thematic structure: Its role in grammar* (pp. 23–46). Dordrecht: Foris.

Baker, M. (2003). *Lexical Categories*. Cambridge, Cambridge University Press.

Baker, P., & Kriegel, S. (2013). Mauritian Creole structure dataset. In S. M. Michaelis, P. Maurer, M. Haspelmath & M. Huber (Eds.), *Atlas of Pidgin and Creole Language Structures Online*, Leipzig, Max Planck Institute for Evolutionary Anthropology. (Available online at http://apics-online.info/).

Bakker, P. (2003). Pidgin inflectional morphology and its implications for creole morphology. In G. Booij & J. van Marle (Eds.), *Yearbook of morphology 2002* (pp. 3–33), Dordrecht, Kluwer.

Baldi, B., & Savoia, L. M. (2019). Possessives in North-Calabrian dialects. *QULSO -Quaderni del Dipartimento di Linguistica*, 7, 19–40.

Baldi, B., & Savoia, L. M. (2021). Possessives, from Franco-Provencal and Occitan systems to contact dialects in Apulia and Calabria. *Languages*, 6(2), 63.

Barat, C., Carayol, M., & Vogel, C. (1977). *Kriké kraké: recueil de contes créoles réunionnais*. Paris, CNRS.

Barker, C. (1995). *Possessive Descriptions*. Stanford, CSLI Publications.

Bartning, I. (1980). *Remarkes sur la syntaxe et la semantique des pseudo adjectif de nominaux en francais*. Stockholm, Almvist & Wiksell International.

Barwise, J., & Cooper, R. (1981). Generalized quantifiers and natural language. *Linguistics and Philosophy*, 4, 159–219.

Bassaganyas-Bars T. (2015). The rise of *haver* as the existential predicate and the perfect auxiliary: the case of Old Catalan. *Proceedings of Sinn und Bedeutung* 19, 107–124.

Baxter, A. N. (1988). *A grammar of Kristang (Malacca Creole Portuguese)*. Canberra, Pacific Linguistics, Australian National University.

Baxter, A. N. (2013). Papiá Kristang structure dataset. In S. M. Michaelis, P. Maurer, M. Haspelmath & M. Huber (Eds.), *Atlas of Pidgin and Creole Language Structures Online*, Leipzig, Max Planck Institute for Evolutionary Anthropology. (Available online at http://apics-online.info/).

Beavers, J. (2011). On affectedness. *Natural Language and Linguistic Theory*, 29(2), 335–370.

Beck, S., & K. Johnson. (2004). Double objects again. *Linguistic Inquiry*, 35, 97–124.

Belletti, A. (2004). Aspects of the low IP area. In L. Rizzi (Ed.), *The Structure of IP and CP* (pp. 16–51). Oxford, Oxford University Press.

Belletti, A. (2005). Extended doubling and the VP periphery. *Probus*, 17, 1–35.

doi   Belletti, A. (2017). Labeling (Romance) causatives. Manuscript. Universities of Geneva & Siena.

Bellucci, G. (2017). Oblique subjects: theoretical and experimental perspectives. Ph.D. Dissertation, Università di Firenze.

Belvin, R. S. (1996). Inside Events: The Non-Possessive Meanings of Possession Predicates and the Semantic Conceptualization of Events. Ph.D. dissertation, University of Southern California.

doi   Belvin, R. S., & den Dikken, M. (1997). *There, happens, to, be, have. Lingua*, 101, 151–183.

doi   Bentley, D. (2013). Subject canonicality and definiteness effects in Romance "there" sentences. *Language*, 89, 675–712.

doi   Bentley, D. (2017). Copular and existential constructions. In A. Dufter, & E. Stark (Eds.), *Manual of Romance Morphosyntax and Syntax* (pp. 332–366). Berlin, De Gruyter.

doi   Bentley, D., Ciconte, F. M., & Cruschina, S. (2015). *Existential and Locatives in Romance Dialects of Italy*. Oxford: Oxford University Press.

Benveniste, É. (1966). *Problèmes de linguistique générale* 1. Paris, Gallimard.

Berwick, R., & Chomsky, N. (2011). The biolinguistic program: The current state of its evolution and development. In A. M. DiSciullo, & C. Boeckx (Eds.), *The Biolinguistic Enterprise* (pp. 19–41). Oxford, Oxford University Press.

Biagui, N. B., & Quint, N. (2013). Casamancese Creole structure dataset. In S. M. Michaelis, P. Maurer, M. Haspelmath & M. Huber (Eds.), *Atlas of Pidgin and Creole Language Structures Online*, Leipzig, Max Planck Institute for Evolutionary Anthropology. (Available online at http://apics-online.info/).

Bickerton, D. (1981). *Roots of Language*. Ann Arbor, Karoma.

doi   Bickerton, D. (1984). The language bioprogram hypothesis. *Behaviour and brain sciences*, 7(2), 173–221.

doi   Bickerton, D. (1989). Seselwa serialization and its significance. *Journal of Pidgin and Creole Languages*, 4, 155–183.

Bisang, W. (1992). *Das Verb im Chinesischen, Hmong, Vietnamesischen, Thai und Khmer. Vergleichende Grammatik im Rahmen der Verbserialisierung, der Grammatikalisierung und der Attraktorpositionen*. Tübingen, Gunter Narr.

doi   Bisang, W. (1996). Areal typology and grammaticalization: Processes of grammaticalization based on nouns and verbs in East and Mainland South East Asian languages. *Studies in Language*, 20, 519–597.

Bisang, W. (1998). Adverbials: The view from the Far East. In J. van der Auwera & D. P. O´Baoill (Eds.), *Adverbial constructions in the languages of Europe* (pp. 641–812). Berlin: Mouton de Gruyter.

doi   Blake, B. (2001). *Case*. Cambridge, Cambridge University Press.

doi   Bobaljik, J. (2012). *Universals in Comparative Morphology: Suppletion, Superlatives, and the Structure of Words*. Cambridge, MA, The MIT Press.

doi   Boeckx, C. (2009). The nature of merge. Consequences for language, mind and biology. In M. Piatelli Palmarini (Ed.), *Of minds and language* (pp. 44–57). Oxford, Oxford University Press.

Boleda, G., Evert, S., Gehrke, B., & McNally, L. (2012). Adjectives as saturators vs. modifiers: Statistical evidence. In M. Aloni, V. Kimmelman, F. Roelofsen, G. Weidman Sassoon, K. Schulz, & M. Westera (Eds.), *Logic, language and meaning – 18th Amsterdam Colloquium, Amsterdam, The Netherlands, December 19–21, 2011, Revised Selected Papers* (pp. 112–121). Dordrecht, Springer.

Bollée, A. & Marcel, R. (1994). *Parol ek memwar. Récits de vie des Seychelles*. Hamburg, Buske.

Boneh, N., & Sichel, I. (2010). Deconstructing possession. *Natural Language and Linguistic Theory*, 28, 1–40.

Boneh, N., & Nash, L. (2012). Core and non-core datives in French. In B. Fernández & R. Etxepare (Eds.), *Variation in datives: A Microcomparative Perspective* (pp. 22–49). Oxford, Oxford University Press.

Borer, H. (2003). Exo-Skeletal vs. Endo-Skeletal Explanations: Syntactic Projections and the Lexicon. In J. Moore & M. Polinsky (Eds.), *The Nature of Explanation in Linguistics Theory* (pp. 31–67). Stanford, CLSI Publications.

Borer, H. (2005). *In name only, Structuring sense, vol I*. Oxford: Oxford University Press.

Borer, H. (2014). Derived Nominals and the Domain of Content. *Lingua*, 141, 71–96.

Borschev, V. & Partee, B. (2001). The Russian genitive of negation in existentials sentences: The role of Theme-Rheme structure reconsidered. *Prague Linguistic Circle Papers / Travaux du cercle linguistique de Prague*, 4, 185–250.

Bosque, I. & Picallo, C. (1996). Postnominal adjectives in Spanish DPs. *Journal of Linguistics*, 32, 349–385.

Bossong, G. (1985). *Differentielle Objektmarkierung in den Neuiranischen Sprachen*. Tübingen, Gunter Narr.

Bowden, J. (2001). *Taba: description of a South Halmahera language*. Research School of Pacific and Asian Studies, The Australian National University, Pacific Linguistics.

Bresnan, J., & Moshi, L. (1990). Object asymmetries in comparative Bantu syntax. *Linguistic Inquiry*, 21, 147–185.

Bruening, B. (2012). By phrases in passives and nominals. *Syntax*, 16, 1–41.

Bruyn, A., Muysken, P., & Verrips, M. (1999). Double-object constructions in the creole languages: development and acquisition. In Michel DeGraff (Ed.), *Language creation and language change: Creolization, diachrony and development* (pp. 329–373). Cambridge, MA, MIT Press.

Buell, L., & Sy, M. (2006). Affix ordering In Wolof applicatives and causatives. In J. Mugane, J.P. Hutchison, & D.A. Worman (Eds.), *Selected Proceedings of the 35th Annual Conference on African Linguistics* (pp. 214–224). Somerville, Cascadilla Proceedings Project.

Bunting, J. (2009). 'Give' and 'take': How dative *gi* contributed to the decline of ditransitive *taki*. *Journal of Pidgin and Creole Languages*, 24, 199–217.

Caha, P. (2009). *The nanosyntax of case*. PhD dissertation, CASTL & University of Tromsø.

Caha, P. (2016). GEN.SG = NOM.PL: A mystery solved? *Linguistica Brunensia*, 64, 25–40.

Caha, P. (2017). How (not) to derive a *ABA: the case of Blansitt's generalisation. *Glossa: a journal of general linguistics*, 2(1), 84–115.

doi　Calabrese, A. (1998). Some remarks on the Latin case system and its development in Romance. In J. Lema, & E. Treviño (Eds.), *Theoretical advances on Romance Languages* (pp. 71–126). Amsterdam, John Benjamins.

doi　Calabrese, A. (2008). On absolute and contextual syncretism. In A. Nevins & A. Bachrach (Eds.), *The bases of inflectional identity* (pp. 156–205). Oxford, Oxford University Press.

doi　Capistrán Garza, A. (2015). *Multiple object constructions in P'orhépecha: Argument realization and valence-affecting morphology*. Leiden, Brill.

doi　Cardinaletti, A. (1998). On the deficient/strong opposition in possessive systems. In A. Alexiadou, & C. Wilder (Eds.), *Possessors, Predicates and Movement in the Determiner Phrase* (pp. 17–53). Amsterdam, John Benjamins.

doi　Cardinaletti, A. & Starke, M. (1999). The typology of structural deficiency. A case study of the three classes of pronouns. In H. van Riemsdijk (Ed.), *Clitics in the Languages of Europe* (pp. 145–233). Berlin, Mouton-De Gruyter.

doi　Cardinaletti, A., & Giusti, G. (2016). The syntax of the Italian indefinite determiner *dei*. *Lingua*, 181, 58–80.

Cardinaletti, A., & Giusti, G. (2018). Micro-variation in the Possessive Systems of Italian Dialects. In J. Emonds, M. Janebová, & L, Veselovská (Eds.), *Language Use and Linguistic Structure. Proceedings of the Olomouc Linguistics Colloquium* (pp. 137–154). Olomouc, Palacký University Press.

Cardoso, H.C. (2009). *The Indo-Portuguese language of Diu*. Utrecht, LOT.

Carlson, G. (1977). Reference to Kinds in English. PhD dissertation, University of Massachusetts at Amherst.

doi　Carlson, R. (1991). Grammaticalisation of postpositions and word order in Senufo languages. In E. C. Traugott & B. Heine (Eds.), *Approaches to grammaticalization. Vol. 2: Focus on types of grammatical markers* (pp. 201–223). Amsterdam, John Benjamins.

doi　Carstens, V. (2002). Antisymmetry and word order in serial constructions. *Language*, 78(1), 3–50.

doi　Champollion L., & Krifka, M. (2016). Mereology. In M. Aloni, & P. Dekker (Eds.), *The Cambridge Handbook of Formal Semantics* (pp. 369–388). Cambridge, Cambridge University Press.

doi　Chappell, H.M. (2015). *Diversity in Sinitic languages*. Oxford, Oxford University Press.

doi　Chierchia, G. (1998a). Plurality of mass nouns and the notion of 'semantic parameter. In S. Rothstein (Ed.), *Events in Grammar* (pp. 53–104). Kluwer, Dordrecht.

Chierchia, G. (1998b). Partitives, reference to kinds and semantic variation. In A. Lawson (Ed.), *Proceedings from Semantics and Linguistic Theory* (SALT 7) (pp. 73–98).

doi　Chierchia, G. (2010). Mass nouns, vagueness and semantic variation. *Synthese*, 174: 99–149.

Chomsky, N. (1981). *Lectures on government and binding*. Dordrecht, Foris.

Chomsky, N. (1995). *The Minimalist Program*. Cambridge, MA, MIT Press.

Chomsky, N. (2000). Minimalist inquiries: The framework. In R. Martin, D. Michaels, & J. Uriagereka (Eds.), *Step by step, essays on minimalist syntax in honor of Howard Lasnik* (pp. 89–155). Cambridge, MA, MIT Press.

doi　Chomsky, N. (2001a). Derivation by Phase. In M. Kenstowicz (Ed.), *Ken Hale: A Life in Language*, (pp. 1–54). Cambridge, MA: MIT Press.

Chomsky, N. (2001b). Beyond explanatory adequacy. *MIT Occasional Papers in Linguistics* 20. Cambridge, MA: MIT, Department of Linguistics and Philosophy, MITWPL.

Chomsky, N. (2013). Problems of projection. *Lingua*, 130, 33–49.

Chomsky, N. (2015). Problems of projection: Extensions. In E. Di Domenico, C. Hamann, & S. Matteini (Eds.), *Structures, strategies and beyond -studies in honour of Adriana Belletti*, (pp. 3–16). Amsterdam, John Benjamins.

Chomsky, N. (2020). The UCLA Lectures (April 29 – May 2, 2019). <https://ling.auf.net/lingbuzz/005485>

Chomsky, N., Gallego, Á, J., & Ott, D. (2019). Generative Grammar and the Faculty of Language: Insights, Questions and Challenges. *Catalan Journal of Linguistics*, Special Issue, 229–261.

Chumakina, M. (2011). Nominal periphrasis. A canonical approach. *Studies in Language*, 35, 247–274.

Cinque, G. (1994). On the Evidence for Partial N-Movement in the Romance DP. In G. Cinque, J. Koster, J-Y. Pollock, L. Rizzi, & R. Zanuttini (Eds.), *Paths Towards Universal Grammar. Studies in Honor of Richard S. Kayne*, 85–110. Washington, DC, Georgetown University Press.

Cinque, G. (2007). La natura grammaticale del diminutivo e del vezzeggiativo. In R. Maschi, N. Penello, & P. Rizzolatti (Eds.), *Miscellanea di studi liguistici offerti a Laura Vanelli da amici e allievi padovani* (pp. 229–236). Udine, Forum.

Cinque, G. (2010a). Mapping Spatial PPs: an Introduction. In G. Cinque & L. Rizzi (Eds.), *Mapping Spatial PPs, The Cartography of Syntactic Structures, Vol. 6* (pp. 3–25). New York, Oxford University Press.

Cinque, G. (2010b). *The Syntax of Adjectives: A Comparative Study*. Cambridge, MA, MIT Press.

Cinque, G. (2015). Augmentative, pejorative, diminutive and endearing heads in the extended nominal projection. In E. Di Domenico, C. Hamann, & S. Matteini (Eds.), *Structures, strategies and beyond -studies in honour of Adriana Belletti* (pp. 67 81). Amsterdam, John Benjamins.

Cinque, G., & Rizzi, L. (2010). The cartography of syntactic structures. In B. Heine, & H. Narrog (Eds.), *The Oxford handbook of linguistic analysis* (pp. 51–65). Oxford, Oxford University Press.

Clements, J.C. (2013). Korlai structure dataset. In S.M. Michaelis, P. Maurer, M. Haspelmath & M. Huber (Eds.), *Atlas of Pidgin and Creole Language Structures Online*, Leipzig, Max Planck Institute for Evolutionary Anthropology. (Available online at http://apics-online.info/).

Cole, P. (1983). The grammatical role of the causee in Universal Grammar. *International Journal of American Linguistics*, 49, 115–133.

Collins, C. (1997). Argument sharing in serial verb constructions. *Linguistic Inquiry*, 28(3), 461–497.

Collins, C. (2005). A smuggling approach to the passive in English. *Syntax*, 8, 81–120.

Colot S, & Ludwig, R. (2013a). Guadeloupean Creole structure dataset. In S.M. Michaelis, P. Maurer, M. Haspelmath & M. Huber (Eds.), *Atlas of Pidgin and Creole Language Structures Online*, Leipzig, Max Planck Institute for Evolutionary Anthropology. (Available online at http://apics-online.info/).

Colot S, & Ludwig, R. (2013b). Martinican Creole structure dataset. In S. M. Michaelis, P. Maurer, M. Haspelmath & M. Huber (Eds.), *Atlas of Pidgin and Creole Language Structures Online*, Leipzig, Max Planck Institute for Evolutionary Anthropology. (Available online at http://apics-online.info/).

Comrie, B. (1976). *Aspect*. Cambridge, Cambridge University Press.

Comrie, B. (1999). Spatial cases in Daghestanian languages. *Sprachtypologie und Universalienforschung*, 52, 108–117.

Comrie, B. & Polinsky, M. (1998). The great Daghestanian case hoax. In A. Siewierska & J. J. Song (Eds.), *Case, Typology and Grammar: In Honor of Barry J. Blake* (pp. 95–114). Amsterdam, John Benjamins.

Corbett, G. (2011). *Number*. Cambridge, Cambridge University Press.

Corne, C, Coleman D., & Curnow, S. (1996). Clause reduction in asyndetic coordination in Isle de France creole: The 'serial verbs' problem. In P. Baker & A. Syea (Eds.), *Changing meanings, changing functions* (pp. 129–154). London, University of Westminster Press.

Coupe, A. (2008). *A Grammar of Mongsen Ao*. Berlin, Mouton De Gruyter.

Craig, C., & Hale, K. (1988). Relational Preverbs in Some Languages of the Americas: Typological and Historical Perspectives. *Language*, 64, 312–344.

Creissels, Denis (2006). Encoding the distinction between location, source, and destination. In M. Hickmann & S. Robert (Eds.), *Space in Languages: Linguistic Systems and Cognitive Categories* (pp. 19–28). Amsterdam, John Benjamins.

Creissels, D. (2010). Benefactive applicative periphrases: a typological approach. In F. Zúñiga & S. Kittilä (Eds.), *Benefactives and malefactives: Typological perspectives and case studies* (pp. 29–69). Amsterdam, John Benjamins.

Creissels D. (2014). Existential predication in typological perspective. Ms., Université Lyon.

Crocco Galèas, G. (1991). *Gli etnici italiani: studio di morfologia naturale*. Padova, Unipress.

Cruschina, S. (2015). Patterns of variation in existential constructions. *Isogloss. A journal on variation of Romance and Iberian languages*, 1(1), 33–65.

Cuervo, M. C. (2003). Datives at large. Ph.D. dissertation, Massachusetts Institute of Technology.

Cuervo, M. C. (2010). Two types of (apparently) ditransitive light verbs constructions. In K. Arregi, Z. Fagyal, S. A. Montrul, & A. Tremblay (Eds.), *Romance Linguistics 2008. Interaction in Romance. Selected Papers from the 38th. Linguistic Symposium on Romance Languages. Urbana-Champaign, April 2008* (pp. 139–154). Amsterdam, John Benjamins.

Dahl Ö., & Koptjevskaja-Tamm, M. (2001). Kinship in grammar. In I. Baron, M. Herslund & F. Sørensen (Eds.), *Dimensions of Possession*, (pp. 201–243). Amsterdam, John Benjamins.

Dardano, M. (2008). *Costruire parole*. Bologna, Il Mulino.

David, A. (2014). *Descriptive Grammar of Pashto and its Dialects*. Berlin, Mouton De Gruyter.

De Belder, M. (2011). A morphosyntactic decomposition of countability in Germanic. *Journal of Comparative Germanic Linguistics*, 14 (3), 173-202.

De Belder, M., Faust, N. & Lampitelli, N. (2014). On a low and a high diminutive. In A. Alexiadou, H. Borer, & F. Schäfer (Eds.), *The syntax of roots and the roots of syntax* (pp. 149–163). Oxford, Oxford University Press.

Déchaine, R-M., Girard, R., Mudzingwa, C., & Wiltschko, M. (2014). The internal syntax of Shona class prefixes. *Language Sciences*, 43, 18–46.

DeGraff, M. (2001). On the Origin of Creoles: A Cartesian Critique of Neo-Darwinian Linguistics. *Linguistic Typology*, 5(2–3), 213–310.

DeGraff, M. (2003). Against Creole Exceptionalism. *Language*, 79(2), 391–410.

DeGraff, M. (2007). Kreyòl Ayisyen or Haitian Creole. In J. Holm, & P. Patrick (Eds.), *Comparative creole syntax. Parallel outlines of 18 creole grammars* (pp. 101–126). London/Colombo: Battlebridge.

Demirdache, H., & Uribe-Etxebarria, M. (2000). The primitives of temporal relations. In R. Martin, D. Michaels, & J. Uriagereka (Eds.), *Step by step, essays on minimalist syntax in honor of Howard Lasnik*, 157–186. Cambridge, MA, MIT Press.

Den Dikken, M. (1991). Serial Verbs, 'Object Sharing', and the Analysis of Dative Shift. *Linguistics in the Netherlands*, 8, 31–40.

Den Dikken, M. (1995). *Particles*. New York, Oxford University Press.

Den Dikken, M. (2006). *Relators and linkers: A study of predication, predicate inversion and copulas*. Cambridge, MA, MIT Press.

Den Dikken, M. (2010). On the functional structure of locative and directional PPs. In G. Cinque & L. Rizzi (Eds.), *Mapping Spatial PPs, The Cartography of Syntactic Structures*, Vol. 6 (pp. 74–126). New York, Oxford University Press.

Den Dikken, M., & Dékány, É. (2018). Adpositions and case: Alternative realisation and concord. *Finno-Ugric Languages and Linguistics* 7(2).

Devonish, H., & Thompson, D. (2013). "Creolese". In S. M. Michaelis, P. Maurer, M. Haspelmath & M. Huber (Eds.), *The survey of pidgin and creole languages. Vol. I: English-based and Dutch-based languages* (pp. 49–60). Oxford, Oxford University Press.

Di Garbo, F. (2014). Gender and its interaction with number and evaluative morphology: An intra- and intergeneralogical typological survey of Africa. PhD Dissertation. Stockholm University.

Durie, M. (1988). Verb Serialization and 'Verbal Prepositions' in Oceanic Languages. *Oceanic Linguistics*, 27(1–2), 1–23.

Durie, M. (1997). Grammatical structures in verb serialization. In A. Alsina, J. Bresnan, & P. Sells (Eds.), *Complex predicates* (pp. 289–354). Stanford, CSLI Publications.

Ehrhart S., & Revis, M. (2013). Tayo structure dataset. In S. M. Michaelis, P. Maurer, M. Haspelmath & M. Huber (Eds.), *Atlas of Pidgin and Creole Language Structures Online*, Leipzig, Max Planck Institute for Evolutionary Anthropology. (Available online at http://apics-online.info/).

Ehrhart, S. (1993). *Le créole français de St-Louis (le tayo) en Nouvelle-Calédonie*. Hamburg, Helmut Buske.

Emonds, J. (1985). *A Unified Theory of Syntactic Categories*. Dordrecht, Foris.

Fábregas, A. (2007a). (Axial) parts and wholes. *Nordlyd*, 34, 1–32.

Fábregas, A. (2007b). The internal syntactic structure of Relational adjectives. *Probus*, 19(1), 1–36.

Fábregas, A. (2015a). Una nota sobre locativos y acusativos." *Archivum*, LXV, 57–74.

Fábregas, A. (2015b). Direccionales con *con* y Marcado Diferencial de Objeto. *Revue Romane* 50, 163–190.

Fábregas, A. (2020). *Morphologically Derived Adjectives in Spanish*. Amsterdam, John Benjamins.

Faraclas, N. (1996). *Nigerian Pidgin.* London, Routledge.

Farquharson, J.T. (2013). Jamaican structure dataset. In S.M. Michaelis, P. Maurer, M. Haspelmath & M. Huber (Eds.), *Atlas of Pidgin and Creole Language Structures Online,* Leipzig, Max Planck Institute for Evolutionary Anthropology. (Available online at http://apics-online.info/).

Feist, T.R. (2010). A Grammar of Skolt Saami. Ph.D dissertation, University of Manchester.

Filbeck, D. (1975). A grammar of verb serialization in Thai. In J.G. Harris, & J.R. Chamberlain (Eds.), *Studies in Tai linguistics in honor of William J. Gedney* (pp. 112–129). Bangkok, Central Institute of English Language.

Filchenko, A.Y. (2007). A Grammar of Eastern Khanty. PhD dissertation, Rice University.

Filip, H. (1999). *Aspect, situation types and noun phrase semantics.* New York, Garland.

Fillmore, C.J. (1968). The case for case. In E. Bach & R.T. Harms (Eds.), *Universals in linguistic theory* (pp. 1–88). New York, Holt, Rinehart, and Winston.

doi Fillmore, C.J. (1986). Pragmatically controlled zero anaphora. In *Proceedings of the Twelfth Annual Meeting of the Berkeley Linguistics Society,* 95–107. Berkeley, CA, BLS.

Finney, M.A. (2013). Krio structure dataset. In S.M. Michaelis, P. Maurer, M. Haspelmath & M. Huber (Eds.), *Atlas of Pidgin and Creole Language Structures Online,* Leipzig, Max Planck Institute for Evolutionary Anthropology. (Available online at http://apics-online .info/).

doi Folli, R., & Harley, H. (2007). Causation, obligation, and argument structure: on the nature of little v. *Linguistic Inquiry,* 38(2), 197–238.

doi Folli, R. (2008). Complex PPs in Italian. In A. Asbury, J. Dotlačil, B. Gehrke, & R. Nouwen (Eds.), *Syntax and Semantics of Spatial P* (pp. 197–220). Amsterdam, John Benjamins.

doi Folli, R., Harley, H., & Karimi, S. (2005). Determinants of event structure in Persian complex predicates. *Lingua,* 115, 1365–1401.

Forman, M.L. (1972). *Zamboangueño texts with grammatical analysis. A Study of Philippine Creole Spanish.* Ph.D. dissertation, Cornell University.

doi Frajzyngier, Z. (2012). *A Grammar of Wandala.* Berlin, De Gruyter.

Francez, I. (2007). Existential propositions. Ph.D. dissertation, Stanford University.

doi Francez, I. (2009). Existentials, predication, and modification. *Linguistics and Philosophy,* 32: 1–50.

doi Francez, I., & Koontz-Garboden, A. (2016). A note on possession and mereology in Ulwa property concept constructions. *Natural Language & Linguistic Theory,* 34, 93–106.

doi Francez, I., & Koontz-Garboden, A. (2017). *Semantics and morphosyntactic variation: Qualities and the grammar of property concepts.* Oxford, Oxford University Press.

doi Franco, L. (2013). Before strikes back: An *ABA constraint on temporal expressions. *Acta Linguistica Hungarica,* 60(3), 265–301.

doi Franco, L. (2015a). The morphosyntax of adverbs of thecarpone/i type in (Old and Modern) Italian. *Probus,* 27(2), 271–306.

doi Franco, L. (2016). Axial Parts, phi-features and degrammaticalization. *Transactions of the Philological Society,* 114, 149–170.

Franco, L. (2018). On Nominalization: Genitives, Datives, and Elementary Predicates in Italian. In A. Bloch-Rozmej, & A. Bondaruk (Eds.), *Studies in Formal Linguistics Universal Patterns and Language Specific Parameters* (pp. 73–90). Frankfurt, Peter Lang.

Franco, L. (2020). (Im)proper prepositions in (Old and Modern) Italian. In L. Franco & P. Lorusso (Eds.), *Linguistic Variation: Structure and Interpretation* (pp. 249–272). Berlin, De Gruyter Mouton.

Franco, L., Baldi, B. & Savoia, L.M. (2020). Collectivizers in Italian (and beyond). The interplay between collectivizing and evaluating morphology (and the Div paradox). *Studia Linguistica*, 74, 2–41.

Franco, L., Bellucci, G., Dal Pozzo, L., & Manzini, M.R. (2017). Locatives, Part and Whole in Uralic. In J. Emonds & M. Janebovà (Eds.), *Language Use and Linguistic Structure – selected proceedings of OLINCO 2016* (pp. 283–304). Olomouc, Palacky University Press.

Franco, L., & Lorusso, P. (2019). The expression of proper location and beyond: motion-to and state-in in Italian spatial adpositions. In M. Baird & J. Pesetsky (Eds), *NELS 49: Proceedings of the Forty-Ninth Annual Meeting of the North East Linguistic Society: Volume 1* (pp. 279–290). GLSA, University of Massachusetts, Amherst.

Franco, L., & Lorusso, P. (2020). Aspectual datives (and instrumentals). In A. Pineda & J. Mateu (Eds.), *Dative constructions in Romance and beyond* (pp. 175–194). Berlin, Language Science Press.

Franco, L., & Lorusso, P. (2022). Derivational Relators in Italian. *Languages*, 7(2): 130.

Franco, L., Manzini M.R., & Savoia, L.M. (2015a). N Class and Its Interpretation: The Neuter in Central Italian Varieties and Its Implications. *Isogloss. A Journal on Variation of Romance and Iberian Languages*, 1, 41–68.

Franco, L., Manzini M.R., & Savoia, L.M. (2015b). Linkers and agreement. *The Linguistic Review*, 32(2), 277–332.

Franco, L., Manzini M.R., & Savoia, L.M. (2021). Locative PS as general relators. Location, direction, DOM in Romance. *Linguistic Variation*, 21, 135–73.

Franco, L., & Manzini, M.R. (2017a). Genitive/'of' Arguments in DOM Contexts. *Revue Roumaine De Linguistique*, LXII, 427–444.

Franco, L., & Manzini, M.R. (2017b). Instrumental prepositions and case: Contexts of occurrence and alternations with datives. *Glossa*, 2(1), 8.

Freeze, R. (1992). Existentials and other locatives. *Language*, 68(3), 553–595.

Gallego, Á. (2010). *Phase Theory*. Amsterdam, John Benjamins.

Ganfi, V., & Piunno, V. (2017). Preposizioni complesse in italiano antico e contemporaneo. Grammaticalizzazione, schematismo e produttività. *Archivio Glottologico Italiano*, CII(2), 184–204.

Garzonio, J., & Rossi, S. (2016). Case in Italian Complex PPs. In E. Carrilho, A. Fiéis, M. Lobo & S. Pereira (Eds.), *Romance Languages and Linguistic Theory 10: Selected papers from 'Going Romance' 28, Lisbon* (pp. 121–138). Amsterdam, John Benjamins.

Gavarro, A. & Heshmati, Y. (2014). An investigation on the comprehension of Persian passives in typical development and autism. *Catalan Journal of Linguistics*, 13, 79–98.

George, I. (1975). Typology of verb serialization. *Journal of West African Languages*, 10(1), 78–97.

Gerdts, D., & Hinkson, M. (2004). The grammaticalization of Halkomelem 'face' into a dative applicative suffix. *International Journal of American Linguistics*, 70(3), 227–250.

Ghomeshi, J. (1997). Non-Projecting Nouns and the Ezafe: Construction in Persian. *Natural Language & Linguistic Theory*, 15, 729–788.

Giusti, G. (2015). *Nominal Syntax at the Interfaces. A Comparative Study of Languages with Articles*. Newcastle upon Tyne, Cambridge Scholars Publishing.

Givón, T. (1975). Serial verbs and syntactic change. In C. N. Li (Ed.), *Word order and word order change* (pp. 47–112). Austin, University of Texas Press.

Goury, L. & Migge, B. (2003). *Grammaire du nengee: Introduction aux langues aluku, ndyuka et pamaka*. Paris, Editions IRD.

Grandi, N. (2001). Su alcune presunte anomalie della morfologia valutativa. *Archivio Glottologico*, 86, 25–56.

Grandi, N. (2003). Mutamenti innovativi e conservativi nella morfologia valutativa dell'italiano. Origine, sviluppo e diffusione del suffisso accrescitivo *-one*. In N. Maraschio, & T. Poggi Salani (Eds.), *Italia linguistica anno Mille – Italia linguistica anno Duemila. Atti del XXXIV Congresso Internazionale di Studi della Società di Linguistica Italiana* (pp. 243–258). Roma, Bulzoni.

Grimm, S. (2011). Semantics of Case. *Morphology*, 21, 515–544.

Grimm, S. (2012). Inverse Number Marking and Individuation in Dagaare. In D. Massam (Ed.), *Count and Mass Across Languages* (pp. 75–98). Oxford, Oxford University Press.

Grimshaw, J. (1990a). Extended projection. Ms., Brandeis University.

Grimshaw, J. (1990b). *Argument structure*. Cambridge, MA, MIT Press.

Hagège, C. (2010). *Adpositions*. Oxford, Oxford University Press.

Hagemeijer, T. (2000). *Serial verb constructions in São-Tomense*. MA thesis, University of Lisbon.

Hagemeijer, T. (2011). The Gulf of Guinea creoles. Genetic and typological relations. *Journal of Pidgin and Creole Languages*, 26(1), 111–154.

Hagemeijer, T. (2013). Santome structure dataset. In S. M. Michaelis, P. Maurer, M. Haspelmath & M. Huber (Eds.), *Atlas of Pidgin and Creole Language Structures Online*, Leipzig, Max Planck Institute for Evolutionary Anthropology. (Available online at http://apics-online .info/).

Hagemeijer, T. & Ogie, O. (2011). Edo influence on Santome: evidence from verb serialization and beyond. In C. Lefebvre (Eds.), *Creoles, their substrates, and language typology* (pp. 37–60). Amsterdam, John Benjamins.

Haig, G. (2008). *Alignment Change in Iranian Languages: A Construction Grammar Approach*. Berlin and New York, Mouton de Gruyter.

Hajek, J. (2006). Serial verbs in Tetun Dili. In A. Y. Aikhenvald & R. M. W. Dixon (Eds.), *Serial Verb Constructions: a Cross-Linguistic Typology* (pp. 239–253). Oxford, Oxford University Press.

Häkkinen, K. (1996). *Suomalaisten esihistoria kielitieteen valossa. Tietolipas* 147. Helsinki, SKS.

Hakulinen, L. (1979). *Suomen kielen rakenne ja kehitys*. (4th revised ed.). Otavan korkeakoulukirjasto. Helsinki, Otava.

Hale, K. & Keyser, S. J. (1993). On argument structure and the lexical expression of grammatical relations. In K. Hale & S. J. Keyser (Eds.), *The view from building* 20 (pp. 53–109). Cambridge, MA, MIT Press.

Hale, K. & Keyser, S. J. (2002). *Prolegomenon to a Theory of Argument Structure*. Cambridge, MA, MIT Press.

Halle, M. (1997). Distributed Morphology: Impoverishment and Fission. In B. Bruening, Y. Kang, & M. McGinnis (Eds.), *PF: Papers at the Interface, MIT Working Papers in Linguistics* 30, (pp. 425–449). Cambridge, MA, MITWPL.

Halle, M. & Marantz, A. (1993). Distributed Morphology and the Pieces of Inflection. In K. Hale & S. J. Keyser (Eds.), *The view from building* 20 (pp. 111–176). Cambridge, MA, MIT Press.

Hanske, T. (2007). Ditransitive constructions in Vietnamese: How to integrate serial verb constructions and systemic zero-anaphora in a typology of alignment patterns. Paper Presented at the *Conference on Ditransitive Constructions*, 23–25 November 2007. Leipzig, Max Planck Institute for Evolutionary Anthropology.

Harley, H. (2002). Possession and the Double Object Construction. *Linguistic Variation Yearbook*, 2, 29–68.

Harley, H. (2008). When is a Syncretism more than a Syncretism? In D. Harbour, D. Adger & S. Béjar (Eds.), *Phi-Theory: Phi-features across Interfaces and Modules* (pp. 251–294). Oxford, Oxford University Press.

Harley, H. (2009). The morphology of nominalizations and the syntax of vP. In A. Giannakidou & M. Rathert (Eds.), *Quantification, Definiteness and Nominalization* (pp. 321–343). Oxford, Oxford University Press.

Harley, H. (2013). *External arguments and the Mirror Principle: On the distinctness of Voice and v. Lingua*, 125, 34-57.

Haspelmath, M. (1993). *A Grammar of Lezgian*. Berlin: Mouton de Gruyter.

Haspelmath, M. (2013). Expletive subject of existential verb. In S. M. Michaelis, P. Maurer, M. Haspelmath & M. Huber (Eds.), *Atlas of Pidgin and Creole Language Structures Online*, Leipzig, Max Planck Institute for Evolutionary Anthropology. (Available online at http://apics-online.info/).

Haspelmath, M. (2019) Differential place marking and differential object marking. *STUF - Language Typology and Universals*, 72(3), 313-334.

Haspelmath, M., & Michaelis, S. (2008). Leipzig fourmille de typologues: Genitive objects in comparison. In G. Corbett, & M. Noonan (Eds.), *Case and grammatical relations: Studies in honor of Bernard Comrie* (pp. 149–166). Amsterdam, John Benjamins.

Heine, B. (1997). *Possession. Cognitive sources, forces, and grammaticalization*. Cambridge, Cambridge University Press.

Heine, B. & König, C. (2010). On the linear order of ditransitive objects. *Language Sciences*, 32, 87-131.

Heine, B., & Kuteva, T. (2002). *World lexicon of grammaticalization*. Cambridge, Cambridge University Press.

Hemmings, C. (2013). Causatives and applicatives: The case for polysemy in Javanese. *SOAS Working Papers in Linguistics*, 16, 167–194.

Higginbotham, J. (1985). On Semantics. *Linguistic Inquiry*, 16, 547–621.

Higginbotham, J. (2009). *Tense, Aspect, and Indexicality*. Oxford, Oxford University Press.

Hoekstra, T. (1999). Parallels between nominal and verbal projections. In D. Adger, S. Pintzuk, B. Plunkett, & G. Tsoulas (Eds.), *Specifiers: Minimalist approaches* (pp. 163–187). Oxford, Oxford University Press.

doi Hohnerlein-Buchinger, T. (1996). *Per un sublessico vitivinicolo. La storia materiale e linguistica di alcuni nomi di viti e vini italiani.* Tübingen, Niemeyer.

Holm, J., & Patrick P. L. (2007). *Comparative Creole Syntax* (Eds.). London/Colombo, Battlebridge.

Holmberg, A. (2002). Prepositions and PPs in Zina Kotoko. In B. Kappel Schmidt, D. Odden, & A. Holmberg (Eds.), *Some Aspects of the Grammar of Zina Kotoko* (pp. 162–174). Munich, Lincom Europa.

Hualde, J. I. (1992). *Catalan* (Descriptive Grammars). London, Routledge.

doi Huang, C.-T. J., Li, Y.-H. A., & Li, Y. (2009). *The Syntax of Chinese.* Cambridge, Cambridge University Press.

doi Huumo, T., & Ojutkangas, K. (2006). An introduction to Finnish spatial relations: Local cases and adpositions. In M-L. Helasvuo & L. Campbell (Eds.), *Grammar from the human perspective: Case, space and person in Finnish* (pp. 11–20). Amsterdam, John Benjamins.

Intumbo, I., Inverno, L. & Holm, J. (2013). Guinea-Bissau Kriyol structure dataset. In S. M. Michaelis, P. Maurer, M. Haspelmath & M. Huber (Eds.), *Atlas of Pidgin and Creole Language Structures Online*, Leipzig, Max Planck Institute for Evolutionary Anthropology. (Available online at http://apics-online.info/).

Itkonen, T. (1997). Reflections on PreUralic and the Saami-Finnic protolanguage. *Finnisch-Ugrische Forschungen*, 54, 229–266.

Jackendoff, R. (1983). *Semantics and Cognition.* Cambridge, MA, MIT Press.

doi Jacob, J., & Grimes, C. (2011). Aspect and directionality in Kupang Malay serial verb constructions: Calquing on the grammars of substrate languages. In C. Lefebvre (Ed.), *Creoles, their substrates, and language typology* (pp. 337–366). Amsterdam: John Benjamins.

Jakobson, R. (1936). Contribution to the General Theory of Case: General Meanings of the Russian Cases. In L. Waugh & M. Halle (Eds.), *Roman Jakobson. Russian and Slavic Grammar: Studies 1931–1981* (pp. 59–103). Berlin, Mouton De Gruyter.

Jansen, B, Koopman, H., & Muysken, P. (1978). Serial verbs in the creole languages. *Amsterdam Creole Studies*, 2, 125–159.

doi Jeong, Y. (2007). *Applicatives: Structure and interpretation from a minimalist perspective.* Amsterdam, John Benjamins.

doi Jerro, K. (2017). The causative–instrumental syncretism. *Journal of Linguistics*, 53, 751–788.

Jóhannsdóttir, K. (2012). Aspects of the progressive in English and Icelandic. PhD Dissertation, University of British Columbia.

Johns, A. (1992). Deriving ergativity. *Linguistic Inquiry*, 23, 57–87.

Johns, A. & Thurgood, B. (2011). Axial Parts in Inuktitut and Uzbeki. *Proceedings of the 2011 annual conference of the Canadian Linguistic Association.*

Josselin de Jong, J.P.B. de. (1926). *Het huidige Negerhollandsch* (teksten en woordenlijst). Amsterdam, Koninklijke Academie van Wetenschappen te Amsterdam.

doi Jurafsky, D. (1996). Universal tendencies in the semantics of the diminutive. *Language*, 72(3), 533–578.

Karimi, S. (1997). Persian complex predicates and LF incorporation. *Proceedings of the Chicago Linguistic Society* (CLS), 33, 215–229.

Karimi, S, & Brame, M. (1986). A generalization concerning the Ezafe construction in Persian. *West Coast Conference in Linguistics* (WECOL 86), Vancouver, Canada

Kayne, R. (1975). *French syntax: the transformational cycle*. Cambridge, MA, MIT Press.

Kayne, R. (1984). *Connectedness and binary branching*. Dordrecht, Foris.

Kayne, R. (1994). *The Antisymmetry of Syntax*. Cambridge, MA, MIT Press.

Kayne, R. (2004a). 'Here and There'. In C. Leclère, É. Laporte, M. Piot, & M. Silberztein (Eds.), *Lexique, syntaxe, et lexique-grammaire (Syntax, Lexis, and Lexicon-Grammar): Papers in Honour of Maurice Gross (Lingvisticæ Investigationes Supplementa*, 24) (pp. 275–285). Amsterdam, John Benjamins.

Kayne, R. (2004b). Prepositions as Probes. In A. Belletti (Ed.), *Structures and Beyond: The Cartography of Syntactic Structures, vol. 3* (pp. 192–212). New York, Oxford University Press.

Kayne, R. (2005). Movement and Silence. Oxford, Oxford University Press.

Kayne, R. (2007). A Short Note on Where vs. Place. In R. Maschi, N. Penello, & P. Rizzolatti (Eds.), *Miscellanea di studi liguistici offerti a Laura Vanelli da amici e allievi padovani* (245–257). Udine, Forum.

Kayne, R. (2010). *Comparisons and contrasts*. Oxford, Oxford University Press.

Keenan, E. (1987). A semantic definition of indefinite NP. In E. Reuland & A. ter Meulen (Eds.), *The representation of (in)definiteness* (pp. 286–317). Cambridge, MA, MIT Press.

Kenesei, István, Vago, R. M., & Fenyvesi, A. (1998). *Hungarian*. London, Routledge.

Kim, K. (2012). Argument Structure Licensing and English have. *Journal of Linguistics*, 48(1), 71–105.

Kimenyi, A. (1980). *A Relational Grammar of Kinyarwanda*. University of California Press.

Kiparsky, P. (2001). Structural Case in Finnish. *Lingua*, 111, 315–376.

Kittilä, S. & Ylikoski, J. (2011). Remarks on the coding of Goal, Recipient, and Vicinal Goal in European Uralic. In S. Kittilä, K. Västi, & J. Ylikoski (Eds.), *Case, Animacy and Semantic Roles* pp. (29–64). Amsterdam: John Benjamins.

Klingler, T. A. (2003). *'If I could turn my tongue like that': The Creole Language of Pointe Coupee Parish, Louisiana*. Baton Rouge/London, Louisiana State University Press.

Koopman, H. (1984). *The syntax of Verbs: from Verb movement rules in the Kru languages to Universal Grammar*. Dordrecht, Foris.

Koopman, H. (2000). Prepositions, postpositions, circumpositions, and particles. In Hilda Koopman (Ed.), *The Syntax of Specifiers and Heads* (pp. 204–260). London, Routledge.

Kouwenberg, S. (2013). Papiamentu structure dataset. In S. M. Michaelis, P. Maurer, M. Haspelmath & M. Huber (Eds.), *Atlas of Pidgin and Creole Language Structures Online*, Leipzig, Max Planck Institute for Evolutionary Anthropology. (Available online at http://apics-online.info/).

Kracht, M. (2002). On the semantics of locatives. *Linguistics and Philosophy*, 25, 157–232.

Kripke, S. (1980). *Naming and Necessity*. Cambridge, Harvard University Press.

Kulikov, L. (2009). Evolution of Case Systems. In A. Malchukov & A. Spencer (Eds), *The Oxford Handbook of Case* (pp. 439–457). Oxford, Oxford University Press.

Künnap, A. (1999). *Enets*. München, Lincom Europa.

Kuo, P-J. (2010). Transitivity and the *ba* construction. *Taiwan Journal of Linguistics*, 8(1), 95–128.

La Fauci, N. & Loporcaro, M. (1993). Grammatical relations and syntactic levels in Bonorvese morphosyntax. In A. Belletti (Ed.), *Syntactic Theory and the Dialects of Italy* (pp. 155-203). Torino, Rosenberg & Sellier.

Laalo, K. (2009). Acquisition of Case and Plural in Finnish. In U. Stephany & M. Voeikova (Eds.), *Development of Nominal Inflection in first Language Acquisition: a Cross-Linguistic Perspective* (pp 49–90). Berlin, Mouton de Gruyter.

Landman, F. (1992). The progressive. *Natural Language Semantics*, 1, 1–32.

Larson, R., & Yamakido, H. (2008). Ezafe and the deep position of nominal modifiers. In L. McNally & C. Kennedy (Eds.), *Adjectives and adverbs: Syntax, semantics and discourse* (pp. 43–70). Oxford, Oxford University Press.

Larson, R., & V. Samiian (2020). The Ezafe construction revisited. In R. Larson, S. Moradi & V. Samiian (Eds.), *Advances in Iranian Linguistics* (pp. 173–236). Amsterdam, John Benjamins.

Larson, R. (1988). On the double object construction. *Linguistic Inquiry*, 19(3), 335–392.

Laury, R. (1997). *Demonstratives in interaction: The emergence of a definite article in Finnish.* Amsterdam, John Benjamins.

Lazard, G. (1957). *Grammaire du persan contemporain.* Parigi, Klincksieck.

Ledgeway, A. (2020). The causative construction in the dialects of southern Italy and the phonology syntax interface. In L. Franco, & P. Lorusso (Eds.), *Linguistic Variation: Structure and Interpretation* (pp. 371–400). Berlin, Mouton De Gruyter.

Lefebvre, C. (1991). Take serial verb constructions in Fon. In C. Lefebvre (Ed.), *Serial verbs: Grammatical, comparative and cognitive approaches* (pp. 37–78). Amsterdam, John Benjamins.

Lefebvre, C. (1998). *Creole genesis and the acquisition of grammar: The case of Haitian Creole.* Cambridge, Cambridge University Press.

Legate, J.A. (2014). *Voice and v: Lessons from Acehnese.* Cambridge, MA, MIT Press.

Lehmann, C. (2018). Foundations of Body-Part Grammar, manuscript, University of Erfort.

Lehtinen, T. (2007). *Kielen vuosituhannet.* Helsinki, SKS.

Lekakou, M. & Szendrői, K. (2012). Polydefinites in Greek: Ellipsis, close apposition and expletive determiners. *Journal of Linguistics*, 48, 107–149.

Leonetti, M. (2008). Definiteness Effects and the Role of the Coda in Existential Constructions. In H. Hoeg-Müller & A. Klinge (Eds.), *Essays on Nominal Determination* (pp. 131-162). Amsterdam: John Benjamins.

Levi, J.N. (1978). *The Syntax and Semantics of Complex Nominals.* New York, Academic Press.

Levinson, L. (2011). Possessive WITH in Germanic: HAVE and the role of P. *Syntax*, 14(4), 355–393.

Li, C.N., & Thompson, S, A. (1976). Subject and topic: a new typology of language. In C.N. Li (Ed.), *Subject and Topic* (pp. 457–461). Austin, University of Texas Press.

Li, C.N., & Thompson, S, A. (1981). *Mandarin Chinese: a Functional Reference Grammar.* Berkeley, University of California Press.

Li, Y. (1993). Structural head and aspectuality. *Language*, 69(3), 480–504.

Lim, L. & Ansaldo, U. (2013). Singlish structure dataset. In S. M. Michaelis, P. Maurer, M. Haspelmath & M. Huber (Eds.), *Atlas of Pidgin and Creole Language Structures Online*, Leipzig, Max Planck Institute for Evolutionary Anthropology. (Available online at http://apics-online.info/).

doi Link, G. (1983). The Logical Analysis of Plurals and Mass Terms: A Lattice-theoretical Approach. In R. Bäuerle, C. Schwarze & A. von Stechow (Eds.), *Meaning, Use, and Interpretation of Language*, (pp. 302–323). Berlin, De Gruyter.

Longobardi, G. (1994). Reference and Proper Names: A Theory of N-Movement in Syntax and Logical Form. *Linguistic Inquiry*, 25, 609–665.

Longobardi, G. (1996). The Syntax of N-Raising: A Minimalist Theory. *OTS Working Papers*. Utrecht, Utrecht University.

doi Longobardi, G. (2001). Formal syntax, diachronic minimalism, and etymology: The history of French *chez. Linguistic Inquiry*, 32, 275–302.

doi Longobardi, G. (2005). Toward a Unified Grammar of Reference. *Zeitschrift für Sprachwissenschaft*, 24, 5–44.

doi Longobardi, G. (2008). Reference to individuals, person, and the variety of mapping parameters. In A. Klinge & H. Høeg Müller (Eds.), *Essays on Nominal Determination: from morphology to discourse* (pp. 189–211). Amsterdam, John Benjamins.

Lord, C. (1989). Syntactic reanalysis in the historical development of serial verb constructions in languages of West Africa, PhD dissertation, University of California, Los Angeles.

doi Lord, C. (1993). *Historical Change in Serial Verb Constructions*. Amsterdam, John Benjamins.

doi Lorusso, P., & Franco, L. (2017). Patterns of syntactic agreement with embedded NPs. *Lingua*, 195, 39–56.

Lovestrand, J. (2017). Temporal iconicity and verb order in instrumental SVCs. Hand-out of a talk given at SLE, 10 September 2017.

Lovestrand, J. (2018). Serial verb constructions in Barayin: Typology, description and LexicalFunctional Grammar. PhD dissertation, University of Oxford.

Ludwig, R. (1996). *Kreolsprachen zwischen Mündlichkeit und Schriftlichkeit. Zur Syntax und Pragmatik atlantischer Kreolsprachen auf französischer Basis*. Tübingen, Gunter Narr.

doi Luraghi S. (2003). *On the Meaning of Prepositions and Cases. A Study of the Expression of Semantic Roles in Ancient Greek*. Amsterdam, John Benjamins.

doi Luraghi S. (2011). The coding of spatial relations with human landmarks: From Latin to Romance. In S. Kittilä, K. Västi, & J. Ylikoski (Eds.), *Case, Animacy and Semantic Roles* (pp. 209–234). Amsterdam, John Benjamins.

Lyons, J. (1967). A note on possessive, existential and locative sentences. *Foundations of Language*, 3, 390–396.

McGinnis, M. (1998). Locality in A-movement. PhD dissertation, MIT.

doi Malchukov, A. (2008). Animacy and asymmetries in differential case marking. *Lingua*, 118(2), 203–221.

Manzini, M. R., & Wexler, K. (1987). Parameters, Binding Theory, and Learnability. *Linguistic Inquiry*, 18, 413–444.

doi Manzini, M. R., & Savoia L. M. (2002). Parameters of subject inflection in Italian dialects. In P. Svenonius (Eds.), *Subjects, Expletives and the EPP* (pp. 157–199). New York, Oxford University Press.

Manzini, M. R., & Savoia L. M. (2005). *I dialetti italiani e romanci. Morfosintassi generativa* (3 volumes) Alessandria, Edizioni dell'Orso.

Manzini, M. R., & Savoia L. M. (2007). *A unification of morphology and syntax. Studies in Romance and Albanian varieties.* London, Routledge.

Manzini, M. R., & Savoia L. M. (2011a). *Grammatical categories.* Cambridge, Cambridge University Press.

Manzini, M. R., & Savoia L. M. (2011b). Reducing 'case' to denotational primitives: Nominal inflections in Albanian. *Linguistic Variation*, 11(1), 76–120.

Manzini, M. R. (2014). Grammatical categories: Strong and weak pronouns in Romance. *Lingua*, 150, 171–201.

Manzini, M. R. & Savoia, L. M. (2014) From Latin to Romance: case loss and preservation in pronominal systems. *Probus*, 26(2), 217-248.

Manzini, M. R., Savoia, L. M., & Franco, L. (2015). Ergative case, Aspect and Person splits: Two case studies. *Acta Linguistica Hungarica*, 62(3), 297–351.

Manzini, M. R., & Franco, L. (2016). Goal and DOM datives. *Natural Language and Linguistic Theory*, 34, 197–240.

Manzini, M. R. (2017). Passive, smuggling and the by-phrase. In N. LaCara, K. Moulton & A-M. Tessier (Eds.), *A Schrift to Fest Kyle Johnson* (pp. 233–244). University of Massachusets – Amherst.

Manzini, M. R., & Savoia L. M. (2017a). N morphology and its interpretation: The neuter in Italian and Albanian varieties. In A. Bloch-Rozmej & A. Bondaruk (Eds.), *Constraints on Structure and Derivation in Syntax, Phonology and Morphology* (pp. 213–236). Frankfurt am Main, Peter Lang.

Manzini, M. R., & Savoia L. M. (2017b). Gender, number and inflectional class in Romance: Feminine/plural –a. In J. Emonds & M. Janebova (Eds.), *Language Use and Linguistic Structure* (pp. 263–282). Olomouc, Palacky University Olomouc.

Manzini, M. R., & Savoia L. M. (2018). *The Morphosyntax of Albanian and Aromanian Varieties.* Berlin, Mouton De Gruyter.

Manzini, M. R., & Franco, L. (2019). 'Agreement of structural obliques' parameter. *Lingvisticae Investigationes*, 42(1), 82–101.

Manzini, M. R., Franco, L., & Savoia, L. M. (2019). Suffixaufnahme, Oblique Case and Agree. In L. Franco, M. Marchis Moreno, & M. Reeve (Eds.), *Agreement, Case and Locality in the Nominal and Verbal Domains* (pp. 211–255). Berlin, Language Science Press.

Manzini, M. R., Savoia, L. M., & Franco, L. (2020). DOM and Dative in Italo-Romance. In A. Bárány & L. Kalin (Eds.), *Case, agreement, and their interactions: New perspectives on Differential Object Marking*, Berlin, De Gruyter.

Manzini, M. R. (2020). The morphosyntactic structure of number in Italian and Albanian. High and low plurals. *Catalan Journal of Linguistics*, 19, 127–157.

Marantz, A. (1984). *On the nature of grammatical relations.* Cambridge, MA, MIT Press.

Marantz, A. (1993). Implications of asymmetries in double object constructions. In S. Mchombo (Ed.), *Theoretical aspects of Bantu grammar* (pp. 113–150). Stanford, CA, CSLI.

Marantz, A. (1997). No escape from syntax: Don't try morphological analysis in the privacy of your own lexicon. In A. Dimitriadis (Ed.), *UPenn working papers in linguistics, vol. 4.2* (pp. 201–225). Philadelphia, University of Pennsylvania.

Marantz, A. (2007). Phases and words. In S. H. Choe (Ed.), *Phases in the Theory of Grammar* (pp. 191–222). Seul, Dong-In Publishing Company.

Marchis Moreno, M. (2010). Relational adjectives at the Syntax/Morphology Interface in Romanian and Spanish. PhD Dissertation, Stuttgart University.

Marchis Moreno, M. (2015). Relational adjectives at interfaces. *Studia Linguistica*, 69(3), 304–332.

Marchis Moreno, M. 2018. *Relational Adjectives in Romance and English Mismatches at Interfaces*. Cambridge: Cambridge University Press.

Marchis Moreno, M., & Franco, L. (2020). Intervention in agreement and case assignment: the role of doubling. *Quaderni di Linguistica e Studi Orientali – QULSO* 6, 125–159.

Markey, T. L. (1982). Afrikaans: Creole or Non-Creole? *Zeitschrift für Dialektologie und Linguistik*, 49(2), 169–207.

Marten, L. (2002). *At the Syntax-Pragmatics Interface*. Oxford, Oxford University Press.

Masi, S. (2020). Variation in the Possession of kinship terms in the Dialects of Italy. *Proceedings of the 2020 CLA – Canadian Linguistic Association meeting*.

Mathieu, E. (2012). Flavors of division. *Linguistic Inquiry*, 43, 650–679.

Matisoff, J. A. (1991). Areal and universal dimensions of grammatization in Lahu. In E. C. Traugott & B. Heine (Eds.), *Approaches to grammaticalization, Vol.* 2 (pp. 383–453). Amsterdam & Philadelphia, John Benjamins.

Matushansky, O. (2009). On the linguistic complexity of proper names. *Linguistics and Philosophy*, 31, 573–627.

Maurer, P. (1995). *L'angolar. Un créole afro-portugais parlé à São Tomé. Notes de grammaire, textes, vocabulaire*. Hamburg, Buske.

Maurer, P. (2009). *Principense. Grammar, texts, and vocabulary of the Afro-Portuguese Creole of the Island of Príncipe, Gulf of Guinea*. London/Colombo, Battlebridge.

Maurer, P. (2011). *The former Portuguese Creole of Batavia and Tugu (Indonesia)*. London/Colombo, Battlebridge.

Maurer, P. (2013). Angolar structure dataset. In S. M. Michaelis, P. Maurer, M. Haspelmath & M. Huber (Eds.), *Atlas of Pidgin and Creole Language Structures Online*, Leipzig, Max Planck Institute for Evolutionary Anthropology. (Available online at http://apics-online .info/).

Mazzoli, M. (2015). Complexity in gradience: the serial verb *take* in Nigerian Pidgin. In A. D. M. Smith, G. Trousdale & R. Waltereit (Eds.), *New Directions in Grammaticalization Research* (pp. 231–260). Amsterdam, John Benjamins.

McDonnell, B. J. (2013). Toward an integrated typology of causative/applicative syncretism. Hand-out of a talk given at Max Planck Institute for Evolutionary Anthropology, Leipzig, Germany, October 9, 2013.

McNally, L. (1992). *An interpretation for the English existential construction*. New York, Garland.

McNally, L., & Boleda, G. (2004). Relational adjectives as properties of kinds. In O. Bonami & P. Cabredo Hofherr (Eds.), *Empirical Issues in Syntax and Semantics vol. 5* (pp. 179–196). http://www.cssp.cnrs.fr/eiss5

McNally, L. (2011). Existential sentences. In C. Maienborn, K. von Heusinger & P. Portner (Eds.), *Semantics: An International Handbook of Natural Language Meaning, vol. 2* (pp. 1829–1848). Berlin, De Gruyter.

McWhorter, John H. (2005). *Defining Creole.* New York, Oxford University Press.

McWhorter, J. H. (2011). Tying up Loose Ends: The Creole Prototype after all. *Diachronica,* 28(1), 82–117.

Merlini Barbaresi, L. (2004). Alterazione. In M. Grossmann & F. Rainer (Eds.), *La formazione delle parole in italiano* (pp. 264–292). Tübingen: Niemeyer.

Meyer-Lübke, W. (1911). *Romanisches etymologisches Wörterbuch.* Heidelberg, C. Winter. Available online at: www.archive.org.

Michaelis, S. M., & Haspelmath, M. (2003). Ditransitive constructions: Creole languages in a cross-linguistic perspective. *Creolica* <http://www.creolica.net/Ditransitive-constructions -Creole>

Michaelis, S. M., & Marcel, R. (2013). Seychelles Creole. In S. M. Michaelis, P. Maurer, M. Haspelmath & M. Huber (Eds.), *The survey of pidgin and creole languages. Vol. II: Portuguese-based, Spanish-based and French-based languages* (pp. 261–270). Oxford, Oxford University Press.

Michaelis, S. M., Maurer, P., Haspelmath, M. & Huber M. (Eds.) (2013). *Atlas of Pidgin and Creole Language Structures Online.* Leipzig: Max Planck Institute for Evolutionary Anthropology. http://apics-online.info

Milsark, G. L. (1974). Existential Sentences in English. PhD Dissertation. MIT.

Montaut, A. (2004). Oblique main arguments in Hindi as localizing predications. Questioning the category of subject. In P. Bhaskararao & K. V. Subbarao (Eds.), *Non nominative subjects* (pp. 33–56). Amsterdam, John Benjamins.

Moro, A. (1997). *The Raising of Predicates.* Cambridge: Cambridge University Press.

Moro, A. (2017). Existential Sentences and Expletive There. In M. Everaert & H. C. van Riemsdijk (Eds.), *The Wiley Blackwell Companion to Syntax, Second Edition* (pp. 1483-1508). Hoboken, NJ, John Wiley & Sons. .

Moyne, J. (1974). The so-called Passive in Persian. *Foundation of Language,* 12, 249–267.

Müller, G. (2007). Notes on Paradigm Economy. *Morphology,* 17(1), 1–38.

Munro, P. (2000). The Leaky Grammar of the Chickasaw Applicatives. *Chicago Linguistic Society,* 36, 285–310.

Muysken, P. (1981). Halfway between Quechua and Spanish: The case for relexification. In A. Highfield & A. Valdman (Eds.), *Historicity and variation in creole studies* (pp. 52–78). Ann Arbor, Karoma.

Muysken, P. (1988). Parameters for serial verbs. In V. Manfredi (Ed.), *Niger-Congo Syntax and Semantics,* 1, 65–75. Boston, Boston University African Studies Center.

Muysken, P., & Veenstra, T. (1995). Serial verb constructions. In J. Arends, P. Muysken & N. Smith (Eds.), *Pidgins and creoles: an introduction* (pp. 289–301). Amsterdam, John Benjamins.

Muysken, P. (1999). Three processes of borrowing: Borrowability revisited. In G. Extra & L. Verhoeven (Eds.), *Bilingualism and Migration* (pp. 229–246). Berlin, Mouton de Gruyter.

Muysken, P., & Veenstra, T. (2006). Serial verbs. In M. Everaert & H.C. van Riemsdijk (Eds.), *The Blackwell Companion to Syntax, Vol. IV* (pp. 234–270). Malden, Blackwell.

Myler, N. (2014). Building and Interpreting Possession Sentences. PhD Dissertation, New York University.

Myler, N. (2016). *Building and Interpreting Possession Sentences*. Cambridge, MA, MIT Press.

Naderi, N. (2010). Semantic and Pragmatics of Grammatical Voice in Farsi. MA Thesis, Leiden, Leiden University Center for Linguistics (LUCL).

Næss, Å. (2008). *Prototypical transitivity*. Amsterdam, John Benjamins.

Nemati, F. (2013). On the syntax-semantics of passives in Persian. In A. Alexiadou, & F. Schäfer, (Eds.), *Non-Canonical Passives* (pp. 261–280). Amsterdam, John Benjamins.

Nichols, J. (1986). Head-marking and dependent-marking grammar. *Language*, 62, 56–119.

Nikolaeva, I. (1999). *Ostyak*. München, Lincom Europa.

Nikolaeva, I. (2014). *A Grammar of Tundra Nenets*. Berlin, De Gruyter.

Nikolaeva, I., & Spencer, A. (2013). Possession and modification: A perspective from Canonical Typology. In D. Brown, M. Chumakina, & G. Corbett (Eds.), *Canonical morphology and syntax* (pp. 207–238). Oxford, Oxford University Press.

Nishina, Y. (2001). Comitative and Instrumental in Japanese. *STUF-Language Typology and Universals*, 54, 346–364.

Nordlinger, R. (2019). From body part to applicative: Encoding 'source' in Murrinhpatha. *Linguistic Typology*, 23(3), 401–433.

Noyer, R. (1992). Features, Positions and Affixes in Autonomous Morphological Structure. PhD Dissertation, MIT.

Ott, D. (2011). Diminutive-formation in German. Spelling out the Classifier Analysis. *Journal of Comparative Germanic Linguistics*, 14, 1–46.

Oyelaran, O. (1982). On the scope of the serial verb construction in Yoruba. *Studies in African Linguistics*, 13(2), 109-146.

Palancar, E. (2002). *The Origin of Agent Markers*. Berlin, Akademie Verlag.

Paul, D. (2004). The passive in Persian. *SOAS Working Papers in Linguistics*, 13, 221–235.

Pantcheva, M. (2006). Persian Preposition Classes. *Nordlyd*, 33, 1–25.

Pantcheva, M. (2010). The syntactic structure of Locations, Goals, and Sources. *Linguistics*, 48, 1043–1081.

Pantcheva, M. (2011). *Decomposing Path: The Nanosyntax of Directional Expressions*. Ph.D. dissertation, University of Tromsø.

Parsons, T. 1979. An Analysis of Mass Terms and Amount Terms. In F. J. Pelletier (Ed.), *Mass terms: some philosophical problems* (pp. 137–166). Dordrecht, Springer.

Partee, B.H. (2007). Compositionality and Coercion in Semantics: The Dynamics of Adjective Meaning. In G. Bouma, I. Kramer, & J. Zwarts (Eds.), *Cognitive Foundations of Interpretation* (pp. 145–161). Amsterdam, Royal Netherlands Academy of Arts and Sciences.

Peck, S. M. Jr. (1988). Tense, aspect and mood in Guinea-Casamance Portuguese Creole. Ph. D. Dissertation, University of California.

Percus, O. (2011). Gender features and interpretation: a case study. *Morphology*, 21, 167–196.

Pesetsky, D. (1995). *Zero syntax*. Cambridge, MA, MIT Press.

Peterson, D. (2007). *Applicative constructions*. Oxford, Oxford University Press.

Pfänder, S. (2013). Guyanais structure dataset. In S. M. Michaelis, P. Maurer, M. Haspelmath & M. Huber (Eds.), *Atlas of Pidgin and Creole Language Structures Online*, Leipzig, Max Planck Institute for Evolutionary Anthropology. (Available online at http://apics-online .info/).

Pham, M. (2011). Are Vietnamese kinship terms pronouns? Ms. University of Chicago.

Pineda, A. (2014). (In)transitivity borders. A study of applicatives in Romance languages and Basque. PhD Dissertation, UAB.

Plank, Frans. (1995). (Re-)Introducing Suffixaufnahme. In F. Plank (Ed.), *Double Case. Agreement by Suffixaufnahme* (pp. 3–112). Oxford, Oxford University Press.

Post, M. (1995). Fa d'Ambu. In J. Arends, P. Muysken, & N. Smith (Eds.), *Pidgins and creoles: an introduction* (pp. 191–204). Amsterdam, John Benjamins.

Post, M. (1999). *Crioulos de Base Portuguesa*. Lisboa, Associação Portuguesa de Linguística, FLUL.

Post, M. (2013). Fa d'Ambô structure dataset. In S. M. Michaelis, P. Maurer, M. Haspelmath & M. Huber (Eds.), *Atlas of Pidgin and Creole Language Structures Online*, Leipzig, Max Planck Institute for Evolutionary Anthropology. (Available online at http://apics-online .info/).

Pylkkänen, L. (2002). Introducing arguments. PhD Dissertation, MIT.

Pylkkänen, L. (2008). *Introducing arguments*. Cambridge, MA, MIT press.

Rainer, F. (1996). Copernicano e luterano: sul ruolo del latino nella derivazione deantroponimica italiana. *Lingua Nostra*, 57, 48–49.

Quine, W. (1960). *Word and object: An inquiry into the linguistic mechanisms of objective reference*. John Wiley.

Rainer, F. (2004). Etnici. In M. Grossmann & F. Rainer (Eds.), *La formazione delle parole in italiano* (pp. 402–408). Tübingen, Niemeyer.

Rainer, F. (2013). Can relational adjectives really express any relation? An onomasiological perspective. *SKASE Journal of Theoretical Linguistics*, 101, 12–40.

Ramchand, G. (2011). Licensing of Instrumental Case in Hindi/Urdu Causatives. *Nordlyd*, 36, 1–38.

Reinhart, T. (2003). The theta-system – an overview. *Theoretical Linguistics*, 28, 229–290.

Ricca, D. (2004). Conversione in avverbi. In M. Grossmann & F. Rainer (Eds.), *La formazione delle parole in italiano* (pp. 550–553). Tübingen, Niemeyer.

Richards, N. (2013). Lardil "Case Stacking" and the Timing of Case Assignment. *Syntax*, 16, 42–76.

Richards, N. (2010). *Uttering trees*. Cambridge, MA, MIT Press.

Rickford, J. R. (1987). *Dimensions of a creole continuum: History, texts, and linguistic analysis of Guyanese Creole*. Stanford, CA, Stanford University Press.

Riese, T. (2001). *Vogul*. München, Lincom Europa.

Rigau, G. (1997). Locative sentences and related constructions in Catalan: "ésser/haver" alternation. In A. Mendikoetxea & M. Uribe-Etxebarría (Eds.), *Theoretical Issues at the Morphology- Syntax Interface* (pp. 395–421). Bilbao, Universidad del País Vasco.

Rizzi, L. (1978). A Restructuring Rule in Italian Syntax. In S. J. Keyser (Ed.), *Recent Transformational Studies in European Languages* (pp. 113–158). Cambridge, MA, MIT Press.

Rizzi, L. (1988). Il sintagma preposizionale. In L. Renzi, G. P. Salvi, & A. Cardinaletti (Eds.), *Grande grammatica italiana di consultazione* (pp. 507–531). Bologna, Il Mulino.

Rizzi, L., & Cinque, G. (2016). Functional Categories and Syntactic Theory. *The Annual Review of Linguistics*, 2, 139–163.

Roberts, S. J., & Bresnan, J. (2008). Retained inflectional morphology in pidgins: A typological study. *Linguistic Typology*, 12(2), 269–302.

Rohlfs, G. (1969). *Grammatica storica della lingua italiana e dei suoi dialetti, III. Sintassi e formazione delle parole*. Torino, Einaudi.

Rohlfs, G. (1968). *Grammatica Storica Della Lingua Italiana e dei Suoi Dialetti. Morfologia*. Torino, Einaudi.

Romaine, S. (1988). *Pidgin and creole languages*. London & New York, Longman.

Romeu, J. (2013). The nanosyntax of Path. Ms. Madrid.

Ross, J. (1967). *Constraints on variables in syntax*. PhD. dissertation, Massachusetts Institute of Technology.

Roy, I. (2006). Body part nouns in expressions of location in French. *Nordlyd*, 33, 98–119.

Roy, I., & Svenonius, P. (2009). Complex prepositions. In F. Jacques, E. Gilbert, C. Guimier, & M. Krause (Eds.), *Autour de la préposition, Actes du Colloque International de Caen (20–22 septembre 2007)* (pp 105–116). Caen, Presses Universitaires de Caen.

Rugna, G., & Franco, L. (2022). Prepositions as relators in Italian Prepositional Compounds. In M. Bril, M. Coene, T. Ihsane, P. Sleeman & T. Westveer (Eds.), *RLLT 19*, Special Issue of *Isogloss. Open Journal of Romance Linguistics*, 8(5), 11, 1–21.

Safir, K. (1983). Small clauses as constituents. *Linguistic Inquiry*, 14(4), 730–735.

Samiian, V. (1983). Structure of phrasal categories in Persian: An X-bar analysis. Los Angeles, CA: UCLA dissertation.

Samiian, V. (1994). The Ezafe construction: Some implications for the theory of X-bar syntax. In M. Marashi (Ed.), *Persian Studies in North America* (pp. 17–41). Bethesda, MD, Iranbooks.

Savoia, L. M., Manzini, M. R., Franco, L., & Baldi, B. (2017). Nominal evaluative suffixes in Italian. In R. D'Alessandro, G. Iannàccaro, D. Passino, & A. M. Thornton (Eds.), *Di tutti i colori. Studi linguistici per Maria Grossmann,*. avalable at Leiden University Repository: https://openaccess.leidenuniv.nl/

Savoia, L. M., Manzini, M. R., Baldi, B., & Franco, L. (2018). A Morphosyntactic Analysis of Evaluatives in Italian. *SILTA – Studi Italiani di Linguistica Teorica e Applicata*, XLVI, 413–440.

Scalise, S. (1990). Constraints on the Italian suffix –*mente*. In W. U. Dressler, H. C. Luschützky, O. E. Pfeiffer, & J. R. Rennison (Eds.), *Contemporary morphology* (pp. 87–98). Mouton De Gruyter, Berlin.

Schäfer, F. (2012). Two types of external argument licensing – the case of causers. *Studia Linguistica*, 66, 128–180.

Schlücker, B. & Ackermann, T. (2017). The morphosyntax of proper names: an overview. *Folia Linguistica*, 51, 309–333.

Schumann, C. L. (1783). *Neger-Englisches Wörterbuch*. Ms. Early creole lexicography: A study of C.L. *Schumann's manuscript dictionary of Sranan*, ed. by A. Kamp, 44–305.

Schwegler, A. (2013). Palenquero structure dataset. In S. M. Michaelis, P. Maurer, M. Haspelmath & M. Huber (Eds.), *Atlas of Pidgin and Creole Language Structures Online*, Leipzig, Max Planck Institute for Evolutionary Anthropology. (Available online at http://apics-online.info/).

Sebba, M. (1987). *The Syntax of Serial Verbs: An Investigation into Serialisation in Sranan and Other Languages*. Amsterdam: John Benjamins.

Seidl, C. (2004). Deantroponimici. In M. Grossmann & F. Rainer (Eds.), *La formazione delle parole in italiano* (pp. 411–419). Tübingen, Niemeyer.

Serianni, L. (1988). *Grammatica italiana. Italiano comune e lingua letteraria. Suoni, forme, costrutti*. Torino, Utet.

Seuren, P. (1990). Still no serials in Seselwa: a reply to "Seselwa serialization and its significance." *Journal of Pidgin and Creole Languages*, 5, 271–292.

Shibatani, M. & Pardeshi, P. (2002). The causative continuum. In M. Shibatani (Ed.), *The Grammar of Causation and Interpersonal Manipulation* (pp. 85–126). Amsterdam, John Benjamins.

Siewierska, A. (1984). *The Passive: a comparative linguistic analysis*. London, Croon Helm.

Siloni, T. (1997). *Noun Phrases and Nominalizations: The Syntax of DPs*. Kluwer, Dordrecht.

Simoncsics, P. (1998). Kamassian. In D. Abondolo (Ed.), *The Uralic Languages* (pp. 580–601). London: Routledge.

Siro, P. (1964). *Suomen kielen lauseoppi*. Helsinki, Tietosanakirja.

Sneddon, J. N. (1996). *Indonesian Reference Grammar*. St Leonards, NSW, Allen and Unwin.

Snyder, William, & Stromswold, K. (1997). The Structure and Acquisition of English Dative Constructions. *Linguistic Inquiry*, 28(2), 281–317.

Spencer, A., & Nikolaeva, I. (2017). Denominal adjectives as mixed categories. *Word Structure*, 10, 79–99.

Sperber, D., & Wilson, D. (1995). *Relevance: Communication and Cognition*. Oxford, Blackwell.

Starke, M. (2009). Nanosyntax: A short primer to a new approach to language. *Nordlyd*, 36, 2–6.

Starke, M. (2017). Resolving (DAT = ACC) ≠ GEN. *Glossa: a journal of general linguistics*, 2(1), 104.

Stassen, L. (2009). *Predicative possession*. Oxford: Oxford University Press.

Steinkrüger, P. O. (2013). Zamboanga Chabacano structure dataset. In S. M. Michaelis, P. Maurer, M. Haspelmath & M. Huber (Eds.), *Atlas of Pidgin and Creole Language Structures Online*, Leipzig, Max Planck Institute for Evolutionary Anthropology. (Available online at http://apics-online.info/).

Stewart, J. M. (1963). Some restrictions on objects in Twi. *Journal of African Languages*, 2(2), 145–149.

Stolz, T. (2001). To be with X is to have X: Comitatives, instrumentals, locative, and predicative possession. *Linguistics*, 39(2), 321–350.

Stolz, T., Levkovych, N., & Urdze, A. (2017). Die Grammatik der Toponyme als typologisches Forschungsfeld: eine Pilotstudie. In J. Helmbrecht, D. Nübling & B. Schlücker (Eds.), *Namengrammatik*, 121–146. Hamburg, Buske.

Stolz, T., Stroh C., & Urdze, A. (2006). *On comitatives and related categories.* Berlin, De Gruyter.

Stowell, T. (1978). What Was There Before There Was There. *Proceedings of CLS*, 14, 458–471.

Stump, G. (2001). *Inflectional morphology: A theory of paradigm structure.* Cambridge, Cambridge University Press.

Stump, G. (2002). Morphological and syntactic paradigms: Arguments for a theory of paradigm linkage. In G. Booij & J. van Marle (Eds.), *Yearbook of Morphology* 2001, 147–180. Dordrecht, Kluwer.

Sulkala, H., & Karjalainen, M. (1992). *Finnish.* London, Routledge.

Sun, C. (1996). *Word order change and grammaticalization in the history of Chinese.* Stanford, CA, Stanford University Press.

Suñer M. (1982). *Syntax and Semantics of Spanish Presentational Sentence-Types.* Washington, DC: Georgetown University Press.

Suutari, T. (2006). Body part names and grammaticalization. In M-L. Helasvuo & L. Campbell (Eds.), *Grammar from the human perspective: Case, space and person in Finnish* (pp. 101–128). Amsterdam, John Benjamins.

Svenonius, P. (2002). Icelandic case and the structure of events. *Journal of Comparative Germanic Linguistics*, 5(1–3), 197–225.

Svenonius, P. (2003). Limits on p: filling in holes vs. falling in holes. *Nordlyd*, 31, 431–445.

Svenonius, P. (2006). The emergence of axial parts. *Nordlyd*, 33, 1–22.

Svenonius, P. (2007). Adpositions, particles and the arguments they introduce. In E. Reuland, T, Bhattacharya, & G. Spathas (Eds.), *Argument Structure* (pp. 63–103). Amsterdam, John Benjamins.

Svenonius, P. (2008). Projections of P. In A. Asbury, J. Dotlačil, B. Gehrke & R. Nouwen (Eds.), *Syntax and Semantics of Spatial P* (pp. 63–84). Amsterdam, John Benjamins.

Svenonius, P. (2010). Spatial P in English. In G. Cinque & L. Rizzi (Eds.), *Mapping Spatial PPs, The Cartography of Syntactic Structures, Vol.* 6 (pp. 127–160). New York, Oxford University Press.

Svenonius, P. (2012). Structural decomposition of spatial adpositions. Presented at The Meaning of P, Universität Bochum. http://ling.auf.net/lingbuzz/001776.

Swolkien de Sousa, D. (2012). The Cape Verdean Creole of São Vicente: its genesis and structure. Ph.D Dissertation, University of Coimbra.

Sybesma, R. (1999). *The Mandarin VP.* Dordrecht, Kluwer.

Syea, A. (2013). Serial verb constructions in Indian Ocean French Creoles (IOCs) Substrate, universal, or an independent diachronic development? *Journal of Pidgin and Creole Languages*, 28(1), 13–64.

Syea, A. (2014). *The Syntax of Mauritian Creole.* London, Bloomsbury.

Syea, A. (2017). *French Creoles: A Comprehensive and Comparative Grammar.* London, Routledge.

Tai, J. H.-Y. (1985). Temporal sequence and Chinese word order. In J. Haiman (Ed.), *Iconicity in Syntax* (pp. 49–72). Amsterdam, John Benjamins.

Takamine, K. (2017). *Putting Adpositions in Place.* Amsterdam, John Benjamins.

Talmy, L. (1985). Lexicalization patterns: semantic structure in lexical forms. In T. Shopen (ed.), *Language typology and syntactic description. Vol. 3: grammatical categories and the lexicon*, (pp. 57-149) Cambridge, Cambridge University Press.

Talmy, L. (1988). The relation of grammar to cognition. In B. Rudzka-Ostyn (Ed.), *Topics in cognitive linguistics* (pp. 165-205). Amsterdam, John Benjamins.

Talmy, L. (2000). *Toward a cognitive semantics. Concept structuring systems, Vol. 1*. Cambridge, MA, MIT Press.

Thomas, F. (1940). Le suffixe Latin -aster/ -astrum. *Revue des Études Anciennes*, 48, 520–528.

Todd, L. (1982). *Cameroon*. Heidelberg, Julius Groos Verlag.

Topping, D. (1973). *Chamorro reference grammar*. Honolulu, University of Hawaii Press.

Torrego, E. (2010). Variability in the Case Patterns of Causative Formation in Romance and Its Implications. *Linguistic Inquiry*, 41, 445–470.

Tortora, C. (2005). The Preposition's Preposition in Italian: Evidence for Boundedness of Space. In R. Gess, & E. Rubin (Eds), *Theoretical and Experimental Approaches to Romance Linguistics* (pp. 307–327). Amsterdam, John Benjamins.

Ursini, F-A., & Long, H. (2018). On spatial nouns and adpositions in Mandarin. *Language and Linguistics*, 81, 193–226.

Vainikka, A. (1989). Deriving Syntactic Representations in Finnish. PhD dissertation, University of Massachusetts/Amherst.

van der Voort, Hein. (2004). *A grammar of Kwaza*. Berlin, Mouton De Gruyter.

van Hout, A., & Roeper, T. (1998). Events and aspectual structure in derivational morphology. In H. Harley (Ed.), *Papers from the UPenn/MIT roundtable on argument structure and aspect* (pp. 175–200). MITWPL32.

van Pareren, R. (2013). Body part terms as a semantic basis for grammaticalization: a Mordvin case study into spatial reference and beyond. *Language Sciences*, 36, 90–102.

van Riemsdijk, H. (1978). *A case study in syntactic markedness: The binding nature of prepositional phrases*. Lisse, The Peter de Ridder Press.

Veenstra, T. & den Besten, H. (1994). Fronting. In J. Arends, P. Muysken & N. Smith (Eds.), *Pidgins and creoles: an introduction* (pp. 303–315). Amsterdam, John Benjamins.

Veland, R. (2012). Le locuzioni preposizionali a(d) opera di, per opera di, per mano di in italiano contemporaneo: funzionamento sintattico e proprietà semantiche. *Zeitschrift für romanische Philologie*, 128, 537–552.

Viitso, T-R. (1998). Estonian. In D. Abondolo (Ed.), *The Uralic Languages* (pp. 115–148). London, Routledge.

Villalba, X. (2013). Eventive existentials in Catalan and the topic-focus articulation. *Italian Journal of Linguistics/Rivista di Linguistica*, 25(1), 147–173.

Von Fintel, K. (1994). Restrictions on quantifier domains. Ph.D. dissertation, University of Massachussets.

von Heusinger, K., & Kaiser, G.A. (2011). Affectedness and differential object marking in Spanish. *Morphology*, 21(3–4), 593–617.

Wälchli, B., & Zúñiga, F. (2006). Source-Goal (in)difference and the typology of motion events in the clause. *Sprachtypologie & Universalienforschung*, 59, 284–303.

Wandruszka, U. (2004). Aggettivi di relazione. In M. Grossmann & F. Rainer (Eds.), *La formazione delle parole in italiano* (pp. 382–394). Tübingen, Niemeyer.

Williams, E. (1983). Against small clauses. *Linguistic Inquiry*, 14(2), 287–308.

Williams, E. (1984). There-insertion. *Linguistic Inquiry*, 15, 131–153.

Williams, E. (1994). *Thematic Structure in Syntax*. Cambridge, MA, MIT Press.

Wiltschko, M. (2006). Why should diminutives count? In H. Broekhuis, N. Corver, Norbert, R. Huijbregts, U. Kleinhenz, & J. Koster (Eds.), *Organizing Grammar. Linguistic Studies in Honor of Henk van Riemsdijk* (pp. 669–679). Berlin, Walter de Gruyter.

Windfuhr, G., & Perry, J. J. (2009). Persian and Tajik. In G. Windfuhr (Ed.), *The Iranian Languages* (pp. 416–444). London, Routledge.

Winford, D. & Migge, B. (2008). Surinamese Creole: Morphology and syntax. In Edgar W. Schneider (Ed.), *Varieties of English, Vol. 2: The Americas and the Caribbean* (pp. 693–731). Berlin, Mouton de Gruyter.

Winkler, E. 2001. *Udmurt*. München, Lincom Europa.

Wood, J. (2015). *Icelandic Morphosyntax and Argument Structure*. Dordrecht, Springer.

Wood, J. & Marantz, A. (2018). The Interpretation of External Arguments. <http://psych.nyu.edu/morphlab/publications/Wood%20&%20Marantz%20

Woolford, E. (1997). Four-way Case systems: Ergative, nominative, objective, and accusative. *Natural Language and Linguistic Theory*, 15, 181–227.

Woolford, E. (2006). Lexical Case, Inherent Case, and Argument Structure. *Linguistic Inquiry*, 37, 111–130.

Yamada, M. (2010). Plurality, reciprocity, and plurality of reciprocity. PhD Dissertation, University of Delaware.

Ylikoski J. (2011). A Survey of the Origins of Directional Case Suffixes in European Uralic. In S. Kittilä, K. Västi, & J. Ylikoski (Eds.), *Case, Animacy and Semantic Roles* (pp. 235–280). Amsterdam, John Benjamins.

Zamparelli, R. (2000). *Layers in the Determiner Phrase*. New York, Garland.

Ziegeler, D. P. (2000). A Possession-Based Analysis of the *Ba*-construction in Mandarin Chinese. *Lingua*, 110, 807–842.

Zwarts, J. (1995). Lexical and Functional Direction in Dutch. In M. den Dikken, & Kees Hengeveld (Eds.), *Linguistics in the Netherlands*, 12 (pp. 227–238). Amsterdam: John Benjamins.

Zwicky, A. (1990). What are we talking about when we talk about serial verb constructions? In B. D. Joseph & A. M. Zwicky (Eds.), *When Verbs Collide: Papers from the (1990) Ohio State Mini-Conference on Serial verb constructions, The Ohio State University Working Papers in Linguistics* 39, 1–13.

Subject index